ACT OF LOVE

ACT OF LOVE
The Killing of George Zygmanik

by Paige Mitchell

ALFRED A. KNOPF   NEW YORK

In Memory of
George Zygmaniak

I gave it a lot of thought. You don't know how much thinkin' I did on it. I had to do somethin' I knew would definitely put him away. And the only thing I knew that would definitely do that would be a gun. And the gun I used—I had to think about usin' that particular gun. See, I have other guns in this house. I have twelve-gauge shotguns with big lead pellets which would be my preference, really. Those are the ones you'd use if you were going to shoot a deer. I wanted to make sure this was done fast and quick. I knew, I felt . . . I'd have one chance to do this. I gave it a lot of thought. You understand? I wanted to make sure he would definitely die.

—*Lester Zygmanik*

June 1973

Lester Zygmanik* is twenty-three years old. He drives a bulldozer. He has lived in New Jersey virtually all of his life—having arrived as an infant among those thousands of postwar immigrants who live here unabsorbed and unacknowledged. Under ordinary circumstances, Lester probably would have lived his life in anonymity. On June 20, 1973, however, under extraordinary circumstances, he committed an act which made him the object of national controversy. He committed a public murder.

Overnight, Lester's strange Polish name was mispronounced by every newscaster on coast-to-coast television. Newspaper headlines read: ZYGMANIK HELD IN APPARENT MERCY KILLING. On radio, Cronkite said, "There, but for the grace of God, go I." Everywhere, the public reacted with indignation, identification, and speculation. An anonymous American had embodied one of the major tragedies of modern life.

Like thousands, I followed the immediate facts through the media. Lester's story haunted me.

On July 3, I flew into Jersey. I spent nearly five months with Lester, his family, and the attorney who defended him for murder, Robert Ansell. Among my own philosophic baggage was a belief in the sanctity of life at any cost, a conviction that an act of violence is irreparable, and an anger at the corruption of human values which runs wild in America. In those five months, all preconceptions shattered. Neither life nor death will permit itself to be boxed into theories or systems of thinking; truth is always contradictory.

Here—from observation, participation, and months of interviews— the events have been recorded, reconstructed, and re-created as they occurred. The story of Lester Zygmanik is uniquely his own.

* Originally spelled Zygmaniak.

I

June 20, 1973
Monmouth County, New Jersey

Along a rocky stretch of eastern seaboard, the Jersey shore borders an Atlantic as gray and treacherous as the lives of the poor in Monmouth County. Here, in June, a vacation is a trip to the boardwalk of Asbury Park, where a room with a view is a view of a Ferris wheel, and endless streams of hard-worked men and women, pale as flounder, confirm a staunch belief in good clean fun. Released from winter's confinement, the blacks and the immigrants emerge from ghettos and farms, and the affluent arrive from Rumson and Deal and East Orange, to mingle where discrepancies are lit by neon and the potential for violence rolls in with the fog.

By the summer of 1973, East Jersey was accustomed to violence. Crime and corruption, barely shrouded in respectability, still ruled vigorously. Disruptions were frequent, tensions flared as bright and swift as fireworks, ferment was a fact of life—still unresolved were the issues that had set Asbury Park ablaze with race riots only three years earlier. Yet, on the night of June 20 the boardwalk glittered, barkers shouted, "Break a bill, try your skill," and those who were likely to meet nowhere else—the disenchanted and the dispossessed— engaged in the common pursuit of organized pleasure.

Not far away was Jersey Shore Medical Center, an undistinguished place—a sturdy, red brick, warehouse-shaped building in the town of Neptune. Inside, it had the joyless look of any other institution. Doctors walked quickly, nurses were preoccupied, and visitors spoke softly, whispering in the presence of pain and the proximity to death. It was a place where life was fragile.

On the night of June 20, no noises from the surrounding ghetto disturbed the halls, though interns and nurses were aware of the dangers of going out for an idle walk and a cigarette. Shortly before 11:00 p.m., the hospital was quiet. Not far away, even the ocean seemed as opaque and spiritless as the amateur seascapes which adorned the hospital lobby. And in the rooms, the rules of life applied: only those patients who could afford windows facing the shore were privileged to listen for an imperceptible lapping of waves.

It was Wednesday. At 10:57, Juanita Johnson, technician, hurried to the third floor, assigned to night duty in Intensive Care. She was young, black, extraordinarily pretty, blessed with high cheekbones, Afro curls, and a soft drawl acquired in Moultrie, Georgia. In Ward 321, she found Robert Blannett, male nurse, completing a patient-check. Blannett, twenty-eight years old, wore gold-rimmed spectacles, a Fu Manchu mustache, and suffered from a slight limp. Together, the two employees went over the charts, murmuring; neither had worked long enough to be inured to tragedy. At 11:00, six critical patients slept—among them, a heart case, a junkie, a recent paraplegic. Within seven minutes, one of the occupants of this quiet ward would be the victim of a murder.

At 11:03, in the corridor, Katherine Kealy, a tidy young registered nurse, was returning a chart to the next ward when she recognized a young man heading toward Intensive Care. She said, "Hello." Katherine Kealy's voice was normally soft and childlike, so when the young man didn't answer, she thought he hadn't heard her.

At 11:05, in the cafeteria downstairs, a young security guard, Alexander Lee Smith, relaxed over coffee with an older colleague, Robert Glick, who had come to relieve him. Both men wore uniforms, pistols, and an air of self-esteem—for a white man over forty and for a black man without a high-school diploma, jobs were scarce. Glick had occupied his position for three months. He considered it man's work—not the best pay, but decent, clean, and steady. For Alexander Smith, the job's appeal lay in the unlikelihood of having to shoot or being shot at; the ill made little trouble.

At 11:06, in Intensive Care, Juanita Johnson greeted the young man as he entered the ward. Again, the young man didn't answer.

Instead, he crossed the room and halted beside the fifth bed, where curtains had been partially drawn. Neither Blannett nor Johnson attempted to stop him. Both took for granted that a hospital was an inviolate place where all were committed to life. The ethic decreed: if the price could be met, life was presumed to be worth saving. Nor was the quality of healing within their domain.

The young man stood there quietly. Blannett and Johnson remained seated at their desk. Had either been paying attention, the young man's reflection might have been seen in a window as he bent over the patient in the fifth bed. Then, an ear-shattering blast rocked the ward.

Katherine Kealy hurried from the corridor toward Room 321, under the impression a bed had collapsed. Inside, Blannett and Johnson rushed toward the patient, believing the respirator had blown. It was Blannett who saw the truncated rifle on the floor. Johnson was the first to observe the gaping wound in the patient's left temple.

The young man shook his head, then turned and walked slowly past Katherine Kealy into the hall.

In the cafeteria, a walkie-talkie summoned Alexander Lee Smith and Robert Glick. They took the stairs. The possibility of violence did not occur to Glick—he assumed that somebody had simply created a "hassle" on the third floor. But Smith, conditioned by generations of Southern black ancestors, paused at the top to ready himself for any contingency. Coming toward him was a young man who appeared to be unarmed, hands visible, walking slowly, making no move to escape. Smith filed a mental description: ". . . a white fellow, wearing a brown felt coat and a flower-colored shirt, about 6 feet, blond hair, long hair . . . in his early twenties, heavyset build." Then several nurses appeared behind the young man, pointing, and one of them called out, "A patient's been shot in the head."

Smith and Glick moved forward.

The young man stopped. "I'm the one you're lookin' for," he said.

"What's wrong?" Smith said.

"I just shot my brother," the young man said.

2

June 17, 1973

He woke feeling cold and damp, and with a sense of something terrible about to happen. So he lay still, trying to figure it out because he believed everything could be figured out. Then pain washed over him, lonely and dark, like the ache of a child—and he was embarrassed by it and a little frightened.

He sat up. Next to him, the girl was asleep. She was young, dark-haired—he couldn't remember her name, only her breasts, and that, like his mother, she had asked too many questions. He saw she was smaller than his brother's wife, prettier, nothing unusual but his brother would have liked the way she looked; he imagined telling his brother how she looked. Then he figured out where he was: in Trenton, her apartment, two flights up a narrow stairway, hot and humid, New Jersey in June. He remembered last night, picking her up in a bar, Saturday night, and not giving her his right name— Lester Zygmanik. Then he realized what the day was—and that the terrible thing had already happened. It was Father's Day. It was four months since his father's sudden death.

The recognition seemed to belong to somebody else. From outside, he could hear the sounds of Sunday traffic, a woman shouting in Spanish, skateboards grating on the sidewalk. Death seemed unreasonable.

The shades were down. His watch said twenty past eight. He noticed that somebody had done a bad paint job, and that the girl had folded his clothes over a chair, making him remember once telling his brother: *The minute you touch a girl, they want to take care of you.*

He got out of bed. In the bathroom mirror, he studied his reflection—fair and blond, a sturdy face, a muscular chest—wearing manhood like an ill-fitting suit, borrowed or handed down. He was twenty-three years old and he drove a bulldozer. When his father was alive, he had worked eighteen hours a day, had laughed all the time, chased girls, felt good all the time, in control. Now, sometimes he had the feeling he might disappear.

Then he saw the girl. She was standing in the doorway, wearing a yellow robe, pale like his brother's wife who never went out in the sun, looking as if she had something to ask him—like, maybe, was she good in bed? He couldn't remember. Instead, for no reason, he remembered the time he had broken his collarbone and his father had cried for a day and a half. They were like that, he and his brother and his father. He didn't know anybody else who was like that.

He splashed cold water on his face, aware that the girl was still watching him. Last night he had told her he was on his way to Canada, cutting out, to get rich. It was only an idea. Sometimes he had peculiar ideas—like feeling his father might be watching him, even though George had said, "Pop's not coming back, kid," and it was only the two of them now, he and his brother.

"Will you write me?" she asked, in a small, nervous voice.

He turned around. He saw what she wanted. She didn't want to be left alone. Everybody was afraid of being left alone.

"I'll call you," he said, knowing he wouldn't but he wanted to please her.

"You don't have the number," she said.

He lied. "I took it off the phone." He didn't like to hurt anybody.

He took highway 33, heading east, going home. Construction had halted for weekend traffic, families going to church. He switched on the radio, a rock station, loud.

Half an hour later, he turned south, winding along the narrow Perrineville road. Inland, the air seemed still and the farms grew familiar, land already scorched by summer. In Perth Amboy, he had spent his summers on the waterfront, member of a gang called the Angels. He had grown up on the streets of an industrial city. Then, four years ago, they had moved to Perrineville, to the eighteen acres where his father had raised nothing, believing land was honorable, of itself, to itself—believing land was a return to what had been lost in Poland to war. Lester saw what it was, woods and scrub, but it was all he had left—the land and his brother.

"Tits—that big," he said, cupping his hands around an invisible basketball.

George laughed. "You swear to God?" In the sunlight, George looked like his father, dark and strapping like his father.

Twenty-six years old, George had been married since he was twenty. His four-year-old son trundled around in the gravel drive on a plastic motorcycle, screaming, "Zoom, zoom!"

"Blonde?" George said.

Lester shook his head. He realized his brother was wearing his navy-blue suit, dressed for church, though George rarely went to church.

"Tall?"

"Not too tall. But *stacked*."

"You're a lucky kid," George said. "I mean, don't get me wrong, you know? I love my wife. But sometimes, like I'm walking down the street and I see this good-lookin' chick, you know? And I think about how it might be, just in my mind, you know? I mean, a man can't get killed for lookin'—right?" Something weary or angry passed over George's face.

"She wasn't that outstanding," Lester said. For no reason, he threw his arms around his brother in an impulsive, brusque embrace.

"Hey, kid, what's the matter?" George said.

From down the road, the church bell in St. Joseph's began to ring. "Happy Father's Day," Lester said.

In the afternoon, the sun burned away his uneasiness. Sweating, he liked the feel of the truck, being in control, moving earth. The truck wasn't as agile as a big machine but it was obedient—and soon the truck would pay for itself, hauling dirt; then they'd buy another secondhand truck, he and his brother.

Next to him, the girl talked constantly in a high, scattered voice. Two and a half years ago, he had met Diane Haus on Friday the 13th. Now, whenever he tried to break it off, she cried and cried.

Not listening to her, he worked until sunset, when he quit to wait for his brother. Then the sky turned red and a light breeze stirred the woods and he knew little Georgie's birthday party was over, so he kept saying to Diane, "You can expect my brother to be here any minute." But a long time went by before he heard the car approaching and saw it wasn't George's car that slowed and stopped on the side of the road. He jumped down from the truck. An aging man emerged from the car, then a big woman in a bright, flowered dress, coming toward him. He recognized Mr. and Mrs. Koprowski, his mother's friends from Perth Amboy.

"There was an accident." Mrs. Koprowski began to cry.

"A motorcycle accident." Mr. Koprowski took out a handkerchief and wiped his eyeglasses.

Lester had an image of his brother's son on the plastic motorcycle. "What happened to little Georgie?"

"It's not little George," Mr. Koprowski said. "It's big George."

Lester felt the ground give way beneath him. "What happened? What happened to my brother?"

"He broke his shoulder." Mrs. Koprowski lapsed into Polish, gesturing and weeping.

"The ambulance took him to Freehold Hospital," Mr. Koprowski said.

"You go home," Mrs. Koprowski said. "You go home and see about your mother."

It was after seven o'clock when he reached the town of Freehold.

The hospital corridors seemed endless and the smell of disinfectant burned his eyes. He found his brother's wife, Jeannie, sitting on a bench, crying. "It's gonna be all right," he said. Jeannie stared at him. He saw she had pulled her long, dark hair into a bun, making her face look thin and sharp, and she was already wearing black.

Looking at her, he felt a profound anger, because if she hadn't failed his brother, then he had, somebody had.

His brother was lying on a cot in the hallway, waiting for X-rays. The doctors were walking up and down, hesitant, avoiding his brother.

He knelt beside the cot and managed to grin. "Listen—that chick, you know? Turns out she's got a sister. Knockers twice as big."

George looked pale and frightened.

"I'll figure out somethin'."

"I want you to go to the doctors," George said. "I want you to find out what's the matter with me."

"Right. I'm gonna do that."

"No lies. I want you to tell me the truth."

"Right."

"I want you to swear to God."

"I swear to God," Lester said.

The first doctor said, "We're not going to touch your brother. He needs an expert." Then an expert came, a bone specialist, who got very excited, moving around, telling people what to do, shouting back and forth in the hallway—it was the first time in his life Lester had ever seen a doctor who wasn't calm. Then the bone specialist said, "I don't want to touch your brother, he needs a neurosurgeon."

After that, the neurosurgeon arrived and there was a lot of confused talking in the emergency room. Then his brother was taken away somewhere, he didn't know where, and he found himself surrounded by doctors, assailed by a feeling of helplessness, wanting to plead: *Do something!*—but the words stuck somewhere below his ribs.

He heard the first doctor say, "I don't understand it. The first X-ray looks all right. But the second one shows the bone in the neck is completely splintered as if it exploded."

The second doctor said, "Your brother has a broken neck."

The third doctor said, "This hospital doesn't have the necessary equipment. He has to be moved to Jersey Shore Medical Center. We'll put him in traction and send him over."

The second doctor said, "I don't feel your brother will ever walk again. I may be wrong, but that's how I feel."

He found his own voice, suddenly loud and angry. *"What are you talking about? Who are you talking about?"*

June 18, 1973

Long before daylight, he was awakened by the howling of the beagles —last night, he had forgotten to feed them. Then he felt the pain and he remembered that last night they had put his brother in traction and moved him to a hospital in Neptune.

He got dressed. Outside, the night was enveloped by fog. In the darkness, he walked the perimeter of the eighteen acres. He fed the dogs. They barked and licked his hands. He said, "I'll work out somethin', right?" Nobody answered him. He tried to pray. He made promises he couldn't keep. Feelings of helplessness frightened him. He pretended to be his father, who had strength and the ability to act. He asked himself what his father would do. For no reason, the loneliness of the girl on Sunday came back to him. Then Monday's sun broke the mist and he took it as a sign that everything would be all right.

On Monday night, he stood beside his brother's bed, feeling odd and weightless as if a wind were blowing through him, moving his life toward some dreaded destination. They had put rods in his brother's head. They had his brother in traction, strapped to a swivel bed. George could no longer move his arms or his legs. And George was afraid. "That's my life," George kept saying. "Twenty-six years, that's my life."

Jeannie wept silently. She seemed as old as his mother, who stood beside the bed, looking frail and stubborn. In Polish, his mother said to George, "You don't worry. We'll take you to Poland. Doctors don't cost money in Poland."

Every time they came to turn him over in the swivel bed, George screamed.

In the corridor, the doctor said they couldn't operate for two or three days, until the swelling went down. The doctor said the operation would cure the pressure, but it wouldn't cure George.

When he got back to the ward, George said to him, "Feel my hands. Feel my feet. Is my body there? I don't know if I'm there or not."

Lester turned his head, trying to avoid his brother's eyes because the message was already there, clear and terrible, and he didn't want to see it.

Jeannie sobbed.

Angrily, he said, "Shut up. He's gonna be all right. You shut up!"

All night, Monday night, he tried to make his mind work, but he couldn't hold on to a thought. He tried to figure out what to do, what a man would do, what his father would do. He kept hearing George say, "All I am is a head."

He tried to imagine what kind of man his brother would be. A man who couldn't work, what kind of man would that be? A man who couldn't have sex, what would that be? He felt what George felt —humiliation and the wish to die.

He tried to think about practical things. The farmhouse and the land were paid for, but taxes were $1,500 a year. Where would he get $1,500 a year? When his father was alive, there had been three of them to keep the place going. When his father was alive, his brother had paid for his share of the food and the gasoline. Afterward, his brother had also paid half of the taxes. Afterward, George had said to him, "We're gonna live for today a little more. We're gonna think a little differently about how far in the future we're gonna live for."

He held his head because it ached so, unable to tolerate his brother's pain and the knowledge in his blood of what was coming.

June 19, 1973

By Tuesday, there were five other patients in Intensive Care. His brother made him keep the curtains pulled. His brother kept saying, "Everything I can feel—hurts."

Lester called the nurse. He said, "Do something. Do something about his pain."

The nurse tried to give his brother the hypodermic in his leg, but George stopped her, saying, "Give it to me in my shoulder so I can feel it."

Jeannie wouldn't stop crying.

In the afternoon, George sent Jeannie away. When she left, George said, "I want you to tell me the truth."

Lester nodded. The words came slowly, painfully.

"You're the man now," George said.

"I'll work out somethin'," Lester said.

"After a while, Jeannie won't want me any more because I'm nothing."

"I'll figure out somethin'," Lester said. He tried to use his father's voice.

Jeannie came back. They sat side by side, next to the bed.

"Did they shave off all my hair?" George said.

"No," Lester said.

"Did they shave my sideburns?"

"No."

"My mustache?"

"No. They didn't shave that off either."

George began to spit up. Jeannie wiped him off and gave him a drink of water.

"Whose little boy is little Georgie?" George said.

"He's yours," Jeannie said.

"Whose little boy is he?"

"He's your little boy."

"You swear to God?"

"I swear to God," she said.

On Tuesday afternoon, they performed a tracheotomy.

Lester paced the corridor. Diane walked with him. He kept saying to her, "It's gonna be all right." For no reason, he wanted to kill her.

In the hallway, the nurses smiled, cheerful and optimistic. He stopped one of them. He said, "Why are they doing this?"

The nurse said, "They're going to operate on his neck tomorrow morning. It's going to be a long operation. They want to make sure he can breathe."

"Why can't they do something?"

"We're doing everything we can."

He prayed, not to God, to his father.

On Tuesday night, he sat beside his brother's bed, listening to the respirator, feeling that the machine was attached to himself. It had a strange rhythm. It went: One . . . two . . . three . . . four . . . then it skipped twice. At times, the machine seemed to turn off completely, to be off for a long time, and he'd begin to worry about whether or not to call a nurse; then the machine would go on again.

His brother's face was disfigured. George's lips curled and he ground his teeth. The nerves in George's head began to jump beneath the skin. Once, George said, "What did you do with that ten dollars?"—and then, "Change the channel."

Lester remembered a film he had seen, *Johnny Got His Gun*, about a soldier with no arms or legs in a hospital bed.

Finally, George woke. The tracheotomy pipe in his throat made it difficult to understand him. "I'm cold," he said. Lester pulled the blanket up around his brother. Accidentally, he knocked the pipe. George began to gasp for air. Lester ran down the hall, calling for a nurse. The nurse replaced the pipe. "Don't leave me alone," George said.

All night, they sat beside the bed. Jeannie was silent, tearless. The nurses came and went, doing nothing for George. Finally, George said, "Hold my hand."

Lester took his brother's hand.

"You know what I want you to do," George said.

Lester shook his head.

"Tomorrow, after the operation, if it's still the same . . ."

"No," Jeannie said. She grasped George's other hand and pressed it against her face.

"I want you to promise not to interfere," George said. "I want you to swear to God."

Jeannie closed her eyes. "We have to pray," she said.

Together, the three of them repeated the Lord's Prayer.

In the silence that followed, George said, "You're my brother. I want you to promise to kill me. I want you to swear to God."

At dawn, on Wednesday morning, Lester left the hospital. He was alone. The parking lot was empty. He could hear the ocean.

For a long time, he stood beside the truck, slowly beating his head against the metal roof. Then he climbed inside and curled up on the front seat and cried.

3

June 20, 1973

At 11:15 p.m., fog wrapped the quiet streets of Neptune, blurring the solitary car that sped along the ocean. At intervals, passing street lamps lit the driver, illuminating clean-cut good looks, a squarish, likable face which vaguely resembled any of television's interchangeable cowboy actors. Around James A. Ward's eyes, however, tiny crisscross lines marked him as a man who had mastered enough removal to fit him for the occupation of detective sergeant in the Neptune Township Police.

Ward's serious expression reflected the urgency of the telephone call that had roused him from home—another brutal shooting. Every police officer had learned the statistics: The rise in violent crime in Jersey was sharpest among the nation's twenty-five largest states; between '69 and '72, violent offenses had nearly doubled. Ward belonged to one of the few law-enforcement agencies in Jersey to enjoy a reputation for efficiency and honor. Investigative reports from Neptune, supervised by men like Ward, were known to be thorough, and the force maintained a close relationship with the community, black and white, so that little occurred without their being aware of it. A predictable attitude accompanied their prestige —any offender was seen as a potential threat to an impeccable record.

Ward parked in the newly built Municipal Complex. City Hall was dark, as were the Courthouse and Neptune High School. Only Headquarters blazed, still vigilant. Walking briskly, Ward entered the dreary, modern, cinder-block building where he stopped to pick up a report from Patrolman Charles A. Jones, the first to arrive at the scene of the crime. Jones, a ruddy, bullish man who had the habit of talking without opening his mouth, said, "It's a bitch," as Ward scanned the report.

> June 20, 11:17 p.m. Upon arrival . . . found suspect locked in custody in the Records Room of Jersey Shore Medical Center. . . . Security Guard Alexander Smith turned over an unspent 20 gauge shell found in the prisoner's pocket. . . . Upstairs, in Intensive Care, lying on the floor, was a J. C. Stevens 20 gauge shotgun, bolt action, approximately 13 inches in length, sawed-off at both ends, the stock and the barrel. The patient appeared to have been wounded at close range in the left temple and is in critical condition. The victim's name is George Zygmanik, age 26, Perrineville, N.J. The subject that was apprehended is Lester Mark Zygmanik, age 23, same address, the victim's brother. . . .

Together, Jones and Ward went down the hall to the Monitoring Room, where closed-circuit television kept an eye on the cells and the hallways. There, Ward studied the screen image of the newly arrived occupant in Cell No. 7. Most new inmates paced, enraged at finding themselves trapped. This one sat passively on the edge of a cot, looking awkward and bewildered. He seemed adolescent, younger than twenty-three, in spite of his size. It was a Slavic face, ordinary, clear-eyed, familiar to Ward, no different from hundreds of immigrant faces in Jersey. Ward watched the prisoner. Whatever the deed, it seldom showed in a criminal's face. It was not surprising that Lester Zygmanik didn't look like a kid who had just blown his brother's head apart. Ward found the idea slightly unsettling.

"Let's go," he said.

When he entered the cell with Jones, the prisoner didn't rise, but remained seated, regarding Ward with a baffled expression.

"How are you?" Ward said.

"Okay."

"Do you need anything? Cigarettes?"

"No."

"It's my duty to advise you that you have the right to remain silent," Ward said, beginning the Miranda warning. His words pierced the peculiar intimacy of the cell. "Anything you say can and will be used against you in a court of law. You have the right to have an attorney present during questioning. If you can't afford to hire an attorney, one will be appointed for you." Ward paused. "Do you understand these rights?"

"Yes."

"Is there anything you want to say?"

"Yes. Is my brother dead yet?"

At 11:43, Detective Sergeant Vincent Martin answered the telephone at home. Called Vinnie by his contemporaries, Martin was ten years older than Ward, a tanned, weather-beaten man whose fierce black eyebrows had prevailed over his graying temples. "I'll be right down," he said.

Martin took Main Street, bypassing the gates of Ocean Grove. Lester Zygmanik was incarcerated in an area which provided penance and absolution for the rest of East Jersey, the state's one historical backlash against sin. Directly after the Civil War, in nearby Long Branch, gold-domed gambling casinos arose to claim the title The

Monte Carlo of America. Reacting against dice-rollers, roulette wheels, and other forms of temptation, the Ocean Grove Methodist Camp Ground sprang up to promote Christian holiness. By 1900 the town of Long Branch had fallen to outlawed gambling and the Depression finished off its golden era—while the revival tents of Ocean Grove survived to become an inspirational community dependent on ninety-nine-year renewable leases from Neptune. Like an old chorus girl subsidizing a nun, the town of Neptune had earned its right to virtue. Martin was a man who understood such contradictions.

At the station, he listened to Jones, read the report, then said to Ward, "I don't want to talk to Zygmanik until we've checked out the hospital."

Martin drove. Most of the windows in Jersey Shore Medical Center were dark. Inside, the hallways echoed. Martin interviewed security guards Smith and Glick while Ward rounded up Juanita Johnson, Robert Blannett, and Katherine Kealy. Then, in the tradition originated by the FBI, Ward became the *hard* cop while Martin turned *soft*, compassionate, fatherly, reassuring the three reluctant witnesses in order to make all facts a matter of record.

In Intensive Care, Ward was prevented from taking photographs because several members of the medical staff were working on George Zygmanik. He was able, however, to get color shots of the victim's mangled temple area and arrangements were made for him to return later to photograph the crime scene.

In the corridor, Martin spoke to Dr. Clement Kreider, George Zygmanik's neurological surgeon. Kreider, a burly man with thinning blond hair and a casual manner, reported that the patient had been involved in a motorcycle accident three days earlier which had fractured his neck. Kreider had seen the patient's brother, Lester Zygmanik, on several occasions and had informed him that George Zygmanik would probably be paralyzed for life. The patient was still alive, though the prognosis for survival was slim.

Outside, in the parking lot, north end, Ward located Lester Zygmanik's vehicle parked directly in front of the emergency entrance. It was a 1969 Dodge, two-door, registration UBT-703. The car was unlocked. Martin's search produced nothing. Ward notified Shafto's Garage and asked that the vehicle be towed in. Upon returning to Headquarters, Martin placed the car keys in the prisoner's property bag. There, he examined the weapon which had been found at the scene of the crime and noted that it appeared to be marked with bloodstains on the stock and the barrel. Martin ordered photographs taken of the weapon. Then Patrolman Jones marked and tagged the shotgun and placed it in the overnight evidence locker to be transported to the New Jersey State Police lab for analysis. Also placed in evidence were the prisoner's shirt, brown jacket, pants, and shoes.

It was after midnight when Ward returned to the cell, accompanied by Martin. Again, the prisoner didn't rise, though in the intervening time he appeared to have grown more nervous and uncoordinated. Ward went through the Miranda warning again. Then he said, "Would you tell Detective Martin what you told me a little while ago?"

"About my brother?"

"Yes."

"My brother asked me to do it and so I did it."

"You did what?" Martin asked gently.

"I shot him."

"Will you make a written statement to that effect?" Ward said.

"No."

"Do you want to call an attorney?"

The prisoner turned to look directly at Ward. "My brother's still alive, isn't he?"

The following afternoon, the sun blazed mercilessly on the bleached-out woods of Perrineville. It was farm country, rutted, unkempt. Inside the Zygmanik house, the kitchen was stifling—a long, narrow, cluttered room dominated by a massive stove, its one window closed, only the battered screen door open to the humid day. At the table, Sonia Zygmanik smoked, a small, soft woman with a chamois complexion and badly bleached hair, her cigarette locked in a blue, arthritic hand. Her daughter-in-law, Jean, tapped nervously on the formica, a bony, kinetic girl whose sparrow-colored hair fell to her waist in commemoration of some half-forgotten joyous memory. She looked sallow and distracted, like an out-of-focus photograph of a girl, staring, talking about George, calling him "my husband" while Sonia, nodding, said *"my son."* In the Zygmanik family galaxy, no one was called by name, only by relationship.

When the telephone rang above the sink, Jean rose and answered it, standing awkwardly, listening as a cultured voice on the other end identified itself. The voice, a representative of Jersey Shore Medical Center, explained the purpose of the call: Since George Zygmanik was soon going to die, wouldn't Jean consider making a contribution to the living by donating her husband's kidney?

Jean began to weep silently. Finally, she said, "No—I don't want my husband mutilated."

4

INVESTIGATION REPORT

Neptune Township Police Dept.
Case No. 73-7360

STATE VS.	ZYGMANIK, Lester Mark White male; age 23 date-of-birth: 2/18/50 place-of-birth: England ht: 5'11"; wt. 200 lbs. blue eyes; lt. brown hair
CHARGES:	Carrying a concealed deadly weapon, 2A:151–41 Murder, 2A:113–1 and 2A:113–2
TIME & DATE & PLACE:	11:07 p.m. June 20, 1973 Jersey Shore Medical Center

EVIDENCE:
1. Black flowered shirt, worn by suspect
2. Brown coat, worn by suspect
3. Maroon pants, worn by suspect
4. Brown socks, worn by suspect
5. Maroon shoes, worn by suspect
6. Sawed-off shotgun used to shoot victim
7. Four vials of blood taken from victim
8. Plastic container with pellets taken from skull of victim at autopsy
9. One spent shell and one unused shell
10. Medical reports from JSMC
11. Autopsy report
12. Photographs of crime scene and victim
13. Statements taken from all witnesses

SYNOPSIS: On 6/20/73, at 11:07 p.m., the Neptune Township Police Dept. received a call from Mrs. Reed RN, Jersey Shore Medical Center, Intensive Care Unit. She reported that a man had been shot by another man.

On the arrival of the officers, they were met by two security guards . . . who found, on the third floor, a white male (later identified as Lester Zygmanik) just about to come down the stairway. He (Lester Zygmanik) stopped them and told them he was the fellow they were looking for. . . .

Both men escorted Lester Zygmanik down to the Emergency Room. . . . Lester stated he had just shot his brother. Lester Zygmanik was searched and a 20-gauge shotgun shell was found. Lester Zygmanik was then locked in the records room until the police arrived. . . .

Found lying on the floor in Room 321, Intensive Care Unit, was a J. C. Stevens 20-gauge sawed-off shotgun, 13″ in length, model 238 bolt action. This weapon was on the floor next to the victim's bed. Also found was one 20-gauge spent shotgun shell. . . .

Lester Zygmanik was interviewed at Police Headquarters, advised of his constitutional rights, Miranda warning.

Lester Zygmanik stated that his brother, George Zygmanik, had a motorcycle accident that had fractured his neck and he was paralyzed from the neck down. . . . Lester said that his brother had begged him to shoot him to put him out of his misery. Lester said he felt very bad about seeing his brother suffering—so he went home and took his 20-gauge shotgun, bolt action, make J. C. Stevens, and sawed the gun down. This occurred in the afternoon on 6/20/73. Lester then stated he returned to Jersey Shore Medical Center about 11:00 p.m. and went to the Intensive Care Unit with the sawed-off shotgun under his coat, and walked into Room 321 past two nurses and over to his brother's bedside. Lester spoke to his brother, told him to close his eyes and that he was going to shoot him. Lester then took the sawed-off shotgun from under his coat and placed it approximately three (3) inches away from his brother's head and pulled the trigger. He then dropped the weapon on the floor and walked out to the stairway where he was met by the two security guards. . . .

. . . On 6/22/73 at 10:30 a.m. an autopsy was performed on George Zygmanik by Dr. Charles Gale, first assistant to the coroner at Monmouth Medical Center in Long Branch. Dr. Gale turned over to Det. Sgt. Martin twenty-four (24) pellets (lead) and a wad that was found inside the skull.

REPORT SUBMITTED BY:

Det. Sgt. JAMES A. WARD
Neptune Township Police Dept.

5

Robert Ansell

There's only one difference between a murder case and any other kind of case and that's the sentence. If a jury comes back "Guilty" in any other criminal case, the Judge can decide what the sentence will be. He orders a pre-sentence report from the Probation Department and they go out and investigate the defendant's background, his family and friends. Then the Judge can give that defendant thirty years, or he can give him one year or ten years. In a murder case, it doesn't matter a damn who the defendant is, or whether or not he's irrevocably a bad guy, there's no choice about the sentence. The minute the jury comes back and says "Guilty" the Judge excuses the jury, turns to the defendant, and says, "I hereby sentence you to life."

6

June 23, 1973

Saturday was hot. At 9:00 a.m., humidity steeped the grimy streets of downtown Asbury Park, where only a handful of tourists idly window-shopped. The district was old, unrenovated, halted somewhere in the thirties when the area emerged from the Depression to reclaim the glory of its bootlegging decade and notions of glamour as obsolete as faded marabou. No longer prime real estate, disregarded by the legendary Sicilian Mafia in nearby Long Branch, the section was owned by white businessmen who had moved their families elsewhere to escape an encroaching third-world city, a population nearly two-thirds black, riddled by misery and bursts of violence.

From such contradictions, the law firm of Anschelewitz, Barr, Ansell & Bonello had melded and grown prosperous.

It was a legal establishment noted partly for professional excellence and partly because its founder, Leon Anschelewitz, had sired an infinitely respectable clan: three sons were attorneys and partners, a fourth interned in Boston—facts which inspired local references to the family as the Jewish Kennedys. Within the self-contained world of middle-class Monmouth County, the title seemed appropriate, particularly since Leon Anschelewitz had invited all American possibilities by changing his four sons' names at birth to Ansell.

On Saturday morning, thirty-four-year-old Robert Ansell parked in the alley beside 513 Bangs Avenue, the unassuming brick building which housed the Asbury Park law offices. A rangy man wearing jeans, a burnt-orange turtleneck, and a recently acquired hairbrush mustache, he was one of the best of that earnest late-fifties generation which had grown up in a climate of political drought and the vacuum created by education designed for those who wished to specialize. In the ten years since Yale, he had built a reputation on a special intelligence, a slightly myopic social conscience, and the kind of humility only very tall men can afford. Like his brothers, he had acquired a reasonable life in that world where men still married their college sweethearts, providing them afterward with 2.5 children, a full-time maid, and the requisite virtues of a husband, which were to be neat, discreet, and at least mildly successful. He had security. He was sustained by an arrangement whereby all the law partners received the same generous monthly stipend. This structure Robert thought of as freedom. It permitted him to take cases that might result in little or no fees. It had allowed him to ignore the question of money when he arranged bail for Lester Zygmanik.

George Zygmanik was dead. Twenty-seven hours after the shot was fired, at the moment of death, the charge against Lester Zygmanik had been changed from "Atrocious Assault" to "Murder." On Thursday, when Lester's black employer, Orlando Linn, had telephoned, Robert had accepted the case immediately. The prospect of wide publicity had deprived him of any sense of nobility—he had been attracted as much by that as by the challenge.

Now he paused on the sidewalk to look for Steve Delaney's car. Last night he had telephoned Boston, where Steve—private investigator, good friend, right arm—had agreed to sit in on the initial interview with Lester Zygmanik.

Traffic was sluggish. Next door, in front of the telephone company, an American flag drooped in the heat. Across the street, a department-store mannequin wore the beaded cocktail dress of the fifties. Upstairs, robes and bikinis were available wholesale. Steve's car wasn't around.

Last night he had described the case to Steve. If a trial was a competitive climb between Prosecution and Defense toward the top of a symbolic Mount Everest, then it looked as if Lester's defense would start at the bottom of the Grand Canyon while the State was already sunning itself at the top.

Inside, only his younger brother, Richard, was working on Saturday. Robert waved from the hall and kept going. In his office, he changed the water in a vase of zinnias, lovingly grown in his own garden—the one spot of color except for the photographs of his three young sons, unsmiling. Everything else was chrome, patent leather, and mirror, conceived by a friend, Nick Grandee, from Manhattan. He had done stubborn combat with Nicky to hang on to the riding saddle which perched in the corner, and the desk—a scarred refugee from earlier days. Now, settling behind it, he made notes while he waited for Lester.

He had not yet met Lester. Yesterday morning, at the Monmouth County Courthouse in Freehold, he had spoken to George's widow, Jean, and to her father, Victor Kazma—taking a hard look at both of them, not as family members but as potential witnesses who might appear in the course of a trial. Jean was tallish, spindly, a nervous, giraffe-like girl with terrified eyes. Victor Kazma, a wiry, pugnacious man, had an unpleasant manner, neglected teeth, and appeared to exert a disturbing control over his daughter. Neither remotely approached a lawyer's dream of the ideal witness.

He had left them alone to confer privately with the Prosecutor's staff. Bail of $25,000 was agreed upon and presented to Judge M. Raymond McGowan. After that, Jean and her father drove back to Perrineville to pick up Lester's mother and the deed to the land, which they posted. Lester's mother, the third prospective witness, spoke hardly any English.

Robert had returned to Asbury Park on other matters when Lester was brought from Neptune to the Freehold Courthouse and released. So the first time he saw his client was when he looked up at a quarter to ten and found Lester standing in his doorway.

First meetings were often ceremonial. No man laid his fate in another man's hands without solemnity. But Lester seemed hapless and adolescent, standing awkwardly, taking stock of the office, adding up the symbols of wealth, education, and status—as if he might have absolute faith in everything he did not know, would never experience, could never attain. What Robert saw was a chubby, apparently remorseless, possibly self-destructive boy who said brusquely, "I don't want to spend one day in jail."

"I can't promise you that."

"Right." Lester's was a blunt face, affable, but amorphous, nothing written on it beyond a vague desire to please. He looked unmothered. "How much time do you think I'm gonna get?"

"I don't know yet," Robert said. "Why don't you sit down."

Lester obeyed silently. Robert noted that the hair was too long and decided that the straggly mustache would have to go. There was something about Lester that seemed offensive—the absence of any repentance. Still, twenty pounds lighter, he might have a certain appeal.

"I've got to ask you a number of questions," Robert said.

"Right," Lester said. "Like you want to know a lotta things. That's okay with me. I don't mind talkin'. But then again, I have to be careful who I talk to about these things."

"You're not going to talk to anybody except me."

"Right," Lester said. "Most people, I know what they want to know. Like they're not really interested in the condition of my brother. They're just interested in, like how'd you get the nerve to do something like that? You know?"

"I know."

"Right."

"I want you to level with me," Robert said.

"Right."

"No lies. The minute I catch you in a lie, you've got yourself another lawyer. Do you understand that?"

"Right."

"Any former arrests?"

"Once I was picked up for stealin' hubcaps."

"Where was that?"

"Perth Amboy."

Robert wrote: *No previous arrests.* "Did you live in Perth Amboy?"

"Right."

"For how long?"

"Seventeen years."

"Were you born there?"

"No. England."

"Can you give me a little family history? Take your time."

Lester spoke haltingly, clumsily. He had a hard time with words, as if boundaries had been constructed around his thinking and he kept running into invisible walls. Once he said, "I wish I knew every word in the dictionary." His tone seesawed between apology and arrogance.

Robert took brisk notes, attempting some kind of chronology:

Father, John Zygmanik, age 56, died of heart attack in Feb. '73. Death appears to have had profound effect on L. He is concerned about his mother, Sonia Zygmanik, age 53. . . . Mother and father are both Polish immigrants. Both captured during WW II—details are vague. . . . George Zygmanik, age 26, was born in Germany. Lester was born in England. Family immigrated to America in '51. . . . Appears to have been a close family. . . .

At 10:00 a.m., Steve Delaney let himself in. He was a compact man in his early forties, slightly rumpled, with a square, good-humored face and an Irish grin. Steve had been a submarine-warfare expert, a construction worker, a prison guard, a cop on the Boston Strangler squad, an investigator for F. Lee Bailey. Robert said, "Steve's an investigator. You'll be seeing a lot of him."

"Right," Lester said.

Robert patched the interruption with a few more simple, non-threatening questions. Lester alternated between bursts of volubility and bouts of silence. Finally, he said, "My father worked too hard. My father worked too much and he thought too much. That's definitely what killed my father."

Robert wrote: *Appears to have been deeply attached to his father. He repeats, "I did what my father would have done."* Robert wrote with clinical detachment, politely, with no thought of anything in common between himself and Lester.

"After my father, my brother was the most important person in the world to me," Lester said.

Robert looked up, directly into Lester's eyes, wondering about the kind of feeling that had provoked a deed as real and hazardous as the one Lester had committed. Had it in fact been an act of bravery? What were the other options? Hostility between the brothers—conscious or unconscious? Did Lester have an eye on his brother's wife? Was Lester in fact involved in an affair with his brother's wife? Was there life insurance? Who was the beneficiary—and how much? What was the land worth—and whose name was it in?

Lester fell silent.

"Why don't you start with the day of the motorcycle accident?" Robert said.

7

Lester Zygmanik

One time when I was a kid, my brother wanted to give me a bike. He stole a bike for me—my brother went all the way to Staten Island and he stole a bike for me. One thing I know—my brother would never lead me to do anything that might hurt me. If he thought I was ever doin' anything that might hurt me, he would right away tell me not to do that. My brother didn't want to live. Like if you read the newspapers and it says he was paralyzed, right? Now, to think of somebody bein' paralyzed is to think of someone who can't move, right? They never wrote in the paper what pain he was in and the things that were happenin' to him, what they were doin' to him. I've given it a lotta thought. I can see where some people who had a brother like mine—or a wife, somethin' like that—it'd be just as easy to run away, you know? They might say, "I just don't want to see it any more," and just take off. But I couldn't do that. Before . . . I used to think about my father. You see, I never expected my father to die. Now . . . I think about my brother and my father.

8

June 1973

Though not required by law, it was conventional in New Jersey for any accused person to be given a preliminary hearing before being indicted. Lester's hearing was scheduled for Friday, June 29. On Thursday, June 28, the Monmouth County grand jury formally indicted Lester for murder without the benefit of any preliminaries.

Angrily, Robert issued the following statement to the press: "Aside from pointing out that Lester maintains his innocence, I am ethically bound not to comment upon the merits of or facts of this case. This does not mean I may not express my displeasure at the procedural course pursued by the Prosecutor. I don't know what moved the Prosecutor to set a speed record in this case. . . ."

The press release made it a matter of public record that Lester had been railroaded through an indictment. On Friday, the morning the item appeared, Robert drove to Jersey Shore Medical Center to make arrangements for interviewing witnesses to the shooting, including Juanita Johnson, Robert Blannett, and Katherine Kealy. There, he was informed by the administrator that the Prosecutor's office had advised the hospital not to cooperate with the Defense and so no interviews could be conducted on the premises.

Irritated, Robert filed a motion—interference with his investigation was unlawful. By then, the Prosecution's tactics had made a point: the Prosecution was going to make nothing easy for the Defense.

Robert knew the figures—every two hours a murder took place in the United States; the average victim was male, between twenty and thirty-five years old; the predominant weapon was a gun. Statistically, Lester had committed an average murder. One fact distinguished him. The man Lester had killed was his brother.

In FBI and police files, Lester was listed simply under HOMI-CIDE. No separate category existed for Lester. Under the law, the murder of a brother was equivalent to any other kind of murder. No distinction was made for Lester. Yet the reality of media response and Prosecutor Carton's irate reaction made it obvious that fratricide remained a special kind of deed, a primal act that would provoke as complicated a range of emotions in a jury as it had in the public, the Prosecutor, and himself.

Robert engaged a graduate sociology student at Princeton, a specialist in "cross-cultural deviants," who ran the subject through a computer and returned the following week with remarkably sparse data.

There were the usual Biblical and mythological references, from which emerged one surprising fact—retribution for fratricide was far from inevitable. At least two creation myths stemmed from the perpetrator of a fratricide—Romulus killed Remus and founded Rome, Cain killed Abel and sired Western man; both were immortalized. There were four other Biblical fratricides—Absalom, Solomon, Jehoram, and Abimilech, who killed sixty-nine of his seventy brothers; none met death as a result of his deed. The precedent was: an eye for an eye rarely applied.

None of it answered Robert's question. What was the nature of the emotions that would be generated in the average juror?

History recorded a long line of royal families who had freely practiced fratricide as a means to the throne, culminating in the Ottoman Empire when Mohammed II decreed, "Whoever may come to the Throne should, for securing the peace of the world, order his brothers to be executed."

The rest was contradictory. Where tribes remained primitive, the man who killed his brother was sometimes exiled, sometimes left to the jurisdiction of the family, and often ignored.

Among the Jibaro Indians, fratricide was considered a partial suicide and was always presumed to be accidental.

In England, in 1954, a twenty-three-year-old die-caster inflicted 124 knife wounds on his mentally disturbed brother. He pleaded self-defense, claiming his brother had previously attacked him with a chopper, a chair, and a knife. He was convicted and sentenced to life imprisonment.

Statistics were almost nonexistent. Fratricide was more prevalent among non-Jews than Jews; family murders occurred most frequently in the Southern part of the United States; in 1890 the rate of fratricide was three a year, though in 1878 four men killed their brothers over "personal matters" in Texas alone.

He was left with his question.

A phone conversation with a sociology professor from Monmouth College elicited the following response: "The family of man has always been called a brotherhood. The common reaction to an instance of fratricide constitutes an emotional reading of the current potential for destruction between brothers everywhere."

He knew it was more personal.

He telephoned a friend in New York, a child psychologist, who gave him an official explanation of the term "sibling rivalry." The premise was that few emerged from childhood without having suffered through the fantasy of killing a brother or sister. Theory explained the act which shocked, fascinated, frightened, and embarrassed as the evocation of this disowned impulse.

Brotherhood was a biological bond and a psychological rivalry. It was a relationship which embodied both the impulse to murder and the capacity to love. Law administered order, civilization imposed restraint, religion sold grace—but the conflict remained unsolved.

Was Lester's deed, then, a touchstone to old warring impulses?

Would each juror feel guilt for his own old wishes? Fear of his own capacity for violence? Pity for Lester as a stand-in for himself?

Would each juror be confronted with his own incompatible impulses, his own ongoing duality?

The answer emerged in the form of a question:

Would Lester, then, represent to a jury the one nightmare reconciliation—a murder where the motive was love?

9

July 1973

The summer continued, hot and moist. July came to East Jersey. In Perrineville, the rolling hills turned brown and the stretches of flatland which had once been potato fields withered under a broiling sun, but the woods and ravines remained dark havens for local ghosts such as David Perrine, descendant of a French Huguenot, pioneer settler and Revolutionary War officer, who was buried in the place which had been named for him.

On the Zygmanik property, summer parched the eighteen acres as winter had buried them. It was derelict land, unused. A small area which had been planted in grass failed to maintain the illusion of life.

On the 26th of June, George's funeral had been held in Perth Amboy. Afterward, the cortege had returned to circle the property before going on to the cemetery. Lester, absent from the services on the advice of his lawyer, had stood at the window to watch the procession arrive and depart.

On the 4th of July, in the town of Perrineville, fireworks had flared. On Sweetman's Lane, the land had remained quiet as the survivors engaged in a simple attempt to resume their lives.

By Thursday, July 5th, the photograph of Lester Zygmanik, looking crude and muscular, ill-mannered and childlike, ceased to appear

in the *Asbury Park Press*. On Thursday, reporters no longer tres-
passed the land or invaded the site where he operated a bulldozer
for O. Linn Excavation. And at four o'clock, when Lester picked up
the mail, he found the flood had diminished to less than half a
dozen letters—anger and sympathy, one small check, and a perfumed
note from an airline stewardess who wondered if he ever got to
Queens.

At home, after a beer in the shade, he set up the ladder and,
sweating, continued the task of painting the two-story house barn
red, his transistor on the roof playing rock until dusk. Then his
mother came out to empty the clothesline and his brother's widow
collected her four-year-old son, and the beagles started to howl from
the dog shed as the light disappeared.

In the falling darkness, he handled the beagles with big, gentle
hands, calling each by name. The newspapers had recorded his au-
dacity and violence; none had reported his love for the dogs. On the
night of June 20, given a choice, he would have killed his prize bitch
instead. He had one regret. Two weeks ago, on the night of June 20,
afterward, he had meant to stop at his father's grave in the cemetery
behind St. Joseph's church and say: "Take care of my brother."

He knelt for a long time, playing with the dogs. Then he rose and
looked out toward the woods, frowning. He felt himself to be the
same person he had been before. He did the same jobs, he thought
the same thoughts. So why had Ansell made an appointment for him
with a psychiatrist?

I O

Robert Ansell

*As far as Lester is concerned, I'm not sure what I feel about him,
personally. I find myself going back and forth. I mean, there are*

times when I feel he's too scheming, he's too goddamn aware and wants to know the kinds of things he really shouldn't want to know —this is, if he felt the way he says he did. He just badly wants to see the autopsy pictures, for instance. Then there are other times when he's boyish and charming and he gets to you.

Legally, we're at the bottom of a well. The law is stacked against Lester. Any prosecutor is aware there's going to be a lot of subliminal shit—emotions—going on in that courtroom and he'll cover that. What I'd really like to do is try this case on evidence. That's a difficult decision to make because you've got a bleeding-heart case and so why mess around with evidence? It's dangerous to that extent. It's also premature. You never know what you're going to find when you investigate—or what's going to be important.

For instance, in 1972 I was involved in a murder case where a child died. I defended the wife—somebody else had the husband. Steve was on the case, too. As we investigated the case, we found out her husband was a Satan-worshiper. He dressed up in a cape and recited the Lord's Prayer backward three times over a candle, and all that kind of business. I discovered this when I was taking an ordinary history from her. I found out they had four dogs, two cats, and a mouse, pets at various times that had died. I started out asking her what happened to the first dog. She said, "He died. My husband stabbed him. Then we got another dog." I asked her what happened to that dog. She said, "Well, we were out walking on the ice and the dog kept slipping, so my husband picked him up and threw him to the ground and he broke his leg. Then he didn't walk very well with a broken leg and so my husband got mad and stabbed him. Then we got a cat." What happened to the cat? "My husband strangled the cat." What happened after that? "We had a mouse, and the mouse got out one day and my husband got so mad, he drowned the mouse. In a bucket of water. He felt sorry after he did that, so he took a battery and he hooked up two wires and he tried to get the mouse's heart going again. But it didn't work." After that, they got another cat, which the husband stabbed. The case was really sick. He would beat her. All kinds of crazy things. We ended up testifying for the

State against her husband. The homicide charges were dismissed against her. The really crazy thing was that the husband worked for a veterinarian. He used to bring home ether. He used to give himself ether at night, to go to sleep. He had trouble sleeping.

I I

Poem written to Diane Haus,
August 1970

> *For some time I have had my doubts*
> *But now I know you would be hard to live without.*
> *I want you to be my lover*
> *For without you there could be no other.*
> *If ever you were to leave me*
> *The saddest day of my life it would be.*
> *And with the love we have going*
> *I hope forever it keeps on growing.*
> *And the days when I'm feeling blue*
> *I know your love will see me through.*

From the One Who Really Loves You

Lester

12

July 7, 1973

The problem nagged at Robert Ansell's sleep, woke him at dawn, and stayed with him as he showered and dressed. In the living room, early morning light streaked through glass walls, across pale floorboards, striking velvet and lucite and the sleeping apricot standard poodle named Sascha. The question remained unsolved.

It had begun with the Zygmanik police report, a certainty of something not right, some discrepancy he couldn't locate. Then work had pursued him and not until yesterday, Friday, had he pinned it down to the last paragraph, the autopsy report: *Dr. Gale turned over to Det. Sgt. Martin twenty-four (24) pellets (lead) and a wad that was found inside the skull.*

Last night, he had driven out to Perrineville and had returned with a shotgun shell, Lester's, a duplicate of the one Lester had used to shoot George. Alone in his office, he had examined the shell—an ordinary 20-gauge shell—spilling its contents and counting the pellets. There were more than a hundred pellets. The question had taken shape, loud and clear: Why, if Lester had fired at a range of three inches, did an autopsy show only twenty-four pellets in George Zygmanik's skull?

It was Saturday. Arlene slept. The three boys had spent the night with his mother, the Jamaican maid had not yet emerged from her quarters, and Barney, the black handyman, had not yet arrived to paint the outside beams. In the quiet, Robert thought about Lester. Last night, in his own surroundings, Lester's fear had emerged, as tangible as the poverty of his daily existence. The house had no heating system. The family, all of them, occupied rooms in the cellar, warmed in winter by the kitchen stove. Last night, at the kitchen table, drinking a beer, still dressed in the undershirt he had worn on the bulldozer, a small gold crucifix around his neck, Lester had seemed oddly heroic as he obstinately repeated, "I did the right thing."

In his greenhouse, Robert checked out the seedlings: tomato plants, daisies—hearty, sturdy, non-exotic growths. He had built the greenhouse as a private retreat. Flowers didn't talk back. They responded to care and feeding by blooming silently.

In the yard, he picked a handful of zinnias. Overhead, a mockingbird squawked, making noises like last night's cocktail party, where he had arrived late. Last night, from his office, he had telephoned Boston and asked Steve to come in. In an hour, he would lay it on Steve: What happened to seventy-five shotgun pellets?

He took Ocean Avenue. One block east, he drove alongside the sea. He drove badly, thinking about Lester, past the great Mae West houses that had originally been summer homes for German banking Jews—turrets and gables and porticoes embalmed for three-quarters of a century against a coffin-gray sky. For himself he had built a glass house, one of the few modern houses in Deal. He was part of its year-round community, one of its two thousand inhabitants—second-generation Italian Catholics and Russian Jews, third-highest mean income in the country, no blacks. Deal's elitism had been lately disrupted: an entire block of Syrian Jews from Brooklyn had recently moved en masse, flaunting their wealth and committing the cardinal sin, "noticeability." Deal, humorless, felt invaded.

In Asbury Park, he found Steve in the coffee shop, tackling breakfast. Steve said, "Have some eggs. You're too damned skinny."

"No, thanks," Robert said. "I've just had thirty-four years of chicken soup."

Steve Delaney liked to say his father was looked down upon for marrying an Italian, his mother was looked down upon for marrying an Irishman, and the sum of two cultures was less than either and greater than both. He understood he had emerged from this unlikely union with passion, humor, curiosity, a fascination with the macabre, a love of tall tales, and rampant guilts. He had married young, had been married for eighteen years, had recently left a wife and nine children, saw it as an escape from a boiler factory for which he would pay in hell. At the age of forty, he identified most with his Italian grandfather, a husky old Roman with a white mustache who had served beer, boiled eggs, and wit in the tavern behind which Steve's family had lived. The old Roman had been as convinced that goat's milk built muscles as he had believed in his own version of World War I: "The General rode up to my tent in the evening," the old Roman would say, "and the General said, 'Peter, I'm tired.' So I said, 'Come on in, General.' And the General came into my tent and I gave him wine and cheese and we talked all night. And when the sun came up, the General knew exactly what to do with the battle. . . ."

Steve waited while Robert fooled around with the zinnias. Steve had known Robert for years, knew Robert was capable of rushing him through breakfast and then taking his time. Finally, Robert said, "I want to try something out on you."

"Shoot."

"Suppose George Zygmanik didn't die as a result of the shotgun wound? Suppose he died from other causes?"

"Then Lester would be guilty of assault, not murder?"

"Right."

"What other causes?"

"George's medical records show he had pneumonia. Why couldn't he have died from pneumonia?"

"Because no jury's going to buy it."

"Okay. On Sunday, June 17, the day of the motorcycle accident, George could shrug his shoulders. By Monday, he couldn't. On Sunday and Monday, he could breathe on his own. By Tuesday, he needed a tracheotomy to breathe. What does that mean to you?"

"He was deteriorating."

"Right."

"What are you trying to say? That the original injury from the accident caused his death?"

"It's a medical possibility. George was shot in the temporal lobe of the brain, which has little to do with life-sustaining function—that's why he lived for twenty-seven hours after the shooting. The vital life-sustaining center of the brain is the medulla, located directly above his original injury, and the damage could have crept up."

"I'm a juror," Steve said. "I'm even an intelligent juror who understands everything you just said. And you know what I'm thinking? I'm thinking: that poor guy was in terrible shape and the shotgun blast didn't make him feel a helluva lot better."

"No credibility?"

"Zero."

Robert lowered himself behind the desk and took his time going through his papers.

"I'm on a case," Steve said. "Socialite's body found floating in the river wrapped in her dining-room rug. You didn't get me down here to try out a theory you knew up front was going to alienate a jury."

"I like your company."

"At fifty bucks an hour?"

"Twenty," Robert said. "Arlene'll throw in room and board."

"Your own money again?"

"The Zygmaniks don't exactly qualify for Dun and Bradstreet."

"I'll settle for expenses."

"Who's going to pay your child support?"

"Sold," Steve said.

"It's the autopsy report," Robert said. "Two points. Number one —a wad was found inside George Zygmanik's skull. What would that be?"

"Might be plastic."

"What kind of plastic?"

"In a shotgun shell, behind the pellets, there's a piece of plastic. When you fire the gun, the powder ignites and the plastic forces the pellets up. It's a split-second thing. The plastic usually disintegrates. But, at that kind of close range, it's possible the plastic lodged in the skull."

"Then you think the allegation that the shotgun was fired at a range of three inches is accurate?"

"I'd say that was accurate."

"Number two," Robert said. "They only found twenty-four pellets in George's skull."

"From a twenty-gauge shell?"

"That's right."

"That's impossible," Steve said.

"Could it have been a defective shell? A misfire?"

Steve shook his head. "No."

"Would Lester remove most of the pellets?"

"I don't know."

"What would he gain by that?"

"I don't know."

"We're going to find out," Robert said.

13

Lester Zygmanik

I do a lotta thinkin'. I know a lotta things. Like you might say I was brought up in a city, Perth Amboy, where I seen a lotta things, you know? I done some wrong things—but I used my head when I did them to make sure I wasn't caught. That was the main thing, not gettin' caught.

Like I always wanted to make it, right? Like I needed money. When I was in high school, I was sixteen and I used to go to companies and tell 'em I was eighteen. Like I was a janitor. I used to fix machines at Revlon. I used to cut my last class, shoot down to work, get out of work at eleven o'clock, go home, go to sleep, go back to school. I gave my paycheck to my mother. I was bringin' home a bigger paycheck than my father. I think he was bringin' home ninety or a hundred dollars a week, and I was bringin' home a hundred and twenty. But I still needed money, you know? So I got diet pills from a doctor and I sold them. And I used to steal copper—go to the boxcars, get the copper out of the trains, and sell it. Then I decided to rob copper right out of the Anaconda Copper Company. It was a big thing. It was the middle of the night and I had to swim a river and go over this big barbed-wire fence. I went right inside the company. They had these big slabs of copper. That was my big dream. But I couldn't budge them—I wasn't too old, maybe fourteen, fifteen. But while I was in there, I had to get something. You see, this was a big thing I really planned out. So I saw they had these big coils of wire—each one must have weighed about fifty pounds. I picked 'em up, and I found a place where the fence didn't meet flush with the ground, and I threw about ten or twelve of them into the water so they'd be submerged. Then I got a couple of friends and my brother. I said, "Wait till you see what I've got, pal." We took these things out of the river and we had them all lined up on the beach. Then the cops came. But they didn't catch me or my brother. I figured it out. When a guy ratted, I told them I found the copper on the beach.

I think things out. Like with my brother—I thought about unpluggin' the oxygen machine. But then I thought this machine must be definitely rigged up so if it's shut off or it clicks off, there's gonna be a buzzer or something. That kind of thing, I thought about. Like I said, I think things out.

14

July 7, 1973

The desolate land went by, broken by woods and an occasional farm. It was the hilliest region in Monmouth County, menial land, where crops came hard—blueberries, parakeets, eggs, Jersey corn, and tomatoes. Some grew nothing, as if land were honor and honor were land. Names on the passing mailboxes were Russian, Polish, and Czech— survivors and casualties of Ellis Island, World War II, savage winters, and common dreams.

Robert drove. Steve was silent as he ferreted around for the thing that was bothering him.

Thirty years ago, after failing the fourth grade, Steve had been taken out of parochial school and sent to live with a German aunt. It was World War II. The aunt had come from Hamburg. He had collected magazine pictures of submarines and battled every neighborhood kid who called his aunt a Nazi spy. A woman doctor named Rosie Draper had blamed his appendicitis on too much peanut butter —he was taken to Cape Cop to recuperate. It was the summer the Ruth McGurk slaying occurred on the Cape. He had sneaked into the empty cottage and sat there a long time trying to figure out what the murderer had done. It had marked the beginning of an instinct for aberration. He had become a crime-scene expert. His talent was to sit quietly in the place a criminal had vacated, identify with the most corrupt, the least tolerable, reconstruct the specifics of violence, and emerge with a theory as neat and concise as a housekeeping budget—his own innocence somehow retained.

Now he found himself going back to '71, to the time he had worked with Robert on a murder appeal. The client had been a young woman convicted of manslaughter in the death of her three-year-old son, caused by burns and unhealed wounds. The original trial had turned on the medical examiner, who testified that an autopsy showed a hole in the child's skull big enough to put his little finger through. Robert had questioned the autopsy. The child had been buried for two years. Robert decided to dig up the body.

Together, they had flown into Boston, where they picked up a local medical examiner, purchased a new casket, paid a funeral director $150 to rebury the remains, hired a gravedigger, and invaded the grave. Steve had taken photographs. When the casket was opened, the child's head had come off in the hands of the medical examiner, not much left but the skull. But the long shot had paid off—not even a hairline fracture was found, much less the hole described at the trial. In the resulting fallout, the original medical examiner had been dismissed for incompetence.

What was bothering Steve was why hadn't Robert considered the obvious solution: an autopsy error? Seventy-five shotgun pellets lost or mislaid?

He raised it. Robert took a moment to think it over. Then he said, "I don't think so."

At the top of the rise, Robert drove past St. Joseph's church, a small, stucco, cave-like structure of vaguely Gothic design, the first Catholic church in the area. Behind it, in the meager cemetery, George Zygmanik was buried next to his father.

Last Saturday, Steve had said, "I've seen a lot of conflicts resolved in blood. You have to work backward. What does a murder resolve?"

Neither of them knew the answer to that.

Robert had his own questions. From where had the daring come— to commit an act which had been both cold-blooded and passionate and, above all, individualistic? At the other end of it, why, if the murder had been motivated by love, had Lester chosen so violent a method? Last Saturday, he had felt that every word Lester spoke, every gesture, had been copied from something, aimed at projecting some naïve version of manhood. How did that fit in?

A hundred yards beyond the church, he turned in at the yellow mailbox. A gravel road sloped down through woods. At the bottom, in a bowl-shaped clearing, the house rose, partially painted New England red. Robert parked in the gravel. Sonia Zygmanik appeared at the top of the cellar stairs, a small, benign woman holding a cigarette, a three-legged Chihuahua yapping at her heels. To Steve, Robert said, "You take her."

"You come," Sonia said. She led Steve across the gravel. She wore ill-fitting slacks and a neon-pink sweater from which her arms emerged, aging flesh. Her grip on his arm was surprisingly firm. She stopped at a bed of flowers that had bloomed and died. "My Georgie," she said, weeping silently. He understood that the garden had belonged to George. He understood also that she had an instinct for drama. Robert had found her confused and grief-stricken. Steve saw her as self-dramatizing and tenacious.

"It's a pretty garden," he said. He watched her gauge his response. Her face was like wrinkled tissue, faded, but something of the girl remained, some dream kept intact, and the loss of both husband and son had not diminished it.

Her tears quit suddenly. In a strangely imperious tone, she ordered him to accompany her. She gave him a tour of the eighteen acres, talking in broken English about her husband, John. Steve listened, unable to understand all of it, but realizing she was proud of the land—and felt she had married beneath her. Periodically, he glimpsed a look of peasant shrewdness and some hidden source of superiority. He didn't attempt to question her. Yet, when the house was in sight again, she stopped, folded her arms, and said, "Okay. You say. What you want?"

"I want to see where Lester kept his guns."

She shook her head. "No," she said. "Enough guns."

In the kitchen, the day's heat lingered, oppressive.

"Where's Lester?" Robert said.

"I don't know." Jean continued to wash dishes without looking around. "I think he went somewhere with Diane."

Robert sat at the formica table. A coffeepot perked—glass, with gold stars on it. A fly buzzed crazily over a bowl of sugar cubes. In the absence of voices, exhaustion pervaded the room, as if witness to a life where all had been bearable and nothing had been rewarding.

He calculated the living arrangements. The kitchen was in the cellar, as were the bedrooms. Upstairs, two floors were unoccupied. The one bathroom was at the end of the kitchen, the one telephone was over the sink. Sonia's bedroom was the family passage to everything. Nobody in the household used the phone, the bathroom, or got a drink of water, without Sonia's knowledge. But she claimed to speak little English and to understand even less, so was the toughest witness to interrogate. He had left her to Steve. Jean was easier. She seemed tenuous and distraught, on the verge of blurting something out—but she wouldn't turn around.

"I have to ask you a few questions," Robert said.

Jean shook her head. "I already told you everything I know."

"An ordinary twenty-gauge shotgun shell holds approximately a hundred pellets," Robert said. "The autopsy found only twenty-four in your husband's skull."

He saw Jean's back stiffen. Finally, she turned. Fierce, penciled eyebrows gave her a startled look. He could feel her fear. "I don't know what you're talking about," she said. Behind her, dishes clattered. Robert saw her hands were trembling.

"I want to help Lester," Robert said gently. "I want to help you. You've had a bad break. I understand what you're feeling. I know your son will grow up now without a father. . . ."

Jean stared at him. Tears sprang to her eyes. "I'll never get married again," she said. "I'm just going to take care of my son. My husband would never want another man raising my son." She bit her lip. "Tears hurt the dead." She moved toward Robert, carried along by her own words. "People say the dead can't come back. My father-in-law, he walks here at night. We heard him on Valentine's Day. And one time I was driving on this lonely road at night and I saw my grandmother. She said, 'Pray for me, Jeannie.' The dead want us to pray for them. Do you believe that?"

"Yes."

"My husband—he told me to pray for him to die. When I saw him in the hospital, he said, 'Jeannie, pray for me to die.' How can you pray for your husband to die?" She twisted her hands. "Now, every day I go to the cemetery and I pray for him." She moved close to the table. "You're not a Catholic, are you?"

"No."

"I'm a Catholic," she said, "but when I die, I'd rather be cremated. I think about what happens to you under the ground, how you look—I know it's against being a Catholic, but I'd still rather be cremated." She perched on a chair, tentatively, ready to flee. "You're a Jew, aren't you?"

"Yes."

"Jews are smart," she said. Terror emanated from her, reminding Robert of a girl in high school who had become a novitiate, a morbid, frenetic girl who had lived on fear, hysteria, and revelations. The girl back then had come from a violent home.

"I want to help you," Robert said. "But I can't—unless you cooperate."

She sent him a bleak look. "I don't know," she said.

"I want you to take me out to the dog shed," he said. "I want you to show me the spot where Lester sawed off the gun."

She shook her head. He could feel her despair. Finally, she said, "All right."

In an alcove under the kitchen counter, the doll was propped—no hair, blank eyes, a head too big for its body. Sonia explained it to Steve. In 1951, when they came to America, a friend of Sonia's found eighteen-month-old Lester too beautiful to be a boy, and so gave him the doll. Sonia called the doll Suzannah. For many years, Lester slept with Suzannah. Then, when Lester was four years old and mischievous, Sonia used Suzannah to spank him and the doll broke. Another friend replaced the body. For twenty-two years, Sonia Zygmanik had kept the doll.

The photograph album was open on the kitchen table. She began to select pictures for Steve. It didn't take long for the album to telegraph its message. Captured in Kodak color, the *family* was god, religion, ethic, totem, and beast.

"Let's take a look at Lester's guns," Steve said.

"No." She shook her head. Then she understood he would go without her.

She took him upstairs. On the wall, one shotgun remained, twelve-gauge, for killing large animals. There was a box of shells. Steve went through it and found nothing. He asked to see Lester's bedroom—it was the only occupied room on the upper level, adjoining what was meant to be a dining room. No bigger than a storage closet, with one tiny window, the room was completely filled by a single bed, a television set, a beagle trophy, and an icon of Jesus. In the bookcase head-board was a stereo set with earphones. The room had no closet. Lester kept his clothes directly off Sonia's bedroom. There, Steve went through the simple belongings and found nothing. On the way back through Sonia's bedroom, she showed him her color television set, won in a church lottery for fifty cents. On it was a photograph of George, at nineteen, in his army uniform. In the top drawer of the bureau were Lester's long blond childhood curls.

Outside, Robert crossed the grass with Jean. He could feel her uncertainty. Grief, frustration, and sorrow were buried in fear. "It's a nice piece of land," he said.

"I hate it," she said. "This grass, this five acres, they cleared it by hand, the three of them—my husband and Lester and my father-in-law. They did everything together. It was like they *needed* each other. Then my father-in-law passed away and my husband couldn't tell his mother or his brother, 'I have my own life'—he couldn't do that. My husband and Lester had to work to keep this place going so his mother wouldn't lose it."

Robert said nothing.

"I used to want my own," Jean said. "But me and my husband never lived alone except in Maryland when he was in the army. And even then my husband wanted to come home all the time. Every weekend. Even though I was working in a boot factory and all I made was fifty dollars a week and it cost twenty-two dollars to drive back and forth to Perth Amboy with gas and tolls. But my husband always told me, wherever his father goes, that's where he's going." She stopped. "My husband had his motorcycle accident on Father's Day," she said. Her voice frayed. Robert felt the question in it. He was not equipped to answer.

The dogs were penned. Jean quieted them. It was a homemade shed, makeshift, chicken-wire. The clearing was surrounded by trees. Robert opened an empty pen. Inside were sacks of dog meal. Then he examined a dilapidated grooming table, the most likely place to anchor a shotgun in order to saw it. He knelt and looked over the ground underneath. When he rose, he said, "What happened to the pieces of the sawed-off barrel?"

"I don't know," Jean said. He knew she was lying. She seemed suddenly limp, beaten, like a rag doll dragged around by a malicious child.

"Who feeds the dogs?"

"Lester. Sometimes my mother-in-law." Her face turned pale, broken. He felt her resistance move in, then away. He felt the weight of her burden.

"Don't conceal evidence from me," he said quietly.

She didn't answer him. He could feel her wrestling with the question of trust. He took her choice away, suddenly.

"It's late," he said. "I have to get back to Asbury Park." He turned around and began to walk.

She let him get as far as the edge of the clearing.

"Wait . . ."

He turned around. "What is it?"

She made a helpless gesture. Then her hands fell limp at her sides. The words came slowly at first. Eventually, they rushed from her in a torrent. She told him what happened on the night of June 20. She told him what had happened to seventy-five shotgun pellets.

15

Jean Zygmanik

On Wednesday night—I don't know what time it was—I was downstairs. I heard Lester go upstairs and then I heard him go outside. Then he came back in and he sat down and started reading the newspaper. Outside, the dogs were barking. So my mother-in-law went out to give the dogs some water. Then she came back in and said, "Jeannie, come outside, I want to show you something. Lester took a gun out by the doghouse." I said, "What are you trying to tell me? That Lester's going to take a gun to the hospital?" Lester just sneered. I got the flashlight. Me and her, we walked out there. She took me to the doghouse where he keeps the food. I opened it. I saw the pieces—and the saw. Oh, my God—I started shaking inside. I went back to the house and I said, "Lester, what are you going to do?" He said, "Do you want to see George look like that for the rest of his life?"

I said, "No, but I've got hope. You have to pray."

Then he asked me for a candle. He said, "Where's a candle?" I said, "Upstairs, in the garage, there's a candle." I didn't know what he wanted the candle for.

His mother's just sitting there. And I keep saying to Lester, "I want to see the other part of the gun." Finally, he went outside and I'm sitting there in shock, and he came back in the house and he took the other part of the gun and he threw it on the table. My son saw it and he wanted to grab it. I picked it up and put it on my mother-in-law's bureau.

Then Barbara came from Perth Amboy. I was going to go back to the hospital and my mother-in-law won't stay alone. It was Barbara's motorcycle my husband was riding when he had the accident. They went to high school together. I said to Barbara, "He's got a gun. I don't know what he's going to do." Then the phone rang. It was Linn—Lester's boss. Lester talked to Linn on the phone. Barbara nudged Lester while he was on the phone. She said, "What are you going to do?" She's a big girl, Barbara. But Lester got mad and pushed her—and kept on talking to Linn.

Then he got off. He went upstairs and got the shell. He came back to the kitchen and he started emptying the shell into the ashtray. And he had the candle. He lit the candle and he melted wax into the shell. Then he put some of the pellets back. I said, "I'm going to call the police." He said, "Jean, you're going to the hospital with me." I said, "If you take that, I'm not going."

He went to get his jacket. When he came back, he said to Barbara, "Would you want to live like that?" Then he put on the jacket and he stuck the gun in his pants. He asked me if I could see it. I said, "What are you doing?" He said, "I'm doing this for George." And then he went. He just went.

His mother was laying on the bed. She says she was sleeping. She wasn't. We weren't whispering. It was hysterical. I think she was in shock, because after he left she was quiet, too quiet. I didn't know what to think—she was laying there quiet.

16

Lester Zygmanik

This was Saturday, Saturday night. It was the night before my brother had his accident. And I met this guy, this friend of mine, Al Harper, and he told me to meet him at this bar around twelve o'clock. I'm supposed to be goin' steady with Diane, so I made up something to tell her. I think I told her I had to drop her off and get some sleep because I had to work on Sunday. I did go to work on Sunday because I was working when my brother had his accident.

Anyway, a little after twelve I got to this bar. On weekdays if we go out, we meet at Shay's in Englishtown, or at the Sportsman's Inn, route eight, halfway between our houses. But that Saturday night we went to the Manor, on route one thirty.

It's a big place. Like it looks like a big trailer. There's a pawnshop next door. A couple of blocks away, there's housing developments going up. I notice things like that.

When I got there, Al hadn't showed up yet. So I started lookin' around, you know. They've got seven bars in that place, all floodlighted. Like it's a weekend factory. They get you ready to go back to work on Monday morning. Like there's a big rock band, loud —and tapes and a disc jockey for intermissions. A lot of neon on one wall, except the dance floor's dark, you know? On another wall they're showin' you slides—candid shots of the customers. I watched that a while. Then I stopped at one of the bars. There's a girl sittin' there, not too good-looking, not my type, a legal secretary. Like she comes there every night—it's part of her daily routine. She was crocheting some kind of blanket and she said, "The people here have a lot of class, they buy you a drink before they hand you a line." I wasn't going to buy her any drink. So she said, "The men here are just lookers and goers. They come and they look and they go." Like she says the same thing to everybody. I told her, "Nobody comes to the Manor looking for a wife." I'm definitely not interested in girls who are available to everybody.

So I was lookin' around again, and I had a couple of dances with different girls. It's easy for me. Like if a girl rejects me or I get turned off right away, I just say, "Good-bye, I'll see you later," and I move on to the next one. The Manor is a good place to look for girls. Nobody there is more than twenty-five years old.

So when I came back to the bar, there he is, Al, sittin' alone. So we started talkin'. Al's a talker, you know. Like the other day, I guess a couple weeks after George's accident, I was tellin' Al that I don't sleep too good lately. I can never get to sleep any more until after two a.m. And Al said, "Maybe it's because George passed away after two a.m.—maybe you stay awake to see about George." Al's a school-teacher, definitely rich, smart, and his brother's a Wall Street law-yer, but I don't let Al do my thinkin' for me. I think things out for myself, like I was tellin' you before. Like figuring I wouldn't be able to saw off a twelve-gauge shotgun to bring it into the hospital with-out bein' noticed. I also fixed up the shell. You see, these are the things it took me a lot of time to think about. So I definitely don't listen to Al. Like I met Al at the Holiday Beagle Club and what he likes to talk about is dogs. He was in Vietnam, artillery, but he doesn't talk about that. Not like an infantry guy I know—he used to shoot up people over there, do a job on 'em, then take pictures to show back in the States. The problem with this guy Al is he doesn't like to move around, you know? And I don't believe in this business of sittin'. I was lookin' for action that night. Everybody's talkin', comin' on, tryin' to be somebody. I'm movin' around. This one guy, he's spaced out, he says to this chick, "Watergate sucks. If these guys were cheatin' on their wives, they'd get caught." She's wearin' a tight sweater, bare-midriff type, but she's not too good-looking.

So I come back and Al's still there alone, and the bar is pretty full. I'm sittin' there and this one girl on the opposite side of the bar I noticed, you know. She was wearin' this satin blouse, cut pretty low, cleavage. And I said, "Al, look at the tits on that one." Like she wasn't definitely what I was lookin' for that night, but it was gettin' late and I needed action. No way I was gonna know the next day my brother was going to have his accident, right? So I'm thinkin' about how to handle this when—I don't know what happened but she just looked at me and I waved at her. And for some reason she just walked right up to me. I bought her a drink and I started talkin' to her. She was sayin' something to her friend about they had to get home. So I said, "Don't worry, I'll give you a ride home."

When we got in my truck, I just put my hand on her breast. She seemed to like that, you know? Which was all right with me. Like the only outstanding thing about her was the size of her breasts. Her name was Michele. I don't know her last name. She lived in Trenton. She told me she couldn't take livin' with her mother and father, so she moved out. She was goin' to school and livin' alone. I took her home and I spent the night with her. I liked the way she looked. She was a good-looking girl. But I didn't like the way she thought. I didn't like the fact that I could get in her pants as soon as I met her.

I didn't get home the next day until about ten o'clock. I had this job to do at noon for Linn's brother-in-law. My mother started on me in Polish—she doesn't like it when I stay out all night. My brother was on his way out, like he's goin' to church. It was Father's Day. It was the last time I saw my brother on his feet.

17

Robert Ansell

The average person responds to the drama of a trial, especially a murder trial—the life-and-deathness of it. But everything, including the verdict, is subject to the boundaries of the law and, no matter what kind of defense a lawyer presents, he can't change that. You have to work within the framework. That's why Jean's story, if she's telling the truth, is unbelievably damaging. You have to understand Lester's charge—Murder One. That's legally defined as a murder with malice aforethought. What that means is, in order to convict, the Prosecution has to prove Lester entertained three necessary mental processes: premeditation, deliberation, and willfulness. Then you have to define those:

Premeditation is the formation of a plan to kill.

Deliberation is the weighing of the pros and cons of that plan, which weighing need take only a few seconds.

Willfulness is the intentional carrying out of that plan.

Now—according to Jean—on the night of the shooting, Lester selected a rifle that wasn't powerful enough for the job he meant to do. So, in addition to the damaging act of sawing the gun, he also emptied a shell and packed it with candle wax, which (a) kept the pellets from spraying, (b) compacted the explosion, and (c) made it more deadly.

If Jean's story is accurate, it means Lester absolutely fulfills all three requirements for a Murder One conviction. That could be what I'm dealing with—incredible premeditation, obvious deliberate thinking, planning, a great amount of care taken by Lester to kill his brother. That could be damned rough. That is, if Jean's telling the truth. I tend to believe her. Still, there's a part of me that hopes to hell she's lying.

18

July 8, 1973

Robert slept fitfully.

In his dreams, before a phantom jury a stranger made his closing speech—fragmented, contradictory, and undefined by legal boundaries:

. . . The Zygmaniks were the last immigrant family to come looking for the American dream; the failure of that dream is the secret perpetrator of this murder. . . .

. . . Most acts of violence are committed in the name of love. . . .

. . . They are Polish non-Jews who might have collaborated with the Nazis and this is gothic retribution. . . .

. . . Any family is an incubator for murder. . . .

Arlene was asleep. The bedroom door was open. The house was silent, enclosed by the inaudible prison of air-conditioning.

In the kitchen, he found Kevin, his youngest, flapping around in Steve's pajamas. He gave Kevin a bowl of cereal, then joined Steve in the yard, where he was walking the oversized poodle. The morning was already hot. A warm, damp breeze came in off the ocean. Together, they walked for a while without talking.

"What are you going to do?" Steve said. The dog stopped to scratch around in the zinnias.

"We're going to verify it."

"Okay, we've divided the witnesses, we'll interview 'em. After that, how are you going to deal with it?"

Robert yanked angrily at the poodle's leash. "Get the hell out of my zinnias!"

• • • •

By nine o'clock he was at his desk, making a list of defense possibilities.

He wrote: *Absence of Malice??* . . . Murder One required malice aforethought. Was a motive of love/grief tantamount to the absence of malice? He wrote: *Long shot.*

He played around with the fact that George had consented to his own murder. The seven common-law crimes were murder, rape, sodomy, robbery, arson, mayhem, and bigamy. In each, the lack of consent of the victim was crucial. Was it, then, still legally defined as a criminal action if the victim consented to his own death?

He knew he was reaching.

At ten o'clock he put in a call to Diane Haus and asked for a private meeting. She giggled, saying she lived with her parents and didn't want to talk to him at home. She also didn't want to come to the office without Lester. He suggested Howard Johnson's on the highway to Trenton at eleven o'clock. Still giggling, she agreed.

He called Arlene, woke her, and told her he wouldn't be home until late afternoon. She didn't argue. He always tried to be home for dinner but otherwise he was overworked and inattentive. She was used to it. It occurred to him briefly that he was used to it also.

He went back to making notes. It was a habit left from law school to record anything that might be pertinent to a case. Later he filed the notes in massive loose-leaf folders, called his "trial notebooks."

He wrote: *Accomplice to Suicide?*—trying out that description of Lester's role in George's death. It was a tricky subject, loaded, despite the fact that an estimated thousand people committed suicide every day throughout the world. In Alabama and New York, it was still a felony to aid a suicide and the accessory was charged with manslaughter. In Oklahoma, South Dakota, and Washington, to attempt suicide and fail was a crime. In New Jersey, however, suicide had been taken off the books in the sixties. Therefore, if attempted suicide was no longer a crime in New Jersey, then aiding and abetting a suicide could not be a crime. He wrote: *Possible.*

When the phone flashed, he lit a cigarette before he answered it. The call was long-distance, a name he didn't recognize. He listened, thanked the caller politely, hung up, and switched on the dictaphone to make a record of the message.

He said, "Karen, file the following under Zygmanik. Sunday, July 8th. Received a telephone call from Rabbi Grossman in southern California. The rabbi offers his aid, quotes Pope Pius VII, who evidently said it's not necessary to use extraordinary means to save a human life. . . . The rabbi also suggests we bring a cripple in a wheelchair into the courtroom and let him sit there throughout the trial. . . . Note: Is there a Hertz Rent-A-Cripple?"

The exchange made him feel better.

He went down the block and ordered coffee. He drank it slowly, sitting at a table near the window, looking out on the empty downtown street and thinking about Lester. Was it possible to defend Lester on the basis of what appeared to be the real motive? Would it be viable to defend Lester on the grounds of euthanasia? In practical terms, it meant an attempt to change the law. It meant arguing before a judge, not a jury. Was it a viable alternative?

Mercy killing had never been used as a murder defense in New Jersey.

On what legal basis could the law be challenged? In most cases, morality was not his concern—his business was acquittal. An attempt to change the law on euthanasia would necessarily involve moral questions. What variables would have to be defined? Would the law ever relinquish its jurisdiction over death? How did he feel personally about mercy killing? What kind of law would be human, yet impose control over its misuse? It was a big question. He didn't want to fall into the trap of making decisions for posterity. Yet, a euthanasia defense would be based on the truth—that would be its strength. Would Lester agree to such a defense? More important, what were the real odds for acquittal?

Back at his desk, under *Euthanasia*, he wrote: *Possible*.

His final notes dealt with the possibility of a *Psychiatric Defense*. It was obvious and traditional. Yet, it remained the most complex. In other euthanasia cases where the defense had been temporary insanity, there appeared to be a connection between the method of killing and the verdict—the more violent the method, the more likely a conviction. Could any jury be convinced that a sawed-off shotgun at a range of three inches was not a violent method? Beyond that, the validity of such a defense would rest on the results of a more complete investigation. He wrote: *Decision deferred*, changed the water in the zinnias, turned out the lights, and left.

He was halfway to Howard Johnson's when the crux of Jean Zygmanik's story struck him. If Jean was telling the truth, it proved premeditation. If she was telling the truth, it proved something else.

What about a theory of accomplices?

He invoked a mental picture of the courtroom. Seated at the Defense table with Lester were Sonia and Jean Zygmanik. He watched the Prosecutor rise, then heard him say, "We, the State of New Jersey, accuse the whole damned family of Murder One."

19

July 8, 1973

Howard Johnson's was packed with families dressed for church. A covey of children with slick hair, starched shirts, and polished faces were running wild. Robert spotted Diane in the fourth booth. When he sat down, she blushed and lowered her eyes. It was a china-doll face, pretty, heavily mascaraed, surrounded by a fluff of bright red hair. She wore dark pink slacks, a light pink shirt, pink barrettes, and was drinking a strawberry milkshake.

He ordered coffee. The waitress left. He said, "Is this difficult for you?"

She giggled nervously and studied her milkshake.

"You want to help Lester, don't you?" he said.

She nodded, hid her face and cried a little. Robert leaned back to listen:

Diane Haus
July 1973

Maybe you think I should have met you at home. But my father's strict. He has a temper. Like I'm not allowed to wear bell-bottoms. One time my father came to Greenwich Village looking for me and he saw these guys wearing bell-bottoms and earrings, and he said, "I never want to see you wearing those pants again." So I hide my pants under my jacket and change in the car. Like once a boy came to my house—he had long hair. My father called him a scumbag. I mean Jesus Christ had long hair. Lester has long hair, so I always go to see Lester at his house. Twice a week. I see Lester on Wednesday and Friday. On Monday, I wash my hair.

I'm nervous now. Ever since this happened. I walk in my sleep. It's almost every night now. Once my mother found me on top of a bookcase. I have dreams like I'm in a strange place and I have to get out.

I would have never believed Lester would do such a thing. I met Lester at a bar called Mel's. He saw me and he asked somebody who I was. I first met Lester on Friday the 13th. I've known Lester three years. Lester never loses his temper. He's always calm. Sometimes he yells to get something through to his mother but he never gets mad. Only one time I saw Lester fight. He was drinking a lot at this hillbilly bar on route thirty-three, and this guy, about thirty years old, kept saying loud things to Lester. So they ended up outside, fighting down by the mill. And Lester was boxing, dancing around, not even fighting. And this guy couldn't fight. He shit in his pants.

Lester's very smart. He figures out people. He thinks about a lot of things. Sometimes we argue. Like I used to read the Village Voice and he thought it was trash. Like I was for Kennedy, but Lester doesn't like helpin' the blacks, welfare. Lester liked George Wallace. I don't go for George Wallace.

Lester works hard, twelve hours a day. Lester and George were going to sell trees, start a nursery, but they couldn't get financing. So Lester bought the truck. The whole family was like that, working hard all the time. Especially John, Lester's father. I met John at a wedding. It was Kasmir's son's wedding. John asked me, "Who do you think is uglier, me or my brother?" John was a good dancer. He wanted to dance all the time, the polka. He'd kiss me after every dance. But around the house, John was always working. He worked from three a.m. to three in the afternoon at the dairy. Then he'd come and work, chopping trees. It would be freezing cold and he'd be outside. Him and Lester and George, they were always kidding around. Like they'd be watching TV in the bed and John would say, "Come on" and everybody would lay on the bed, watching TV. John would talk about Siberia and how they caught dogs and killed them. He ate dog meat because they were starving. He used to tell Lester he wanted him to get married, everybody live together, one big, happy family.

I was there when John had the heart attack. It was in February. It was ten o'clock at night. He was lying in the bed still wearing that thermal jacket from outside and having pains. He said to Sonia, "Bring my children here." He made them promise to take care of Sonia. It took the ambulance a half-hour to get there. John insisted on changing from his workpants. Then they couldn't get the stretcher down the stairs, so he walked up all those stairs. I was at the top. He said, "Goodbye, Diane, take care of yourself." Like he knew he was going to die.

The night he died, I stayed over. We all slept together, me and Lester and Sonia, in her bed downstairs.

Since then, the house is spooky, quiet. We heard footsteps upstairs one night. And once when I was in Lester's room, we heard a pounding on the door. I said, "Maybe John wants to get back in." Like I had a Sunday-school teacher once who used to come drunk and tell about how she saw her husband cremated—she watched it and he sat up. Dead people can sit up. They move. Anyway, she saw him sit up and she said, "Stop, Harry's still alive!" After it happened, somebody called Father Valentine and asked him to help find a lawyer. He came to the house and he sat there talking about how he was against what Lester did, saying, "You can't take the law into your own hands." And telling us about a case like George's where the boy walked again. Sonia didn't understand anything he said, but finally Barbara Petruska, she said to him, "You're no help to us, you get out of here." So he left. He drives a pick-up truck.

Lester wasn't there. Lester was in jail, worrying. Like with Lester, his family comes first. Money's important, they drilled it into their heads. They worked all their life to save money to buy that property. George was doing it too. Even in jail, Lester was worrying about the money.

I still can't believe it. I still can't believe that night. You know, the night of the shooting, the dog was howling all night, like he knew someone died. That night Lester told me to come to his house around eleven o'clock. I got there early, so I drove around Perrineville until eleven. I like to do what Lester tells me to do. When I got to the house, there was Barbara Petruska and Jeannie and Sonia. They said, "Lester's not here." I said, "Why would Lester tell me to come here at eleven o'clock if he wasn't going to be here?" They said, "He went to the hospital." I said, "I'll go there." They said, "No, don't go. Stay here." Jeannie said to Barbara, "What would you do?" I left anyway. I drove to the hospital fast. I saw Lester's car and I parked next to it. The side door was locked, so I went into the lobby and I said to the nurse, "I want to see somebody who's visiting upstairs." She had a pad on her desk and I looked down at it and I saw the name: George Zygmanik. I said, "I want to see somebody who's visiting him." She called upstairs and then she said, "Okay. Wait." I waited. Two nurses came down and took me into another room and said, "There's been an incident here tonight. He's at Police Headquarters." I said, "What happened?" They said, "We *can't tell you." I drove to the police station and parked in the back and started pounding on the door—like nothing was the right door. When I finally found the front, I went in, I saw a cop and told him who I was. The cop said, "He tried to do away with his brother." I thought Lester had taken a tube out or something. They took me in another room and they said, "He shot his brother." I couldn't believe it.*

They said I could wait in the reception room. I was waiting and I saw a cop bring out a gun in a suitcase. Finally, they brought Lester out. I ran up to him. Lester said, "Did they tell you what I did?"

I said, "Yeah."

He said it again, "Did they tell you what I did?"

I said, "Yeah—you shot George."

Lester was wearing reddish pants and a red-and-blue shirt. He was wearing George's shirt.

20

July 8, 1973

Orlando Linn took his family to church. Afterward, Steve found Linn at home on his patio, barbecuing chickens from an old Southern family recipe. Linn turned out to be gregarious and voluble, a stocky, energetic man wearing red-white-and-blue striped trousers, a polka-dot shirt, and sneakers, who continually referred to his pride in being black and descended from slaves. He was eleven years old when his mother brought six children up from Alabama for the potato season. Today, he owned O. Linn Excavation Co. and lived in an $80,000 house. A member of the Pentecostal Church, he didn't drink or smoke, believed in good deeds and an accounting after death. Lester had worked for him since March.

Orlando Linn
July 1973

I talked to Lester that very night. Wednesday night. I called him because he stopped by that morning and he told me he was comin' in to the job the next day. Lester hadn't been on the job for three days, not since George's accident on Sunday. I called to verify if he'd be on the job on Thursday like he said. When I called first, Mrs. Zygmanik answered. She told me Lester was at the hospital. So I called back that night.

It was about nine to nine thirty at night and I talked to Lester. I asked him if he'd be on the job the next day. He said yes. But he was very excited. He had been at the hospital and seein' his brother in such pain. He said there was no hope. Lester said, "My brother can't even scratch his ear, I have to scratch it for him."

Lester was very agitated. It was more like he was trying to prevent something that was going to happen. I think Lester was feeling like if you know there's an accident down the road waiting to happen to you, like you would try to avoid it. Lester said to me, "My brother is beggin' me to take his life." I said, "This is not a decision for us to make. God decides." He said, "What kind of God would let my brother suffer like that—won't take his life? And what kind of God—my father was a hard-workin' man—would let my father just vanish away?" He said, "I don't believe in God any more."

I hung up and I said to my wife, "I'm worried about Lester. He's talking crazy."

Steve made notes:

Linn confirms he spoke to Lester by telephone on Wednesday night. This statement may be found on the first portion of the tape. The latter portion of Linn's tape does not relate directly to the day of the shooting, but is definitely relevant in terms of using Linn as a witness to Lester's character and to the relationship between Lester and George.

Orlando Linn

A German taught me how to work my first machine. Every time I made a mistake on the 'dozer, he called me a dumb bastard. One day I thought: You sonofabitch—and I left. It was a hard road up, believe me. I took a lot of chances, financially. My head was stepped on. But I made it. What I want to do is go back to Alabama and buy a farm. Because if I'm drivin' a white Cadillac in New York, some white man on the curb is sayin', "There goes a nigger in a white Cadillac livin' on welfare." But if I go back to Dothan, Alabama, that white man says, "Ain't that Ezell Linn's son—used to work for me for a dollar a day?" Down there, they know who you are.

As far as Lester is concerned, he came out lookin' for a job. Now, I can tell from reactions when a guy answers a newspaper ad and then he sees you, whether he's shocked or surprised that you're black. Lester didn't quibble. He wanted the job. He didn't mind me tellin' him what's right and what's wrong. When he came to work for me, he hadn't worked around heavy equipment in three years. But he seemed like he wanted the job so bad that I let him try it. In two days he was fantastic—he could grade a house almost as well as I could.

He came to work for me in March, right after his father died. I noticed one thing—Lester never got excited. I'm the one gets hot under the collar—the homeowners aggravate me. Lester had a lot of patience with them. Lester and me, we have a pretty good relationship goin'. He's the first guy worked for me that I ever encouraged to buy any equipment—I encouraged him to buy a truck. Like I don't grudge a man who tries to get ahead. I try to help him. I know how it is. My father worked for sixty cents a day. Cotton, they don't work *by the day, they work by the pound. Like two dollars a hundred for pickin' cotton.*

I knew one of these days Lester would be in his own business. So I said to him, "You buy a truck and I'll buy one. We'll have our own trucks on the job." So he talked to George, and him and George got the money up. Then George had been workin' day shift at Reynolds. So George went on nights at Reynolds in order to drive the truck durin' the day. George would leave his Reynolds job at seven o'clock in the morning, then shoot from Woodbridge down to Woodland Green where the job was—and George would be sittin' there in the morning when we got there. George would drive the truck from eight o'clock in the morning to about four o'clock in the afternoon. Then he'd go home and have about two or three hours' sleep. Then he'd shoot back to Reynolds that night at ten. George did this for thirty days. Right until the day of the accident.

Lester never did anything unless George was consulted. It looked to me like they said to themself, "We lost a father and there's only two of us left—and if we don't make it, there's nobody else to make it." It looked to me like what they did—this is just an imagination thing in my mind—that they took a lock and put it on themself and said, "We're gonna do it together." Like they were just one person. George was quieter. Lester was more with the jokes, with the mouth, with the girls—naturally, George was a married man. George was always talkin' about how Lester used to go out, and Lester's drinkin', and Lester's buddies. But George was a family man. Still, I would describe them as bein' one ball of twine that's wound together.

I admire that. I'd like to have that with my brothers. My mother had fifteen kids—nine lived. We always lived in raggly houses. When I went to school, I was ashamed for the bus to stop at my house. I put into my mind this would never happen to my kids. I built this house in a black neighborhood to upgrade my neighborhood. So my people, when they come by, they can say, "Hey, this is a brother livin' here." One night Lester came by with George—Lester was gonna pick up a paycheck. My wife took them on a tour of this house. They thought it was fantastic. They didn't envy me. They stayed until eleven o'clock that night.

I think Lester did the right thing. He did what he had to do. I'd have probably done the same thing. The other workers on the job—everybody feels he did the right thing. Lester said to me when he was in jail, "If I make twenty years, it's nothing compared to what my brother's goin' through." He wanted to see me when he was in jail. I went down there at seven o'clock in the morning. And the first thing he asked me was, "Is my brother still alive?" I said I didn't know. Then the police captain came in and Lester asked him. He said, "No, your brother died last night." I could see Lester's relief. Like somebody took a burden off his shoulders.

When the shooting happened, there was all kind of lawyers callin' up the Zygmanik house, wantin' to sue the hospital. I told Mrs. Zygmanik not to sign anything with anybody. I called Robert Ansell. He didn't know me but I knew him because his brother did my taxes. The family went down to his office and they got along.

I don't know what a jury'll do—probably follow society's traditions. They have to worry about what their friends are gonna say, or what society is gonna say. If Lester had a million dollars, society wouldn't look down on him as a murderer. The rich survive. Your freedom lies in your wallet. The doctors take an oath—then they say, "I can perform this operation but it will cost ten thousand dollars. If you have no money, I have to let him die."

Everything is recorded in the Book of Life. One of these days, John D. Rockefeller is gonna be judged the same as me. If you read your Bible, the King James Version, it tells you there's gonna be war, and earthquakes in diverse places, and hunger, and the way society's gonna turn. It's no surprise to me.

2 1

The Polish word for brother is *tribal*, meaning cousins or distant relatives. The sons of a common father are designated by a particular word which translates as blood-brother. Lester never called George by name, he always said "my brother." Most often he said "my brother and my father," and sometimes "me and my brother and my father." They called themselves the Three Musketeers.

By the summer of '73, only Lester was alive. He seemed a boy, passive, untutored, incapable of originality or boldness. He showed no remorse and expressed no guilt. He had simply acted as his father would have acted.

John Zygmanik died in February. The bond remained. On the night of June 20, John Zygmanik had been dead for four months. His code remained. John was the source. It was he who instilled in his two sons, George and Lester, absolute family allegiance, a primitive tie, and the seeds of tragedy.

Questions persist. How much of their intimate three-way relationship was due to Polish heritage and background? How much sprang from the fact that every family has its own internal laws, that John Zygmanik, not unlike Leon Anschelewitz, defined his sons' perimeters and their relationship with the outside world? How much is attributable to what psychiatrists call a symbiotic relationship—an emotional interdependence which is likened to that between a mother and an unborn child.

What kind of man was John Zygmanik? And George—who was he? What was Lester when his father and his brother were alive? A reconstruction is possible, though bound to be flawed. There is the human tendency to enshrine the dead, the problem of separating fact from wish, truth from myth. Emotions are not verifiable. Still, what emerged from hours of interviews are fragments of three lives.

John

It is fact that John Zygmanik was born in the winter of 1917, in the county of Obfot, Warsaw Province, Poland. It is perhaps myth that the midwife, a displaced Ukrainian, crossed a field of frozen corpses to attend his birth. It is a matter of history that his own father was absent.

The time was World War I; Poland was occupied. Snow fell bitterly on wasted fields and slaughtered livestock. Famine prevailed. World War I, the war to end all wars, would last for three more years on Polish soil.

In the autumn of 1918, when Poland was returned to world independence after 120 years of partition, the Germans departed, but the sounds of war remained. A year after that, when John Zygmanik was two years old, he met his father. The Pole returned from the rebel army, a renegade patriot who had fought the Germans in France. He arrived at night, his right hand torn apart, sprouting two gnarled fingers which a battlefield doctor had set with a metal clip. He arrived wearing big black boots, an icy beard, and carrying, under his thick woolen shirt, a strangled goose.

To John Zygmanik, the Pole remained a stranger. "They sent me home, sir," he often said. "What good, sir, is a soldier who cannot shoot?" Every morning the Pole rose in darkness and washed his grisly beard and went away and came back with something—if not food, firewood. It was late one evening when the thud of hoofbeats moved in from the distance and a knock shattered the peace of the cottage. The Pole rose slowly from his evening meal of boiled potatoes, picked up a hatchet, and set it nearby before he opened the door and faced the Cossack. Ice crystals glittered on the Cossack's fur. In the Cossack's face was what was left of war, now transformed into rage at the Russian revolution, now transmuted into fury at the Polish dispute over the Ukraine, now embodied in the aggression of galloping predators in search of scapegoats. John Zygmanik—two years old—watched the hatchet split the Cossack's head clean as an apple.

Only after they stripped the Cossack's body and buried him by moonlight and waited for the snow to cover the blood, and after his mother began to make coats from the Cossack's fur, and after the Pole rose in darkness and washed his beard and mounted the Cossack's horse in the cold gray light of dawn, did John Zygmanik recognize him as his father.

Lester

It's hard to talk about my experiences. You might not be shocked, but I might be shocked tellin' you—you understand? Like I always had a lot of girlfriends. I like a girl you can tell she's a girl from a mile away. Just walkin' down the street—you know? I like that. Nice looks, nice shape, that's what I look for.

I get around a lot, you know? If I see somethin' in the paper that I like, I go look at it. Like I took a ride through Pennsylvania just because somebody told me it was nice out there. I said, "Well, I'll take a look at it." Like I met this girl in Pennsylvania. Wherever I go, I like to find some action there. Get into somethin'. Then I just cut out of there and shoot back home.

Most girls I meet, maybe one out of thirty gets my right name. Never give 'em my right name. Feels better that way. That way, I'm not really involved with 'em. They know a Bill or a Frank—so let's say they wanted to see me more often, they couldn't. I don't see myself with one girl. I see myself with a lot of different girls. I don't know, I have some weird thoughts.

Like it gets boring after a while. Like it's not as exciting as it used to be. It gets too easy. When you know what kind of girl you're lookin' for and you keep gettin' it, it like wipes it out, you know? Then you've got to think of somethin' new to do. Like I try to make it more difficult, you understand? Like I try to pick out in my mind girls of different nationalities—then you have to find the girl of that particular nationality, the one you want to go out and look for that week. You really have to look around then. It makes it difficult. Or like you decide you want a certain age. Like this week you're lookin' for a German girl thirty years old, something like that—something you haven't had. So there's something different about each one and it's not boring.

I don't know, it's like I always had a life here with my brother and my father, and I always had a life out there. I have to have a private life. It's something that never had anything to do with my father or my brother, only with me.

George

In May of 1973, George planted a marigold garden the size of a grave. It was dusk when he started, after work—a bullnecked, broad-shouldered man wearing army boots, Lester's old trousers rolled to the shin, a St. Christopher medal to preserve him from harm, long, dark sideburns, and a Tartar's mustache, grown last August for his twenty-sixth birthday. He carried the shovel like a rifle.

For more than an hour he dug in the curve of the gravel road, aware that the garden was a luxury, would produce nothing beyond blooms. Last pale rays of East Jersey sun streaked the five-acre clearing, grass that would soon need cutting, green coming up in a vegetable garden that would soon need weeding—in the woods, a spruce to be dug and delivered on Sunday, replanted in a Neptune City lawn; Lester had made the deal, $100. An owl hooted. From the dog shed, Lester's beagles set up an answering howl. Then silence returned, the rustle of leaves, a squirrel, an occasional raccoon. He paused, uneasy with solitude, seldom alone. At Reynolds, he worked with a team of mechanics, somebody always laughing or cursing. Here at home, in the small cellar quarters, somebody was always cooking or weeping or planning; somebody was always mourning.

When the earth was prepared, darkness had fallen. George stopped long enough to pick up little Georgie's motorcycle and set it inside the breezeway. Then he retrieved a toy rifle. Winter habits remained, though winter was finished—the most they'd get through May was rain. He laid out the plants, neatly spaced, so he wouldn't have to thin them later, handling each gently, purposefully, molding the dirt the way his father would have done.

Kneeling, he felt the dirt and calculated that, with luck, the flowers would bloom on Father's Day.

John

By 1922, Poland was free. A village festival proclaimed the end of war. The Pole planted beets, acquired chickens, traded eggs for a bushel of rye. The Pole came home on the Cossack's horse, leading a cow. A brother was born, Kasmir, the first Zygmanik to be born into freedom in over a century. The Pole quoted a poet who wrote, ". . . a new world is trembling under our feet."

In the new world, an agrarian reform broke a few large estates and distributed land to a handful of peasants. In the new world, home became one of the few farms in the Polesie region not owned by the Radziwills—a hundred acres of pine forest and meadow near the Russian border, in Kresija, Brzesc, on the River Bug. Here, John Zygmanik learned the ways of the land. As a boy, he pastured the cattle. All night, through his tenth summer, he grazed the horses, sleeping close to the earth, one eye on the stars. To John Zygmanik came a deep and lasting love of the land. At the age of twenty, he was the son of a landed peasant, meant to inherit a pasture, a mill, a rye field, horses and cows, a plot for a house and a cabbage garden. His life was promised.

He was twenty-two when Hitler invaded Poland.

On September 1, the citizens learned that the German word *Blitzkrieg* meant *lightning war*. Cities were razed. Refugees fleeing along country roads were strafed. Armies arrived, driving tanks.

The Pole accompanied John as far as the wayside shrine in Kresija. At the railway station, a dress band played, women wept, young girls came with flowers. Three days later, under attack, John saw a dead cavalry officer still clinging to a horse which continued to gallop without its head.

On the 17th of September, the Russians crossed the eastern border. Twelve days later, Ribbentrop and Molotov divided Poland. A million Jews, a half-million Poles, were deported, imprisoned, executed.

In a packed and frozen railway car, through the depths of a Russian winter, John was taken to Siberia. John Zygmanik spent three years in Siberia. He retained his sanity by recalling the joys of his childhood, and he prayed to St. George, the patron saint of the harvest—for whom he would name his first son—because that was the only saint he knew well.

In July 1973, his younger brother, Kasmir, would describe that portion of John's life (translated from the Polish):

It was 1939, madam, when they took my brother, Janek, to Siberia. It was horrible. Hundreds of corpses fell daily from hunger, from starvation, from cold and exposure. Janek survived as one in a hundred did. In 1942, finally, General Szykorski took the Poles out of Siberia, what was left of them. Janek traveled to Persia by way of the Indian Ocean, later the Pacific Ocean, somewhere near Gibraltar. He was taken to Scotland and then to England, where he was met by General Szykorski. He became an under-officer in the Royal Air Force. It was the front, madam, it was the war. Later, Janek went into Hanover, Germany, as part of the occupying forces.

We are descended, madam, from a very wealthy family. We had sixty-five hectares of land, approximately a hundred acres. We had eleven hectares of woods, six of meadow, two houses, and so on. We would have lived on that farm forever, but it was lost, all lost. After Janek aided us in coming to America in 1967, he used to say to me, "Kazio, I want to live as our father did. . . ."

Lester

My brother used to worry about me. My brother used to worry about the things I did—like he would worry that his wife would find out. But I didn't tell my brother everything either. Like I didn't want him to feel bad. I'm goin' out, having this good time while he's at home with his wife, you know? My brother felt his responsibilities. He was more concerned with the family than me. He was more like my father.

When I was a kid, I used to want to be a priest. But I forgot that. Then I wanted to go in the FBI but they wanted me to lose weight. After that, I thought about bein' a State trooper, but you can't make it that way. You take the average worker who'll be workin' for fifty years and he ain't gonna get nowhere. I understand that. That's why I tried to make it gambling. I used to go to the racetrack, sports, dice, anything. Around here, it rains a lot. The track was always muddy. So, with some other guys, I shot down to Florida to play the horses. I thought I was gonna make it big. Like I lost a thousand dollars in four days.

Now I've lost all my drive. I used to work—I didn't like workin' but I could take workin'—sixteen hours a day. See, now I can hardly make it to four thirty. Like I operate heavy equipment, bulldozers. It's a boring job. Like you can't talk to anybody, you know? It's just you and that machine. Just like pushing dirt all day.

I definitely miss my father. Like he was the brain. With him alive, we were definitely gonna make it. Then, after he died— But me and my brother, we got over that. We started workin' again, real hard, and things were rollin' again. Like we were thinkin' about buyin' a restaurant, night club, something, you know? Maybe one night club after the next, different things. But then my brother started gettin' nervous again. I don't know why. Like right before his motorcycle accident, he seemed to be very nervous over unimportant things. I no-

ticed he lost quite a bit of weight. And once we were in the truck goin' over to New Brunswick and a cop stopped us and said pull over, he wanted to see the license and registration. And when the cop left, my brother was trembling. Neither one of us ever understood why.

George

In July 1973, George's widow, Jean Zygmanik, would say:

I don't know, it was maybe a month before the accident and my husband woke up that morning and he told me this dream he had. He told me he seen his father in the casket. In the dream, my husband was standing there and his father sat up in the casket. My husband said, "Pop, you're not dead?" and his father said to him, "No, George, I'm alive." Then my husband started to cry and he went over to the casket and his father held him in his arms.

When my husband woke up that morning, he was crying.

22

July 11, 1973

On Wednesday, Steve drove to Perth Amboy to interview Barbara Petruska. George Zygmanik had been riding Barbara's motorcycle when his accident occurred. More important, Barbara had been present in the Zygmanik house during the events which preceded the shooting.

A brief description and history taken by Steve read:

Barbara is 26 years old, 5'10", 180 lbs. Background: Polish. During WW II, her family moved to Belgium where she lived until she was twelve years old. "Because of the Communists," they did not return to Poland, but came to the States. Barbara once spoke Flemish as well as Polish—her English has no trace of an accent. She lives in Perth Amboy with her son and second husband, who is a maintenance man at a chemical plant.

Barbara Petruska

I went to see Lester in jail. His cell was small, like a bathroom. We couldn't say too much because a captain was out in the hallway. Lester was going to be transferred to another jail if he didn't get a lawyer. Orlando Linn, his boss, came in, and he said, "Maybe you don't want any help from a soul brother?" I said, "We'll take any help we can." A reporter was there, big ears, asking questions—I didn't tell him nothing.

I was at the house when Lester got out of jail. It was pouring rain. Then, after that, I saw Lester after the funeral. He was up in his room. He wanted to know how many people came, how many flowers, how many reporters were there.

I knew George better than Lester. Lester was always quiet. Lester's different now. I can't explain it. He's more outgoing now. More outspoken. Like I was over there last week and Lester came in—he was eating, and he said, "How's your diet going?" He would never say something like that. He seems more active now than when George was alive. Painting the house, things like that. He's talking more than he did before. He's more bold.

My husband is completely against what Lester did. After the shooting, Andy called me at the Zygmanik house and told me to come home. Mrs. Z was in tears. I was in tears. There were funeral arrangements. I said to him, "I'm going to stay here whether you like it or not. You can go to hell as far as I'm concerned—but I'm staying here."

I've known George since I was twelve years old. In Perth Amboy, when we were kids, I was at George's house all the time. Mr. Z used to call me Basha—Polish for Barbara. He was great. We used to talk Polish. Mrs. Z and me, we used to talk about the other side. They were always close but they were always friendly, like: Help yourself, the house is yours. They were always working. They bought a new house on Market Street and they were always working on it, new sheet rock, new floors, constantly.

I was in Jean's class in high school. George asked me to introduce him to Jean. I didn't do it. Me and Jeannie weren't even good friends. I didn't even meet her until after I got fed up with the nuns at St. Stephen's—they didn't want me to tweeze my eyebrows, so I changed schools. George's interest was always Jeannie. He didn't date anybody besides Jeannie. When he went into service, they got married. I'm married twice. My first husband, I had to scrape for money, he spent a lot of money. I told him to get the hell out. He went on a merchant-marine ship.

George and me, we always kept in touch. George is my son's godfather. George would always remember Scott's birthday, send ten dollars, something like that. I wouldn't see him all the time, maybe at a wedding or something—my mother gave me hell because I spent all my time talking to George. Me and George, we had a completely different relationship. I don't think I'd ever had that with any other man.

When they moved to Perrineville, I'd go up for picnics, 4th of July, things like that. He'd say, "Come up more often." But it wasn't his house, it was his mother's house—so I didn't go unless she invited me.

This year, I went down two weeks before Father's Day. George was always telling me I didn't know nothing about machines. I wanted to show off—show him how I could ride a bike. He wanted to ride it that day. But I said no. Andy, my husband, told me not to let anybody ride it unless he's around.

We were supposed to be there on Saturday. Saturday was little George's birthday. They changed it to Sunday. I don't know why. My husband came home from work on Sunday around noon and he said, "We'll take the car." I said, "No, we'll take the bikes." I already had my boots on. As soon as I got them off, he said, "We'll take the bikes." I took one, and my husband took one, and my sister on the back. When we got there, my mother and father were there, and Jeannie's father, and her sister and brother, and the girl from the farm next door. Lester wasn't there. He was working. He had a private job.

I had a beer. And me and George were talking. George had gone to church that morning, the first Father's Day Mr. Z wasn't there. George looked tired—he had been working two jobs, Reynolds and driving Lester's truck. We had another beer and then I wanted to go for a walk. They've got a lot of blueberries there and I wanted to see if they were ripe. George said he wanted to go, so we took a walk. George was talking about how he missed his father and then he was showing me Lucky's grave. Lucky was his father's dog from Perth Amboy. The place was all piled up with rocks where the dog was buried.

Then we got back and George said he wanted to ride my bike. George parked the bike on the gravel and he was trying to start it. I said, "You should never start a bike on the gravel." I told him, "Don't go on the gravel in second gear, or even in third—it spins. You lose control." He couldn't start the bike, so I started it for him. I asked him did he want the helmet. I said, "You should wear the helmet." He said, "No, I don't want it." He rode the bike around a couple of times, rode it back in the woods, came back, rode it around again. I thought he was going to quit, but he kept on going. He took the bike back on the gravel. He went on that winding road up to the street. He didn't listen to what I said. He came flying back down that gravel road and went right into that telephone pole that's lying flat by the ravine. He went right over into the ravine.

It was a trail bike. It was a good bike. After the accident, the front wheel was bent, the frame was bent. I was upset. I blamed myself for the accident because he rode my bike.

Monday, I didn't go back there. Tuesday, I didn't go back there. Wednesday, Mrs. Z called and said she needed me to come stay with her while Jean and Lester went to the hospital. This was about eight p.m.

When I got there, Lester was on the phone talking to his boss. Jean and Mrs. Z were drinking coffee. Jean said, "He's going to take a gun to the hospital." I touched Lester's shoulder. He pushed me. He said, "If my father was alive, he'd kill the whole family—letting people ride motorcycles who don't know how." I never saw Lester like that. Lester would never push me. Mrs. Z went to lay down on the bed. Lester went out and came back with a gun. It was sawed-off. He asked Jean for a candle. Jean went and got the candle. Then Jean asked him what he was going to do with the candle. Lester said he knew what he was doing. He lit the candle and melted wax into the bullet. We were all sitting at the table. Nobody said anything. Then he went and got his jacket and asked us if we could see the gun. Then he left.

After he left, somebody said, "Maybe we should call the police." But we didn't want to do that. We didn't really know what he was going to do. I said, "Maybe he'll cool off and come back." Then a car pulled up and we thought it was Lester coming back. But it was Diane. Jean told Diane not to go to the hospital. But Diane left anyway. Then we were sitting there. And Jean was afraid the police would come. There were pellets on the floor and in the ashtray. We flushed the pellets down the toilet and they went down. Then I went outside and threw the pieces of the gun into the woods.

23

July 13, 1973

By Friday, Robert no longer needed further confirmation of Lester's behavior in the hours preceding the shooting. What he was confronted with, instead, was the problem of formulating a defense built entirely of adverse facts. "Somehow we're going to have to deal with the truth," he said.

Steve paced the office. "To try this case on the basis of truth, you have to challenge the law on euthanasia. Are you prepared to do that?"

"I don't know." The last major witnesses to be interviewed were Victor Kazma, Jean's father, and Sonia. He expected neither to provide a miracle. "You have to think of a fact like money in the bank. It depends on what you do with it."

"For instance?"

"Temporary insanity."

"Interpret the facts as evidence of Lester's craziness?"

"That's right."

"Where's your hook?"

"I don't know."

"If that's why you're going out there, you can save yourself the trip. You won't get it from Sonia."

"I know you don't like her."

"I don't trust her. She pretends not to understand—she understands everything. She's shrewd and self-protective. This is just speculation, but I'd say Lester had her approval. Maybe more than that. I don't know how much more than that."

. . .

Directly after the occupation of the city of Poznan during World War II, Sonia Setukanska was taken to Hanover, Germany, as a member of the compulsory Polish workforce. She was assigned to a factory which was probably owned by Krupp or I. G. Farben, two of those industries which engaged in production near or in collaboration with concentration camps. Sonia worked on the assembly line. The product manufactured was gas masks.

She worked seven days a week, eleven hours a day. Her housing and board cost the German authorities ten cents a day. She was supervised by the SS with dogs. She was given one small piece of soap every three months. It is not unlikely that this soap was made from the fat of human corpses at a plant erected for such purposes in Danzig.

As a member of the workforce, she escaped incarceration or death at Belzec, Sobibor, or Treblinka, three Polish concentration camps where nearly half a million dollars of profits accrued from the clothes, possessions, gold teeth, and hair of victims. She worked industriously because the weak and the slow were sent regularly to extermination camps and were replaced by the strong. She was not raped or molested in any manner, though such occurrences were regular. Sonia Setukanska was strong. She survived.

Not far from the factory where she worked was a psychiatric hospital where gas chambers were being installed for the purpose of mass killings of patients under the heading of "euthanasia." The covering rationalization was "the destruction of life devoid of human value." During the five years Sonia spent in Hanover, this principle was extended to include all "superfluous" people, which meant the old, the weak, the handicapped, the disturbed, the epileptic, and the undesirable. The movement was led by prominent German doctors and scientists of impeccable credentials and international reputations. At the beginning, Jews were excluded, ineligible for the "benefits of euthanasia."

In 1945, Sonia Setukanska was set free by English occupying forces. Among their ranks was a young Polish under-officer named John Zygmanik, who took her to a picnic.

Sonia Zygmanik
(translated from the Polish)

I don't speak English. I understand very little—in slow motion. Polish is better. I speak a very good Polish—not a common Polish.

I'll tell you a story about my life. When we were leaving England, my John and me, with our two babies, my friend said to me, "Why are you going to America?" I said, "I'm young. I have to go and look —find the place that's me." She said, "You won't like it. Everything is hurry up, hurry up." I said, "Hurry up and die, too?" She said, "Yes."

That's a true story. I think about it. I'm alone too much. I have too much time to think. Jean has taken the baby and gone to Victor's. I know what's on Victor's mind. He thinks about the money. Jean will have my Georgie's veteran's insurance, ten thousand dollars. Jean will have the ten acres down the road which my Georgie saved his money to buy. Also, Victor likes to make lawsuits. For myself, I have not even hospitalization.

It's a very sad thing. I cry too much. I remember too much. I remember everything. On Father's Day, my Georgie went to mass. He went to the cemetery to see John. Jean was sleeping. When my Georgie came in, he said, "I prayed for you, Mama." He said, "God is everywhere, Mama."

Once he said to me, "Mama, I love you more than my wife, Jeannie."

That's a true story.

My Georgie was a good worker, like my John. Everybody must work for something. Everybody must have a job. A man is a man, he must work. He must be strong. Sometimes Lester is too soft. I don't like that. Always they were close, Georgie and Lester. Maybe too close. When they were small, in Perth Amboy, I was always telling them, "Go out and play with somebody else." It was a nice four-

family house—five and a half rooms in every apartment, four garages, and two entrances. But it was very dilapidated and they wanted twenty-two thousand dollars. I said, "That's too much." Later, they sold it to us for sixteen thousand, and my John fixed it up. I always took care of the money. I paid for everything, cash. I used to say to John, "You just bring me the money." I never spent the money. I always had good tenants. One tenant I like very much. She kept her apartment clean as Hollywood.

My John loved this country. I loved this country. Until last April, I hadn't seen Poland in thirty-three years. Then my children told me, "Mama, we'll give you some money." In April, the fare is half-price. I found nothing in Poland is as it was. I have two sisters still in Poland. There are no communists in my sisters' houses.

There were six children in my family. I was said to be my father's favorite. My father had two butcher shops. In his white coat, he looked very handsome, like a doctor. He never swore. He was a good Catholic, the same as my husband. We lived in a big house, but we didn't own it. In Poland, there was a saying, "The Jews own the house but the Poles own the street." Then the Germans took everything. The city burned. And, afterward, everywhere was written: "Für Deutscher"—for Germans only. My brother worked on a German food barge. German soldiers stole some food and then set fire to the boat. The crew was Polish. My brother was hanged with the rest of the crew.

That is a true story.

I worked in a bistro. It was owned by Jews. The Germans took them away. They ordered me into the Arbeitsam. In Hanover, if I saw something, I looked the other way. I never tried to teach anybody anything. If you do that, later they come back and they ask you, "Why did you teach me that?" For myself, I don't listen to anybody. I have my own brain. God gives every person a brain. You must use it for yourself.

In Hanover, I met John. He was a good Catholic, like my father. He had a nice shape. He knew how to dance well. In England, he won second prize for the tango. We were married in Germany, in a *barracks. They made a church out of it. There was a Polish soldier who was also a priest. My John went to Belgium and bought me a ring and a navy-blue suit. My Georgie was born in Germany, delivered by nuns with forceps. Lester was a caesarian birth. After Lester, I had fever. I had no milk. Then there was a miscarriage. The doctor said, "No more babies." My John was a very good man. No more babies.*

Now I have a dream that comes back and comes back. I don't tell it to Lester. In my dream, my Georgie is calling me. I am running toward the sound of his voice but I can't find him anywhere. Then, suddenly, I see my Georgie on the top of a hill with the sun. There, a carousel goes slowly around. There are three painted horses. My Georgie rides one of them. He calls out to me, "Mama, look what Jeannie and Victor have done to me!"

ROBERT ANSELL'S TRIAL NOTEBOOK

INTERVIEW: Sonia Zygmanik
DATE: 7/13/73

On the night of the shooting (June 20) Sonia says Victor Kazma brought Lester home from the hospital around 6 p.m. Victor then stayed a couple of hours, she is not sure of the time. After Victor left, she says she saw Lester "going this way and that way" and knew something was wrong. At about 9 p.m., she went upstairs and noticed one gun in the room. She knew from cleaning that there were two guns. She took a lamp and went outside. She saw Lester in the area of the doghouse but as she approached, Lester left the area. She observed the pieces of the gun. She then took Jean out to the doghouse and showed her the pieces. When they came back to the house, Barbara Petruska was there. According to Sonia, she said, "You must call the police," and Jean answered, "You are sick and you are tired. There is nothing wrong. Go to sleep." According to Sonia, she took two tablets and lay down on her bed. (Note: Sonia's bed is approximately ten feet from the kitchen table and has a clear view.) About ten minutes later, Sonia asked Jean if she was going to the hospital and Jean answered, "No. Not tonight. I'm tired."

Sonia says she never saw Lester with a gun. She never saw Lester wax a bullet. She did not see him leave. At one point, however, she did say, "Lester is the same as his father. A promise is a promise."

24

Robert Ansell

Death is personal. I can't talk sociologically or politically, I only considered it from a legal standpoint. There's no question in my mind that, personally, I'm in favor of euthanasia. I just can't, as a lawyer, come up with a law that would adequately cover all varying circumstances. There are tremendous jurisprudential problems involved. Like creating a definition that would fit only the kinds of cases you wanted it to fit, and that could still be applied generally across the board. The big problem is—once you create a euthanasia defense, that defense is going to be raised. Any time a murder occurs when two people are alone in a room, the one who survives is going to say the other one begged him to do it.

There are too many variables. Number one is: Whose consent would you need? The first person, of course, is the person who's going to be killed. Do you need that person's consent? Suppose that person is in no condition to give consent? Number two would be the dependents of the sick person—must you get their consent? Don't they have a say in it—if in fact they are dependent? Once you get by whose consent you want, the next variable would be: Whose approval do you need? Must you have approval? Medical? Must you have medical approval? Must you have court approval? Must you have law-enforcement approval? The third thing is: What kind of underlying illnesses would you permit euthanasia in? Must they be painful? Must they be terminal? Or, in fact, must there be an underlying illness at all? Suppose somebody walks into a hospital and says, "I just want to cash my chips in"? And the fourth thing is: What methods would you approve? Must it be injection? Could it be a gun? Would you make up a list of methods and ask the patient to check a, b, or c?

Those are the four areas I'd have to explore if I were sitting down to draft a law. And I can't answer those questions. Yet, I can think of obvious cases—such as Freud, who requested his own death— where you say to yourself, "What's wrong with that?" The one big difference between Hitler's euthanasia law and any other kind is the element of consent. If I could draft a law that would include Dr. Freud, and George, and myself . . . under certain circumstances and excluding other circumstances, I'd be in favor of it.

25

July 13, 1973

Insanity as a legal defense for murder was formulated in 1843 after an Englishman named McNaughton set out to kill the Home Secretary and shot a civil servant by mistake. McNaughton was tried, found not guilty by reason of insanity, and immortalized for future generations of lawyers.

In New Jersey, the McNaughton criteria for insanity still applied: "At the time of the act, was the defendant laboring under a defect of reason from a disease of the mind so as not to know the nature and quality of his act or the difference between right and wrong?"

On Friday afternoon, Robert drove to Point Pleasant, New Jersey, to see Dr. John Motley, psychiatrist—a big, florid man, solidly built, probably Irish and Catholic. To Robert, he seemed like a man who understood that when priests began to dispense penance, somebody was needed to hand out compassion. The office was spartan, adorned only by typical Monmouth County boat paintings.

Motley stuck to generalities. He had seen Lester once. On the basis of that visit, Lester appeared rational, though perhaps confused and disoriented.

Robert asked, "How confused and disoriented?"

"In terms of an insanity plea?"

"Possibly."

"McNaughton's a tough critieria. I'm not sure Lester qualifies."

Gently, Robert pressed. Motley demurred, refusing to be pinned down. Finally, Motley suggested that Lester be submitted to a battery of psychological tests. Robert agreed.

July 14, 1973

On Saturday morning, the following item appeared in the *New York Times*:

Freehold, N.J., July 13—Lester M. Zygmanik, the 23-year-old Perrineville man accused of killing his paralyzed brother in a Neptune Hospital last month, pleaded not guilty by mail to a first-degree murder charge in Superior Court here today.

Under speeded-up court procedure adopted about four years ago in New Jersey, the accused man's lawyer, Robert Ansell of Asbury Park, mailed the form he had signed to the chief Monmouth County Court clerk, John J. Mariglia, who formally filed the plea in Superior Court.

The accused man has been in seclusion since the death of his brother, according to Mr. Ansell who said that he expected to be prepared to go to trial in the man's defense in late September or

*early October in Superior Court here. Malcolm Carton, Assistant
County Prosecutor, declined today to estimate when the case
would be called to trial. According to speculation and heightening
public interest, the issue of mercy killing may be raised by the
case.*

*Mr. Ansell has declined to discuss the case, but court sources
here noted that the next legal move on the part of the defense
could be the submission of a defense motion within 30 days of
today's pleading that would advise the court that a psychiatric defense might be undertaken. This step is not uncommon in homicide cases growing out of unusual circumstances.*

July 16, 1973

On Monday, Robert and Steve constructed a calendar—three days,
from June 17, the day of George's motorcycle accident, through June
20, the night of the shooting. Filling in hour by hour from tapes, interviews, notes, and medical reports, they attempted to get some
sense of the chronology of events. There were gaps in the calendar.
The largest occurred on the day of the shooting. At 5:00 p.m. Lester
had telephoned Diane Haus and asked her to meet him at 11 p.m.
The call raised a question. If Lester had already decided to kill
George, would he have made a date with his girl for that same night?
The afternoon was blank. Between noon and 6:00 p.m., when Victor
Kazma brought Lester home, was penciled in only as time spent at
the hospital. Robert said, "I want to find out how Lester spent those
six hours."

"Where do you want me to start?"

"Start with the hospital—orderlies, nurses, anybody who worked
the eleven-to-seven daytime shift that Wednesday. Maybe somebody
will remember seeing him. After that, check out Victor."

"You think something happened between noon and six p.m. that
made Lester decide to kill George?"

"I don't know."

July 17, 1973

On Tuesday morning, in the Englishtown post office, among Lester Zygmanik's mail, was the following letter:

Dear Mr. Zygmanik,

After reading about you in the newspapers, I feel compelled to write.

Until two years ago, I lived in a commune in the Northwest. There were twelve of us. One brother was a paraplegic. His blood-brother was also a part of our very close family. We lived together for two years. I felt Johnny was the most loved person that I knew. During Johnny's last year, he became very suicidal. He would go for medical trips to get injections to stop muscle spasms. We tried everything to get him out of his suicidal state of mind. He talked with many of us. He wanted to leave well and he wanted us to understand.

One night, he asked to be left alone. He shot himself in the head. After hearing the shot, five people ran back and found his body still in spasms. One brother picked up the gun and fired a second shot. In the morning, we all buried him at sunrise in his favorite place, under a tree on a garden hillside. His brother flew east to tell his parents. After that, we all went through much, I imagine, the same as you. It took a month of homicide accusations and ugly newspaper stories before it was over. After the body was exhumed, and an autopsy was done, we learned the first shot was fatal.

I hope this letter can be of some comfort. I hope the jury will be compassionate. God bless you and Peace.

July 20, 1973

The rule of Court in New Jersey was: "If a defendant intends to claim insanity or mental infirmity either as a defense, or affecting the degree of the crime charged, he shall serve notice of his intention upon the Prosecuting Attorney when he enters his plea or within 30 days." Translated into calendar terms, Robert had twenty-four days in which to test the potential of a psychiatric defense.

He called David Silver in. David, a student at the University of Virginia, was working through the summer while waiting to enter law school. David wore shoulder-length blond hair with his business suit. He was twenty years old. His summer salary was $25 a week. Robert gave him a list of names—Lester's friends and the people Lester worked with. "I want you to interview them. Also the local priest, Lester's high-school teachers in Perth Amboy, principal, get grade records—and anything else you can think of. I want to know more about Lester than he knows himself. Can you do that?"

"Sure."

"One more thing. Any ideas you have about this case, I'm open to them."

He spent the afternoon with Wertham's *Why Men Kill*. According to Wertham, men killed from "negative emotions," from "greed, jealousy, fear, distortion, the frustration of sexual development, hunger for revenge, hostility, sadistic fixations, wild ambition, resentments, unforgiven humiliations and rivalries."

None of it seemed to apply to Lester.

In the hallway, he watched his father go past with New York Supreme Court Justice Irving Saypol, ex-prosecutor of the Rosenbergs, golf partner.

Schmidt's Attorneys' Dictionary of Medicine defined dissociation reaction: "Emotional states in which the person's behavior and general functioning becomes dissociated or separate from his conscious awareness so that he may carry out various acts, including highly complex and organized behavior, without any conscious awareness or later recollection of doing so. During performance of such acts, the patient may appear to be entirely aware of what he is doing, but afterward has no recollection of the behavior."

He made a note to himself: *Do complete time-sequence interview with Lester. Look for memory gaps.*

July 23, 1973

On Monday, at 4:00 p.m., in the afternoon mail, Lester Zygmanik found the following letter:

Dear Mr. Zygmanik,

I know you will never kill anyone again because, upon doing so, our loving God Jehovah would not forgive you a second time. So while you are at home grieving and praying, remember Ezekiel 33, "I take delight not in the death of the wicked one, but that in someone wicked turns around (or turns back) from his ways." During your trial, I know you will want to ask forgiveness and be repentant, so we offer you the opportunity to study the Bible free and with compassion. So, if you'd like to study, just write and request that someone in your area come and talk to you.

July 24, 1973

On Tuesday, Robert scheduled Lester for 5:00 p.m. In the preceding week, Lester had submitted to the series of psychological tests, including Rorschach, Graphic Projectives, Szondi Test, Verbal Scale IQ, WAIS, and a Wide Range Achievement Test. On Tuesday afternoon, Dr. John Motley telephoned to say the results were in. The psychodiagnostic evaluation had been handled by Dr. Alvin Krass,

Ph.D., consulting psychologist. Motley considered the report thorough, professional, and competent. The results were summed up in a sentence which appeared at the end. "*He* [Lester Zygmanik] *presented no clinical evidence during this evaluation to suggest that he was a seriously emotionally disturbed person.*" It was a report that could get Lester at least twenty years.

At 5:15 p.m., Lester showed up with a ticket for speeding. "I'm sending you to another psychiatrist," Robert said.

"I'm not crazy," Lester said.

26

ROBERT ANSELL'S TRIAL NOTEBOOK

Interview: Victor Kazma
By: Steve Delaney

Victor provides new facts concerning the missing hours in the afternoon preceding the shooting, particularly in terms of looking for something which might have affected Lester's state of mind:

Victor began by stating he was with Lester on the day of the shooting from eleven a.m. to nine p.m. He claims Lester was very angry because Victor had gone up to Intensive Care and had taken up one of the visiting spaces, forcing Lester and Jean to wait downstairs. Victor then reported the following incident which occurred in the hospital cafeteria around one p.m.

Victor accompanied Lester to the cafeteria. There, seated at the counter, was a doctor from the operating room. Lester recognized him as the doctor who had come in the morning to take George to surgery. He was also wearing a cap. He was about thirty-five years old, fairly short, stocky, wore a mustache. Victor does not know his name. According to Victor, Lester talked to this doctor for about an hour. Victor overheard the conversation. This is Victor's version:

LESTER: What do you think of the Zygmanik case? What are the chances?

DOCTOR: He's in terrible shape.

LESTER: Well, it's someone close to me. It's my brother.

DOCTOR: Your brother will have to be taken care of twenty-four hours a day and, because of his age, he might live another five or ten years. I've seen twenty of these cases in service and four since I got out and all of them are hopeless. If you want to see how George will live, go to the East Orange Veterans' Hospital. There are men like George who are deteriorating.

According to Victor, the doctor said George would be a "headless body" or a "bodiless head," unable to control any of his body functions. Eventually, George would be "covered with bedsores" and would "dry up and deteriorate."

According to Victor, Lester was very upset. The following conversation is also Victor's version:

VICTOR: Let's give God a chance. We've given the doctors a chance, now let's give God a chance. There's a possibility George will be all right.

LESTER: I don't believe you. I believe the doctors. My brother doesn't have a chance.

According to Victor, he kept trying to calm Lester down, but Lester remained in an agitated state. Then, in the late afternoon, on the way home, Lester kept saying, over and over, "I can't let my brother live like that. I can't let my brother live like that." Victor kept saying maybe it was a mistake and Lester kept denying the possibility of a mistake. (At this point, Victor seemed to be building up his attempts to calm Lester down and to talk him out of what he was going to do—though Victor denies knowing what Lester was going to do.)

When they got home, Victor states Lester received and made a number of phone calls. During these phone conversations, Lester talked in great detail of his conversations with the doctor. Then Lester and Victor had three or four cans of beer. Victor did not think Lester was drunk or changed in any way, but it sounds as if the beer was consumed rather quickly. Victor said he thought he had calmed Lester down and so he decided to go home. At this point, Lester asked Victor to go back to the hospital with him. Victor said he had seen enough of the hospital, he was tired, had not been sleeping, and could not see where anything would be accomplished by going back. According to Victor, Lester asked him more than once to go back to the hospital. Now, of course, in light of what happened later, Victor said he was sorry he didn't stay.

In terms of a psychiatric defense, it seems to me that the conversation in the cafeteria with the doctor might well be some kind of turning point in Lester's state of mind.

In my opinion, however, Victor is likely to be a troublesome witness. His personality is unpleasant and he seems to inspire fear in Jean, who was there with the son. During an emotional scene, Victor began bad-mouthing Lester, referring to him as the "damn fool, the jerk who did that stupid thing." He kept saying he was afraid Lester was "not right." Jean disagreed with him. He feels himself to be the anguished victim of the current situation and insists on recounting the tragedies of his own life. He lists his occupation as electrician but has not worked in some time. He has instituted several lawsuits in the past, particularly one suit for which he was awarded a major sum for Jean's younger sister, who was involved in a minor automobile accident. He is now planning lawsuits against the motorcycle company, the hospital, and the doctors, and has retained an attorney for this purpose. Because of this, his story about "the doctor" should probably be checked thoroughly.

27

Robert Ansell

I don't know if Sonia overtly urged him to do it. Obviously, she's protecting herself at this point, her own involvement, whatever it was. I'm aware that Lester's basically obliging. Sure, he's got what he calls his private life—girls, bars—but, basically, he wants to please you, he wants you to think well of him. In a sense, I feel he was programmed. The belief that a man who can't work and can't have sex isn't a man—that's what he acted on. Most men buy that definition—in that sense, we're all programmed. Yet, none of it wipes out the fact that what he did was very real—that he didn't do it because of Jean or Sonia or Barbara, he did it for George. Whatever he felt for George, whatever he felt he was doing, he felt so deeply and it was so real to him that he acted. Whether you call it fear, love, exploitation, whatever you call it, it was meaningful enough to him and caused him to do something 99.9 percent of us wouldn't do. That's the reality. I didn't buy it right away. I think maybe it's unsettling to feel that somebody like Lester has more courage than you might have, or that he loves somebody in a way you've never experienced.

The irony is—as the facts accumulate, it looks like my best shot is to try to prove he was mentally deranged.

28

Dear Mr. Carton,

On Friday, I came to your office at 1:20 p.m. and was advised you would see me. At 1:45, I was advised you would not be able to see me because of a conference with three judges.

I am sure you are aware that my trip to Freehold to see you in person was made necessary by the fact that my telephone calls went unanswered. It is going to be very difficult to conduct pre-trial matters in this case if our contacts are going to be limited to writings. I know that you are concerned by the amount of publicity generated by this case. Although I do not nurse at the public mammary, I also have a busy schedule.

If I do not hear from you within seven days, I will be obliged to file a motion herein.

Yours very truly,

Robert I. Ansell

Dear Mr. Ansell,

If you read the newspapers as often as you are quoted in them, I assume you are aware that the sentencing of Theophus King Webster will take place on September 14, 1973.

Obviously, I have no intention of doing anything with respect to your client, Lester Zygmanik, until that time.

Very truly yours,

Malcolm V. Carton
Acting Prosecutor

Dear Mr. Carton,

I have your gracious reply and will contact you with respect to Lester Zygmanik after September 14th.

I noticed that you signed your letter as "Acting Prosecutor." Where may I catch your act?

Very truly yours,

Robert I. Ansell

Dear Mr. Ansell,

This will acknowledge your letter in which you inquire about theatre tickets. This will also acknowledge your earlier letter in the Zygmanik case in which you made reference to a public mammary.

I have considered a lengthy reply to both of your letters. However, I have settled for a two-word expression which not only sums up my feelings towards you, but is one which I know you will understand. The first is a verb, the second is a pronoun.

Very truly yours,

Malcolm V. Carton
First Asst. Prosecutor

Dear Mr. Carton,

Thank you very much for your kind letter. I must confess to being somewhat confused, since "love" can be either a verb or a noun. In any event, in your position as Prosecutor, you should make some effort not to verbalize your respect and admiration for me.

Very truly yours,

Robert I. Ansell

29

July 31, 1973

Robert was aware he was spending less time than usual at home, and those moments with his sons, Scott, Brian, and Kevin. He was aware that, for company, Arlene had imported an old high-school friend from Washington who had, in the interim years, become a long-haired divorcee with painted snowflakes on each raspberry toenail. He was further aware that, for the first time in a ten-year career, a case was creating a backlash in his life.

Periodically, he caught himself making comparisons between his own life and Lester's. There was the similarity of a family hierarchy —a life created from obligations. Though his own circumstances were less dramatic, they sometimes seemed as binding and as unquestioned. When he turned a cold, clear barrister's eye on himself, he saw a series of untested roles. Along with priest-of-the-law and dutiful-heir was half-hearted husband.

For all these reasons, he invited Arlene to New York, where he had made a late appointment with a second psychiatrist for Lester— Dr. Samuel Klagsbrun.

It was Tuesday night. They stopped for dinner at the Cypress, a candlelit, wood-paneled place adorned by pen-and-ink caricatures of East Jersey patrons. Howard Rose, manager, stopped at the booth. "You know Nathan Acari?" he said. "Patient in the bed next to the guy who was shot?"

"Heart case?"

"Right. He's my brother-in-law."

Robert picked up the menu. "What kind of champagne have you got?"

"The mercy-killing business must be pretty good," Howard said.

"The champagne's for the lady," Robert said.

In 1957, the girl from Washington had introduced them. Arlene had been in high school, he had worn a college crew-cut. In less than two years, they were pinned, engaged, and married. They hadn't ordered drinks on their honeymoon because neither had been twenty-one. He had gone to law school. She had worked.

She had been one of those indulged, lonely, only children who envied big families. Like his father, he had given her sons.

In fourteen years, Robert had watched her grow elegant and angular, a fanatic on cleanliness and crossword puzzles. A month ago, he had heard her say to someone on the phone, "From the day we got married, I've never seen him."

He took the Garden State Parkway. It was a silent drive. Near the Jersey Turnpike, boxes of plastic geraniums marked the end of bucolic East Jersey. Silhouetted against a black summer sky, oil plants and industry stretched the rest of the way to New York.

The address he sought was a street-level office in the expensive East Sixties of Manhattan. Dr. Samuel Klagsbrun answered the discreet buzzer. He turned out to be a soft-spoken man in his early forties, wearing mod aviator glasses, a vest, and smoking a pipe. Dark, springy curls encircled an expression that was both benevolent and sober, as if he took seriously the power which had been passed from Jehovah to Moses to Freud to himself. He was an expert on death. The term was "thanatology," from the Greek *thanos*, meaning "death"—root of the word "euthanasia," which meant "the good death." A major part of Dr. Klagsbrun's career had been spent working with terminal patients.

The office was comfortable, inviting, lined with books. The remains of a group-therapy session littered the coffee table—iced tea in a plastic pitcher, peanuts, dried apricots, and oatmeal cookies.

Klagsbrun took a rocking-chair. Arlene selected a corner of the couch. Robert took a seat at the opposite end of the couch, momentarily afflicted by the layman's notion that psychiatrists could read minds. He had seen Klagsbrun on a television panel concerning euthanasia. Klagsbrun's position had been pro-euthanasia. He had defined mercy killing as valid under three conditions: when the power to act had been totally taken away; when one was totally dependent; when one was robbed of any opportunity to make a mark or a statement. Robert had telephoned, hoping that Klagsbrun would begin from a position of compassion for Lester.

"It's an interesting case," Klagsbrun said. Robert recognized the tone. It was one he used himself with clients, reassurance without commitment.

Robert began to talk. In an easy, relaxed manner, he started with June 22, the day he had taken on the Zygmanik defense. He outlined the events leading up to the shooting, threw in his own impressions of Lester, described the interviews with the family, friends, witnesses, doctors, hospital employees, summarizing his own discovery of facts. Klagsbrun stopped him, periodically, with a brief question. For the most part, Robert talked for nearly an hour without interruption.

When he finished, Klagsbrun made a tent of his fingers. "Of course, you're saying the family not only approved Lester's course of action, they collaborated."

"I've abandoned that as a trial possibility."

"Why?"

Robert grinned. "The minute I try to get them indicted, I'm fired as a lawyer."

"I see—it's pragmatic?"

"Nine-tenths of the law is pragmatic."

"All right. What I see, then, is a series of hidden accomplices. Going all the way back to the night of the motorcycle accident. For instance, why didn't they operate on George that night? Time sequence is terribly important in administering medical aid. Then, why did the doctors take the risk of moving George from one hospital to another? It's almost as if everybody George encountered helped him on the way to death."

"Number one—it's too difficult a concept for a jury. Number two —I don't want to take on the entire system of medical care in America. I'm only interested in saving one man, Lester." Robert leaned back and studied Klagsbrun. He found him a little academic, but direct, thoughtful, and a master of timing. Klagsbrun probably cared a great deal for his patients and that would come through to a jury.

"What's the legal criteria for insanity in Jersey?"

"McNaughton."

"That's very confining."

"Right. Did he know the nature and quality of his act? Did he know the difference between right and wrong? It's specific. Was Lester aware that pulling a trigger would launch a bullet? That's the *nature* of his act. Was he aware that launching a bullet would cause death? That's the *quality*. Did he understand both the short-range consequences and the long-range consequences of his act? Did he know what he was doing was wrong? Those are the questions that have to be answered."

"I haven't seen Lester," Klagsbrun said. "I can only answer hypothetically, on the basis of your description of him. There are possibilities, however. For instance, are there any past episodes of impulsive behavior on Lester's part? There is in psychiatry a category called 'infantile character disorder.' This is the ability, under stress, to regress to the pre-ethical state of a child, to an 'impulse-ridden state of mind.'"

Robert took notes.

"Also, hypothetically, there's the possibility of what's called a 'fusion fantasy.' That implies someone whose personality is so simply and tentatively constructed that the 'boundaries of identity' are not fixed. It's possible that Lester was unable to separate himself from his brother's pain, and so was, in a sense, killing himself by killing his brother. By relieving his brother of suffering, he thereby relieved himself."

"That's probably the theory closest to the truth," Robert said. "But, again, it's too complicated for a jury. It's difficult for *me* to understand. I don't know how the hell you explain it to *them*."

"Psychiatry's like religion," Klagsbrun said. "People can't be convinced, they have to be converted."

"I only want to convert them long enough to acquit Lester," Robert said.

"I don't know Lester," Klagsbrun said. "I don't know who he is, or what kind of violence he's capable of. Certainly, at face value, I'm sympathetic. But I can't give you what you want. I can't even form an opinion until I've made my own evaluation of Lester."

"When will you see him?"

"When is the trial?"

"I don't know yet. September. October."

"I'll try to work him in once a week."

"Let me level with you," Robert said. "You've got your professional ethic and I've got mine. Yours is to evaluate Lester according to a set of standards I don't understand. Mine is to give Lester the best defense he can get. I don't know if he's crazy or not, but it's the best shot I've got. I think a jury will be sympathetic. I hope so. My business is to give them a *legal excuse* to set Lester free."

Klagsbrun was silent for a moment. Finally, he said, "All right, I'll level with *you*. I'm a Belgian Jew. My father was a diamond merchant. Before we came here, in 1941, I was on the other end of a few bombing raids. They were rounding up Jews. From those experiences came my own need to master death. It's my own way of challenging authority, of showing I'm not going to be intimidated. When I spoke to you on the phone, I assumed you were going for a euthanasia defense." Klagsbrun removed his glasses and wiped them.

"I'm going for Lester," Robert said.

"Hypothetically," Klagsbrun said, "there's another possibility that just occurred to me."

"I'd like to hear it."

"At the Michael Reese Hospital in Chicago, they've done a study on 'intolerable stress.' They studied battle neuroses. It was a phenomenon of World War II. Every man has a stress limit. Under the limit, that man behaves normally. Over the limit, that same man cracks. You've heard of battle fatigue?"

"Yes."

"There were what—three days?—between the motorcycle accident and the shooting?"

"Three days. June 17 through June 20."

"How much sleep did Lester get during those three days?"

"I don't know. Why?"

"Enough sleeplessness might be grounds for a psychotic episode." Klagsbrun stood up. "Hypothetically," he added. The chair continued to rock. "It might be worth looking into," he said.

On the Jersey Turnpike, Arlene said, "I like him. Maybe *you* ought to go to him."

30

August 3, 1973

At 6:00 a.m., Robert telephoned Lester at home. "What time can you leave the job?"

"Four thirty," Lester said. "Maybe four o'clock."

"That's no good. I have to be in the Freehold Courthouse from three o'clock on."

"What's the problem?"

"It'll hold," Robert said. "Come for dinner. Seven o'clock." He gave Lester his Deal address.

By then, Lester had backed up Victor's story concerning the doctor in the cafeteria, but Dr. X couldn't be found. With Steve and Karen Applegate, his secretary, Robert had gone each day to Jersey Shore Medical Center when the shifts changed, to talk to every employee who had been within five feet of Lester or George. Interviews were conducted in the doctors' lounge. Most witnesses were like Juanita Johnson, who began with hostility, irritated at being imposed upon, angry at being involved, and not thrilled with Lester. Robert and Steve turned most of them around, but no new facts emerged— and Dr. X didn't appear among those interviewed. He remained the one crucial witness who couldn't be found, and his discovery now would be difficult because Steve was on his way back to Boston. Before Steve left, he had said, "Are you going to go for broke?"

"I don't know," Robert had answered. "It's up to Lester."

At 7:00 p.m., Lester arrived, wearing his best flowered sportshirt and blue corduroy pants. The Jamaican maid let him in. Arlene greeted him warmly. At the chrome-and-glass dining table, over flowers and candles, Robert's oldest son, Scott, said to Lester, "Gee —I hope you get off."

After dinner, Robert took Lester into the living room. Outside, the grounds were lit. Past the expanse of glass, ten-year-old Brian was walking the apricot poodle. Everywhere, the zinnias bloomed in lavish colors. Robert settled into a brown velvet chair. "This is important," he said. "We have a decision to make and you have to help me."

"Okay." Lester lit a cigarette and began, methodically, to smoke it down.

"All right, let's start from where we are. The Prosecution has charged you with Murder One."

"Right," Lester said.

"I've already explained to you, a conviction under Murder One brings an automatic penalty of life imprisonment. The judge can't say, *This is a nice guy, I'll only give him five or ten years*. Murder One, if we lose, you go to jail for life. Do you remember that?"

"Right. Like I would be in jail . . ." Lester flushed.

"Okay. Now, you know I've sent you to two psychiatrists because I'm considering a psychiatric defense."

"I definitely don't think Klagsbrun thinks I'm crazy."

"I don't know yet what Klagsbrun thinks."

"I'm not crazy."

"I'm trying to explain something to you."

"Right."

"There's one kind of psychiatric defense that attempts to exonerate you—that means you weren't responsible at all for what you did. We go in for Murder One. It's all or nothing. They either let you go free or they send you away for life. Do you understand that?"

"Right," Lester said.

"Okay. Now, Murder One depends on three elements—premeditation, deliberation, and willfulness. It doesn't matter if you don't understand what that means. What's important about it is, in order to get you acquitted, we only have to knock out one of the three. But that's going to be tough to do. There's no way I can promise you we're going to be able to do that."

"What's the other way?" asked Lester.

"The other way," said Robert, "we go in for Murder Two. We also use a psychiatric defense, diminished responsibility—that means you were only partly responsible for what you did. The jury's happy to buy it and you'd probably get a Murder Two conviction. That means the Judge has some choice about the sentence—five years, three years . . ."

"I'd still go to jail, right?"

"The choice is, do we want to gamble on all or nothing? On acquittal versus life imprisonment? Or do we settle going in for a couple of years?"

"I don't want to spend one day in jail," Lester said.

"It could be five or ten years versus the rest of your life."

"It could be twenty, also—right?"

"Yes."

Lester shook his head. "If I have to spend twenty years, I would still do it again because I had to do it, you know? But that doesn't mean I want to spend twenty years. I mean, whatever happens, I guess I could take it. I'm strong. I could take it. But I don't want to take it."

"You'd better think about it," Robert said.

"I don't need to think about it. I'd rather take a chance. Like ten years in jail is the same to me as my whole life. What's the difference? Ten years from now, I'll be thirty-three years old. I won't have my young years left, you know?"

"Thirty-three's not so old," Robert said.

"Not for you. For me, it would be. Like what I think about is maybe goin' into business, maybe havin' three bulldozers, somethin' —so maybe one day I could have a house like this, you know? Maybe not as good as this, but almost as good as this. Like maybe I could have a wife with class, like your wife—all those things like people have who were born in this country, you know? That would take a lot of work. I don't mind workin'. I'd definitely rather take a chance, because if they take ten years of my life, I'm never gonna catch up. You see—" Lester looked at Robert—"you have to make it while you're young."

31

PSYCHIATRIC REPORT

Lester Zygmanik

BY: Dr. Samuel Klagsbrun

NOTE TO ANSELL: I know you've got a Dostoevsky situation, but Lester seems calm, not torn by conflict—he appears to have evenness, gentleness, lack of depth.

In this initial session, Lester seemed guarded and careful, tense, but lounging, trying to be cool. He said he didn't trust psychiatrists, that he couldn't understand "how someone can come into an office and just talk and feel better." Clearly, Lester does not like situations he cannot fully comprehend, or control in some manner.

I said, in order to help him, I needed to understand his background, his current life, and, eventually, something of what happened over the three days which preceded the shooting of his brother. In order to put him at ease, I asked him to start by giving me some information about his background.

Instead, he spent most of the session talking about his father.

Lester sees his father as an extraordinarily hard-working man with an almost invincible aura about him. His father could do no wrong even when he engaged in economically bad ventures. Lester's view of his father is that he was "too good" and was "taken advantage of"—and Lester recalls numerous examples of this.

Lester speaks of his father as if he were not dead.

He describes his father as a man who "likes everybody," then says, "My father only trusts people who came from Polish backgrounds—who came from the war, people like him." He says, "My father lives with the fear that in this country the authorities will turn on him like they did in Poland."

Lester recalls quarrels between his mother and father: his mother's need for security versus his father's desire to change jobs. Lester describes his father as a quiet man, then says, "But my father gets into many arguments." Lester says, "The usual punishment my father would give me was to strap me a few times. Sometimes he would strap me until I was black and blue."

Lester feels this was just.

Lester views his past without rancor or bitterness. He sees his father as a deeply moral man whose sense of loyalty and fairness was innate. One of Lester's main motives in life is to live up to his father's standards and to be like him in every regard. He is not aware he has been presented with totally contradictory images.

NOTE TO ANSELL: Lester's father comes through as a kind of "earth man" who taught Lester an incredible mixture of don't-trust-people while he allowed himself to be taken advantage of. He appears to fall into a category which has been named "the suffering servant of God"—that is, a man who finds recognition through martyrdom. He was, clearly, an angry saint. One of the means to subvert aggression is to do noble deeds, to assert oneself for the other guy, get "clobbered" for the other guy, get recognition, gratitude, and suffering in one move.

The very troubling aspect of Lester's identification with his father was clearly in evidence when I asked Lester how his father would have reacted to the shooting.

Lester replied, "My father would have done the same thing. Except that my father would have killed himself, also." Lester added, "I don't have that kind of courage."

32

Robert Ansell

I have to deal with Lester's head. I don't want him to sit around thinking of all the crazy things he did. I don't want to present him to a jury as somebody who believes he's crazy. I want Lester to be Lester, and let his craziness come from what other people around him felt and observed. I want him to keep his own concept of how rational everything was that he did, and put that in this maelstrom everyone else describes. I think it'll make him appear even more irrational. So I'm trying to preserve his head. I don't want him to sit and talk about it all the time so he gets his recollections mixed up with what other people say. That's very dangerous. I've told him not to talk to his mother or Jean or anybody else. Even I'm very careful in talking to him about it. So, in a way, it's become a cat-and-mouse game.

He's very curious. He wants to know "What did Motley say about me?" or "What did Klagsbrun say about me?" He wants to see the reports. And he continues to ask to see the autopsy and the photographs. I think, underneath, he wants to see if George's spinal cord was really ripped up, the way the doctors described it. He never gave me that reason, but I think if the autopsy report said George's spinal cord was only minimally bruised, Lester might go off a cliff. I don't show him anything and I don't talk to him about my thinking on this case. He's made all the decisions he's entitled to.

He's very concerned about my estimate. He asks me constantly what his chances are. You can't put him in an icebox to preserve him, so I always say, "The worse off we ever were was at 11:07 p.m. on the night of June 20 when you fired that shot." I can't tell him—can I?—that it's possible this case was over on the night of June 20 when he fired that shot.

33

August 1973

In August, the temperature climbed.

In the *Asbury Park Press*, news of Lester Zygmanik gave way to the approaching resurrection of the once-renowned Baby Parade. In the Sunday Supplement, a local celebrity poll selected John Wayne and Julie Andrews as favorite film stars—the second straight year for John Wayne; Julie Andrews replaced Doris Day.

In Perrineville, Sonia Zygmanik was often alone. Jean and four-year-old George, Jr., remained with Victor. On the day they left, in July, little Georgie had said to her, "Lester killed my daddy."

Through August, Sonia continued to rise at dawn, and dress, and make coffee for Lester before he left. In the hours that followed, friends no longer came from Perth Amboy and the phone didn't ring. The old house echoed. She did little housework, was not bored, occupied herself with coffee, cigarettes, memories, and rumination. To Robert, she seemed fulfilled by tragedy. At no time did she nurse the illusion that God was available for bargaining, or the mother's conviction that she could bring her son back. Remembering simply kept her company.

She talked to Robert about her youth, the war, her dead husband, her own thrift, her instinct for property. About Lester's predicament, she remained unwilling to do more than sum up her feelings in some learned phrase, most often slang, saying about her own loneliness, "Oh, boy!"

Robert drove to the farm regularly to spend time with Lester, hanging around while Lester painted the house or trained the beagles—raising issues, feeding Lester cross-examination questions, testing the effect of Lester's simplicity and Lester's confusions, preparing for trial. Lester remained stoic, sustained by a belief in luck and a touching bravado. Robert didn't tamper with any of it. Subliminally, he planned to argue: *The murderer as victim.*

On Thursday, August 9, Robert filed a formal statement of intent to plead temporary insanity.

By then, Lester was going regularly to New York to see Dr. Samuel Klagsbrun. Lester appeared to like Klagsbrun, but, so far, nothing earth-shaking had come out of it. Robert had sent Lester back for one more visit to Dr. John Motley who afterward reported Lester had said, "My lawyer wants to find out if I'm crazy or not. I don't think I'm crazy."

In the evening, Robert walked the beach, wrestling with the ongoing questions:

Could he conceive a psychiatric defense that was more than a traditional, old-fashioned bow to the system? And if he did, how did he make certain it didn't boomerang? How did he dismantle the average juror's feeling that psychiatry was a dupe?

What kind of results would come out of Lester's obligatory examination by a State psychiatrist? Then, even if both Klagsbrun and Motley ended up in his corner, wouldn't the trial come down to one psychiatrist's word against another's? What about the average juror's mistrust of all psychiatrists?

Then, there was Klagsbrun's suggestion concerning the effect of lack of sleep. Preliminary research had located a sleep laboratory at the University of California in Los Angeles, but a telephone call revealed the lab had been closed for two years. Should he continue to pursue it? The most cursory research disclosed it was one of those fields where no two authorities agreed. If he based his defense on that kind of rebuttable premise, what happened if Carton came up with his own sleep expert?

The following night, he drove to the farm and took Lester out for a beer. He chose a nearby bar on highway 33, a dark place, nearly empty, not one of Lester's usual haunts. Over the second beer, he said, "You really loved your brother—is that right?"

"Right," Lester said.

"The two of you never argued?"

"Sometimes. Like about who would cut the grass."

"You didn't argue about other things?"

"No."

"George was your father's favorite, wasn't he?"

"No."

"Didn't you have your eye on Jean?"

"Are you crazy?" Lester said.

"You keep talking about all this love shit," Robert said. "If you loved your brother so damned much, why'd you use a shotgun, like you were going to shoot an animal?"

"What's the matter with you?" Lester said.

"If there's anything you're holding back, I don't want to learn about it when the Prosecutor questions you in court."

"I loved my brother."

"You never argued? About money? About women? Anything?"

"No."

"There's nothing you haven't told me? Nothing you left out—or forgot?"

"No."

"Think about it."

"There's only one thing," Lester said. "About my mother."

"What about her?"

"That night—the night my brother got shot. My mother wasn't sleepin'. My mother took the gun away from me."

"Before you left for the hospital?"

"Right."

"What happened?"

"She took the gun away from me and she put it on top of her dresser."

"Is that the only fact you've held back?"

"Right. When I brought it up, she got mad. She called me a liar."

"Why did you lie?"

"She's my mother."

"I don't give a damn," Robert said.

The next morning, he went to see Sonia.

She kept shaking her head, pretending she didn't understand him.

He repeated his question. "On the night of the shooting, Lester says you took the gun away from him. You said, 'Let God do it.'"

"No," she said. "No gun." She had never seen Lester with a gun.

He wondered if she understood he planned to argue: *Death was a family decision.*

He restated the question. She continued to shake her head. He said, "It's important."

"Why?" she said.

"I want to prove that Lester was *not right*." He tapped his head. "Lester remembers you put the gun on your dresser. Lester doesn't remember taking the gun off your dresser." He hesitated. "If Lester remembers some things and he doesn't remember other things, it would help Lester. Do you understand?"

"No," she said.

"You can help Lester," he said. "Please—the night of the shooting, did you take the gun away from Lester?"

She shook her head. "No," she said.

"Are you sure?"

"I never forget," she said.

34

PSYCHIATRIC REPORT

Lester Zygmanik

BY: Dr. Samuel Klagsbrun

NOTE TO ANSELL: The following is a transcribed portion of our last session. I am including it intact because I feel you should be aware of the nature of Lester's one remaining family relationship.

LESTER:

Like not only is my brother gone, but my mother may not have a Lester any more either. I realize that's the reason my mother wants me home—because there's no one left other than me. Any friend I bring over, if he comes repeatedly, then my mother automatically thinks he is an evil influence on me, that he is taking me away from her, you know? That's what she worries about mostly.

My mother thinks I take dope. One of the reasons she thinks I take dope is because when I was seventeen years old a friend gave me a stick of pot, and she found it, so she considers me a person who takes dope. I go out too much. I smoke too much. She thinks. Like if I go out once a week, she says I go out every night.

She used to do that to my father, accuse my father of all kinds of things, make accusations. She tries to do the same thing to me. But I don't go for that stuff.

My mother doesn't like to stay alone. She's afraid to stay alone. Like I don't really feel she thinks I did the wrong thing, but she worries more about having to stay alone.

When I was a kid, my mother looked pretty good, physically, I mean. She likes to have somebody tell her how good she looks. We lived in an apartment house in Perth Amboy on the second floor until I was five. There was no heat and no hot water. Me and my brother and my mother, we slept together. Like there were no beds.

My mother used to tell my father on me if I did something wrong. She always made things sound worse. It's a good thing I'm a calm person. You know? I don't get aggravated too easily. I worry about her now. It seems to me she's getting lazy. My mother would never believe that, but it's true. I make her do things every day. I give her a job. I keep her busy, so that she knows there are a few things for her to do every day. She keeps tellin' me, Don't worry, everything will be okay, she's spoken to a priest.

35

Robert Ansell

Every racehorse has the same birthday. It doesn't matter when that horse is born, his birthday is listed as January 1. A horse born in March has a six-month advantage over a horse born in September, because both of them are considered yearlings on New Year's Day. In a race for two-year-olds, then, my horse is going to be twenty-one months old while the other guy's horse is really only fifteen months old, so which one is going to have the better chance? As an owner, that's how you increase your odds. Whatever it is—thoroughbreds or a trial—you have to figure out how to increase your odds.

If you're going to compare Lester's case with horseracing, you'd have to say we've got the youngest, weakest horse in the race. Even if you forget all the damaging facts—the sawing of the shotgun, the waxing of the bullet, the twenty-minute drive alone to the hospital. Even if you forget the one good piece of evidence we have—the doctor in the cafeteria, because (a) nobody can find him, and (b) what's he going to say if we do find him? Is he going to take the stand and say, "Hey, I had a conversation with the defendant that sent him over the edge"? So, forget everything else and concentrate on the big problem—my witnesses.

Those twelve people, the jury, are going to be sitting there and I can't tell the story myself. I can only tell it through the mouths of my witnesses. And who do I have? First, I've got Victor to tell the story of the cafeteria incident. How's Victor going to look to a jury? Number one, Victor wasn't happy about his daughter's marriage to George. Number two, he can see money coming out of this whole situation. Number three, he's going to be in the spotlight, which he's going to relish and that's going to come across. Number four, he doesn't have enough teeth, he's grubby-looking, and he speaks in that raspy voice. Now, who the hell is going to like Victor?

Then, there's Diane, Lester's girlfriend. In point of fact, she's harmless and kind of a lady. But she's got a cheap, dyed red hair, floozy kind of look, and that's how she's got to come across.

Then, we've got Sonia. In terms of her role, she could be sensational—she's the mother, she lost a husband and then a son, she could be a very sympathetic kind of witness. But we can't use her. All I can do is put her on so that the jury can look at her and see there's a mother. In terms of what she looks like and even the way she talks, that would be fine, but I have no idea what she's going to say. She could say anything. So, what have we got—a time bomb or a token mother?

Then, there's Jean. On the surface, Jean could be all right. But Jean is Victor's daughter and not only is she Victor's daughter, she's under his control. Who knows what she'll say on a witness stand? Maybe she'll help Lester, or maybe she'll say something Victor planted in her mind. So, there's Jean, a key witness and a dangerous witness.

The trial is set for October 29. That's the line-up. Which horse do you want to put your money on?

36

September 12, 1973

According to New Jersey law, pre-trial preparation included a mandatory exchange of facts between Defense and Prosecution. The regulation was intended to eliminate surprise, to make the trial an honest search for the truth, and to avoid a victory for either side based on secrecy. Like most legalities, it worked best in principle.

Early in the week, Robert had been permitted to inspect the sawed-off shotgun, the shells, and Lester's clothes. He was given copies of all lab reports and the gory autopsy photographs. The autopsy report, in its entirety, again noted the twenty-four pellets in George's skull, but raised no question.

To the Monmouth County Prosecutor's Office, Robert had delivered a statement saying he would forward all doctors' examination reports, both mental and physical. He had included Lester's records from Perth Amboy High. He had sent a list of more than forty witnesses because any names he didn't submit would be prohibited from testifying. He had not included his own discovery of the seventy-five missing shotgun pellets or the waxing of the bullet.

On Wednesday morning, the mail brought copies of all interviews taken by the Prosecution of State's witnesses. The packet included statements from Juanita Johnson, Robert Blannett, Katherine Kealy, and Alexander Lee Smith. All were dated June 21, the day after the shooting—except one. On June 23, a statement had been taken from a Gregory Carver, age twenty-six, anesthesiology student at Jersey Shore Medical Center. Carver's statement began, "On the afternoon prior to the shooting, I was in the cafeteria, having lunch, when the patient's brother approached me. . . ."

At 10:00 p.m. on Wednesday, Robert's desk was littered with coffee cups, the remains of barely touched sandwiches, and an ashtray that overflowed. Slouched in a chair, Lester looked solemn and weary.

"Let's go over it again," Robert said.

"Which night?"

"Start with Saturday, the day before George's accident. Try to figure out exactly how much sleep you got. Two hours? Three hours? Seven hours?" Until this morning, Klagsbrun's reference to sleep-deprivation had been a backup theory. Carton's discovery of Gregory Carver had made it crucial.

"Like I told you," Lester said. "I took this girl back to Trenton. I spent the night with this girl."

"She could testify you didn't sleep?"

"Right."

"What was her name?"

"I think—Michele."

"What's her last name?"

"I don't know."

"Is there anybody who could testify that you took her home?"

"I don't know."

"Think about it," Robert said.

In the past few days, the problems had multiplied. He had spent the better part of Monday looking for a junkie. On June 20, a few hours before the shooting, a heart patient in the bed next to George had been removed and his bed given to an addict. The hospital refused to release the junkie's name. The image that continued to plague Robert was one of the anonymous junkie being arrested two weeks before Lester's trial and deciding that the way to get out of jail might be to bargain some helpful information to the Prosecutor on the Zygmanik case. His image extended itself to the courtroom, to the junkie on the stand, saying he was in the bed next to George and, right before Lester pulled the trigger, George was screaming, "No—no, don't kill me!"

The Prosecution had found Gregory Carver when he couldn't. Would Malcolm Carton also be able to find the junkie?

Lester's eyes looked bloodshot.

Robert settled into an easy chair and propped his feet on the glass table.

"What are my chances?" Lester said. "Fifty-fifty?"

"It's not a horserace," Robert said. "Now—let's get back to Sunday. When you got back from the hospital on Sunday night, what time did you go to sleep?"

"I'm trying to remember."

"Try a little harder."

"What difference does it make, my sleepin' or not sleepin', anyway?"

"Just think about it. Try to answer the question," Robert said.

Red tape and the Prosecutor's acrobatics had swallowed his time. The current issue between them was Nathan Acari, the heart patient who had been replaced by the junkie. Acari was an impact witness, one who could graphically describe George's condition and George's pleas to die. But Acari was scheduled for a heart operation in the Midwest and might not be around for the trial. For a deposition, both Prosecution and Defense had to be present. Carton had remained unavailable. Robert had been forced into another motion. For the third time, Carton had appeared in court, consented, and left.

At 10:45 p.m., Lester circled the office like a caged bear. "What did Motley say about me?"

"Motley hasn't sent a report."

"What did Klagsbrun say? I'd definitely like to know what Klagsbrun has to say."

"There's no report," Robert said. "Go back to Monday. How much sleep did you get on Monday night?"

"I'm thinkin' about it," Lester said.

At 11:00 p.m., the telephone interrupted. On the other end, David Silver said, "I'm at Jersey Shore Medical Center."

"What'd you find out?"

In Steve's absence, David had interviewed Lester's friends, teachers, and compatriots at the Holiday Beagle Club, including fifty-six-year-old Dan Parrotino, who had summed everything up. "The family's not American," Parrotino had said.

"The junkie's in a mental institution," David said.

"How'd you find that out?"

"Off the record. A doctor here is a friend of my father's."

"What about Kales?" Dr. Kales was an expert on the effects of sleep-deprivation, located in Hershey, Pennsylvania.

"Haven't gotten hold of him yet."

Robert hung up. To Lester, he said, "Where were we? Monday night? Let's go over it again. Before we leave here tonight, I want an estimate of how much sleep you got between Saturday night and Wednesday night. The entire three days."

"I don't know," Lester said. "Like I told you. I never sleep much. You know? I just go. I just keep goin'."

At midnight, Robert took everything home. He sat up in bed, papers scattered around him, going over all of it. Arlene insisted on looking at the bloody autopsy photographs while he went through Gregory Carver's statement again. Carver wasn't a doctor. He was an anesthesiology student. Carver's statement predictably contradicted Lester's version of what took place. The statement contained no basis for claiming an emotional turning point. There was no hair-raising description of George's condition, no vivid details which might have spurred Lester into his act. There was nothing.

Carver reported: "He [Lester] *asked me what the outlook was for his brother's recovery and I said there was no way for me to know that. . . . I said as long as there was any possibility for him* [George] *to get better, we would do everything in our power to help him. . . .*"

Carver's statement reeked of piety.

Arlene handed George's autopsy photographs back. All she said was, "He's not circumcised."

It was after midnight when the phone rang. Robert grabbed it.

David said, "I got Kales. You have an appointment at the Sleep Research Center in Hershey, Pennsylvania. Monday afternoon. Two o'clock."

"You're going to make a helluva lawyer," Robert said.

37

PSYCHIATRIC REPORT

Lester Zygmanik

BY: Dr. Samuel Klagsbrun

Today, Lester spoke about the trust he has for Ansell. Lester has a kind of fatalism about the outcome of the trial, and appears to be quietly, and with some nobility, accepting whatever society is going to decide to do with him. He acknowledges the fact that he might go to jail—and I find myself trying to prepare him for such a possibility.

Lester talks a great deal about George, and his own sense of loss. George was essentially the second anchor in Lester's life. (After his father's death, George became the primary anchor.) George figured prominently in Lester's future plans.

For the most part, Lester prefers talking about his girlfriend, Diane, and how to extract himself from that relationship, than about anything else. But he realizes this is foolish, that he is here for other reasons.

In this session, Lester talked a little more about his mother. He said, "My mother said to me the other day maybe my brother would have gotten better. She asked me, 'Do you really feel your brother wanted to get shot?' And I said, 'He didn't want to get shot, he just wanted to die.' "

NOTE TO ANSELL: This was session in which Lester roamed widely over a number of topics. I was able, however, to form a further impression.

It seems to me Lester is like a Léger painting—he is made up of bits and pieces of his father and his brother.

He appears to be what is known as an "as if" personality—that is, one who has little real personality of his own, but behaves *as if* he were manly, strong, courageous—all the things he admires in his brother and father, or, perhaps, in others.

38

September 1973

It was a long session. There were parts Lester couldn't remember, but he started with the night before his brother's accident and he made himself keep on going to the moment when he pulled the trigger. When he finished, he felt freed from something.

At five o'clock, he came out of Klagsbrun's office into the noise of 69th Street. The sky had turned to gunmetal. A ceiling of clouds threw tricky shadows. He could smell the threat of rain. Unwilling to go home, he fell into the rhythm of the street, carried along by the flow of hurrying pedestrians, moving west. He felt dazed and strangely euphoric.

When he reached Park Avenue, he headed downtown, distracted by the symbols of wealth, huge apartment houses, emblazoned doormen, a beribboned poodle in a waiting limousine. A light wind had begun to blow. It was closing time. From the side streets came a stream of people. Up ahead, Grand Central loomed. He thought about taking a train somewhere, but he didn't know where. He had a need to see who he was in the eyes of strangers.

He covered a dozen blocks, walking briskly, measuring his size and shape against the avenue, wondering how it might feel to live in the city, surrounded by people and the awesome sense of endless possibilities. New York had always bewildered him. Now, turning west on 57th, he felt pleased by the darkening sky, the burgeoning traffic, a girl's skirt flashing in the wind, strange shouts, a policeman's shrill whistle. In a brief flash of clarity, he saw he had given up something to Klagsbrun—his conviction of an enclosed destiny. He felt a sudden release of energy and a desire to test his new power.

He crossed Madison and moved on to Fifth. Two blocks uptown, he could see the traffic clogged in front of the Plaza and Central Park. He kept moving, crosstown, past the Russian Tea Room and Carnegie Hall. He felt a kinship with passing strangers. Below Columbus Circle, he stopped to smoke a cigarette. He saw the people were less sophisticated, working people, more familiar. A young man was walking three ducks on a leash. The ducks were wearing baby shoes. He moved on. After a while, he could hear the sounds of the boats on the Hudson.

He started uptown again. On Broadway he toyed with the notion of finding a bar. The street was shabby, in the process of being rebuilt, a haven for winos, junkies, out-of-town salesmen, and prostitutes. The lights were going on, glittering neon. Nobody bothered him. In a store window, it took him a moment to recognize his own reflection. He felt he was on the verge of discovering something. He was close to Lincoln Center when lightning split the sky, thunder rolled, and a light, cool rain began to fall—the end of summer. Ducking under canopies, he searched for a bar, avoiding those that looked intimidating, trying to find a familiar refuge. He felt a sudden need for a girl, a different kind of girl.

Feeling solid and clear-headed, he made a choice. Inside, the place seemed funky, gray and smoke-filled, Ray Charles singing over the noise of an espresso machine, a faded mural on the wall. The patrons were young and seemed to know each other. He noticed that a few wore theatrical make-up. Most looked like hippies. At the bar, he ordered a beer. Nobody spoke to him. After a few minutes, a tall black man made a flamboyant entrance wearing an oversized hat and an iridescent shirt, shouting, "Hello, lover!" at an albino-haired young man, and greeting everybody else with a high, tinkling laugh. Then Lester heard the black man say, "Look out for the narc." Somebody laughed. The exchange made him uncomfortable. A moment later, he felt somebody take the stool next to him, and when he looked around, he saw the girl was slender and small-breasted, wearing a black leotard and faded jeans—a pale translucent face surrounded by marmalade curls, bare arms leaning carelessly across the bar.

"Jesus saves," she said. "What do you do?"

"I'm in construction," he said.

"What do you build? Temples? Pyramids? Stage sets? Old-age homes?" Her voice was deep, husky.

"I build houses," he said.

"Suburban?" she said. "Planned marriage followed by planned parenthood? PTA, paddle tennis, canned religion, charge accounts, custom shirts, and small trips to Bermuda." She rattled it off. "The program reads: *Security*," she said. "I'm a refugee."

He had no idea what she was talking about. "Houses from fifty to eighty thousand dollars," he said.

"In Red China, doctors cart garbage and lawyers carry bedpans," she said. "Are you a narc?"

"No."

"You look like a cop."

"I'm not a cop," he said.

"You look Slavic. Are you Slavic?"

"I'm American." He felt his face flush.

"Chopin was a Polack," she said. "And Paderewski. And Carole Lombard." She smiled at him. "If you could have ten people to dinner who were dead—who would you have?"

"My brother," he said, considering the idea. "And my father."

"I'm sorry . . ." she said.

"That's okay."

"What are you doing here?"

"I came in out of the rain," he said.

39

September 17, 1973

In the morning mail, Robert Ansell found the following letter:

What are you trying to do? Make a name for yourself like the lawyer in the Sam Sheppard case? I happen to have received hand-painted cards from a man and a woman in Florida. Both are paralyzed from the neck down, yet they paint these cards by holding a brush in their teeth. It takes three months to make one design, yet these people support themselves. Who knows if Lester's brother would have recovered? Miracles happen. I believe in the ten commandments. A man is dead. His brother killed him. Your client should go to jail for life.

It wasn't a good start for a Monday morning.

The first phone call of the day advised him that his client Lester Zygmanik had an appointment with the State psychiatrist, Dr. David J. Flicker, on October 4.

The phone call didn't cheer him up either.

A half-hour later, David Silver came in to say the rumors were: Lester had shot his brother because he was having an affair with his brother's wife. Robert snapped, "I wish to hell the Prosecutor would build his case around that."

There were no commercial flights to Hershey, Pennsylvania. At 10:00 a.m., accompanied by his secretary, Karen Applegate, and David Silver, Robert climbed into a chartered plane. The flight cost $90. Karen spent the flight with the pilot, who looked like Robert Redford.

The University of Pennsylvania Hospital was new. In its well-equipped labs, scientists were engaged in exploring uncharted fields—among them, marijuana research and sleep research. Dr. Anthony Kales turned out to be a slender, dark-haired, soft-spoken man in his late thirties, wearing spectacles, shirt sleeves, and a small mustache. Not much of what he represented was theoretical. Kales was the man in the field, in the lab, the man who conducted experiments, who got his hands dirty and stuck his neck out—one of the foremost experts on sleep in the country.

In the privacy of a conference room, Robert sold Lester's position, giving a twenty-minute presentation of the facts in their most sympathetic light. When he had finished, Kales said, "How can I help?"

It was a bumpy flight back.

Kales had given him a crash course on sleep research and enough material to fill a briefcase. Robert began to go through it. Kales had warned him the field was a controversial one. Now he found that contradictions existed even regarding the definition of sleep.

Sleep was defined as:

• a healthy condition of inertia and unresponsiveness

• a complex, dynamic process during which the sleeper is extremely "busy"

• a structured experience, following an orderly progression through drowsiness, light sleep, medium-depth sleep, and deep sleep

• a restorative process, a period of recuperation

• a simple behavioral adaptation, learned and non-vital

• a preventative of destructive wakeful acts

Robert made notes. He passed the material to David. Karen stayed up front with the pilot. The sky turned dark. The plane jolted around like a recalcitrant horse. Robert continued to read.

It was interesting reading:

Nobody clearly understands the function of sleep.

The older a person gets, the less sleep he needs. Babies need sixteen hours. Many of the elderly sleep no more than five hours a day.

In the animal world, predators sleep more than prey, presumably because they feel safer. Cows, sheep, and goats sleep only two or three hours a day because it takes most of the twenty-four hours to eat enough grass food to survive. Oppossum and armadillos sleep twenty hours a day—they can acquire all the food they need in two hours.

New material learned before eight hours of sleep is retained better than new material learned before eight hours of wakefulness.

Strenuous exercise just before going to bed interferes with sleep, though exercise several hours before going to bed enhances sleep.

No definite proof has ever been found that people can learn in their sleep.

Twenty million Americans suffer from some kind of sleep-disturbance.

Not much of it was what he was looking for: *Can sleep-deprivation precipitate a psychotic episode?*

The one fact everybody appeared to agree on was the presence, if not the purpose, of dreaming. By means of an electroencephalogram, scientists had been able to monitor bodily functions during sleep. They had discovered that, at intervals during sleep, volunteers tended to focus their eyes as if they were making observations. These "Rapid Eye Movements" came to be known by their initials, REM, indicating the stage of sleep during which dreaming occurred. "While dreaming, breathing becomes irregular, heart rate is elevated, a rise in adrenal hormone occurs, and brain waves resemble those of waking life."

Dreams occurred only during light and medium sleep.

While awake, individuals exercised "cerebral vigilance," by which means they judged reality. During sleep, the dreamer accepted hallucinatory experiences as real, accepting situations that would seem incongruous if awake.

Experiments had found no non-dreamer, though many people didn't remember their dreams. Most people dreamed for a period of approximately two hours every night; periods of dreaming and non-dreaming alternated during the night.

There were some startling facts:

Dreams do not take place rapidly; dream events occupy about the same amount of time as corresponding natural events.

The younger the child, the more REM sleep; a newborn spends 50 percent of his sleeping existence in REM, or one-third of his life.

During some periods of dreaming, the body burns up more caloric energy than during a bout of heavy exercise.

Kinsey reported that 99 percent of American college-educated males had orgasmic dreams and 70 percent of corresponding females reported frankly sexual dreams.

The dreams of persons suffering from emotional stress reflect their waking life—i.e., soldiers dream of battle.

There was no agreement on the function of dreaming. Some authorities said loss of dreaming time could lead to anxiety, irritability, and personality disturbance. Others claimed that many functioned adequately without dreaming. Whether dreams were a means of solving either deep-rooted problems or those of everyday life was up for grabs. Physically, REM was triggered in the lower center of the brain, which then sent explosive messages to the upper brain and central nervous system. Whether or not this process which resulted in dreaming served as an emotional safety valve had never been determined. However, there was a method to solve the content of one's own dream: (1) Ask yourself what kind of feeling the dream leaves you with, and (2) look at the pictures as visual metaphors.

It was a smorgasbord. He could take his pick and whatever he picked was refutable.

David said, "Can I talk to you about something?"

"Later." The plane danced around as if it had no will of its own. Robert kept reading.

Disagreement widened. On the effects of sleep-deprivation, opinions ranged from those who claimed it had no effect at all to those who claimed that loss of sleep caused alterations of thought—perceptual, visual, and auditory hallucinations, anxiety, aggression, and social affectation.

The longest sleep-deprivation on record was that of a high-school student in San Diego who went without sleep for eleven days and was completely restored after a twelve-hour sleep. . . .

In 1969, Kales and a group of doctors did a study with four healthy adult males, depriving them of sleep for 205 hours. Kales' results indicated they all suffered from "transient ego-disruptive phenomena." At 168 hours, one of the subjects experienced frightening visual hallucinations, screamed in terror, and fell to the floor, sobbing and muttering incoherently about a gorilla. . . .

Science Digest reported on a twenty-seven-year-old disc jockey in Michigan who attempted to establish a new "wake-athon." After seventy-two hours, he grew irritable. After 100 hours, he talked volubly and incessantly in grandiose terms, and was obviously becoming paranoid. By 160 hours, he was plagued by visual hallucinations and dreaming-while-awake episodes. He had blackout periods—and grabbed a companion around the throat with the apparent intention of choking him. . . .

Another theory proposed that a sleep-deprived person tended to keep falling into a light sleep without being aware of it, and so was subject to all the effects of light or borderline sleep, including dreaming-while-awake, abnormalities of thinking, hallucinations, and other similarities to schizophrenia.

There were as many experiments that suggested little or no personality deterioration.

Any prosecutor could take all speculation apart.

"Can I talk to you now?" David said.

"What's on your mind?"

"When I went back to the University of Virginia to register, I stopped in to see the head of the Psychology Department. He told me they did a jury survey before the Harrisburg Seven conspiracy trial, and before the Ellsberg trial. You take a sample from the voting list, then poll that sample on age, occupation, attitudes, that kind of thing. You find out if a Republican is a better juror for us than a Democrat, what age, what religion, everything."

"What's wrong with an impartial jury?" Robert said.

"There's no such thing. *You* taught me that."

"In the first place, the Harrisburg jury panel was predisposed *against* the defendant. In Lester's case, most will start out sympathetic. In the second place, Monmouth County's a small town. Everybody knows me and everybody knows Malcolm Carton. If the Prosecution finds out we're doing a survey, we could end up with judicial repercussions. Or they could decide to do their own survey. No dice."

"Mercy killing's a philosophical question," David said. "We can find out what type of people are predisposed to condemn it, what type might have open minds."

"No."

"It might help me get into law school," David said.

"You're a bright kid. You don't need any help," Robert said. The plane hit an air pocket. He went back to his reading.

"Deep sleep is entered in the earlier part of the night. REM is entered at periodic times during the night and each dreaming period is of longer duration than the previous one. . . .

"Nobody has, as yet, proved the function of sleep in the human being. . . ."

Robert leaned back and closed his eyes, trying to figure out what a jury would understand. What did average people know about sleep from their own experience? What did he know about sleep from his own life? He needed to find a way to present his theory as fact, a means that would be simple, dramatic, and irrefutable. The solution wasn't at his fingertips.

Karen said, "The pilot wants to know if he can come to the trial."

40

October 1973

Autumn arrived.

In a burst of color and a cold, brisk wind, the rich and the poor parted ways.

In rural Jersey, truck farms were plowed under and planted in winter rye to be used next spring as green fertilizer. Dairy farms stocked up with hay for the cattle. The remaining migrant workers moved on to the Finger Lakes grape region or the Hudson Valley orchards or south. Along the shore, striped bass and bluefish on their way from Maine to the Carolinas could be caught by the handful, and in the woods, bird season began, with hunters stalking the marshes with guns and soft-mouthed golden retrievers. In the suburbs, women mulched roses; men raked leaves for the compost bin and laid in the firewood. At the beach clubs, the rich brought their boats into drydock for winter. Fanatics would play golf on country-club greens until the first snow. In the ghettos, children collected insulation in the form of newspapers and rags.

A month ago, on the first Monday in September, the tourists had vanished. The boardwalk had been closed since Labor Day. Now the last of the concessionaires moved south with the chefs and the waiters and those who had run the summer hotels. The old men and women were gone, their benches relinquished to seagulls and the ocean's gray horizon to the smoking garbage scow.

In the final days of the political contest for Governor of New Jersey, both aspirants launched last-minute attacks. Liberal Democrat Brendan T. Byrne denounced conservative Republican Charles W. Sandman as a candidate who would usher in an "era of darkness." Supporters of Sandman distributed literature outside Sunday church services, claiming that Byrne favored abortion. Sandman further accused Byrne of exceeding the $1.5 million campaign-spending limit set by State law.

On Thursday, October 4, Lester was examined by Dr. David J. Flicker, State psychiatrist. The examination took place in Dr. Flicker's office in East Orange. Dr. Flicker, an ex-army psychiatrist and courtroom veteran, took Lester's general history, medical history, and the details of his "present predicament." In the outer office, David Silver timed the interview, which took less than an hour.

The following week, Robert received a copy of Dr. Flicker's findings:

A physical examination showed Lester to be a "well-developed, well-nourished, robust, healthy-looking young male adult."

A neurological examination revealed no specific problems.

A psychiatric examination resulted in the following conclusions:

His [Lester's] answers were relevant and responsible. I could elicit no ideational disturbances, no delusions, hallucinations, phobias, etc. There are no affective disturbances noted. His affect was completely appropriate. . . .

and:

I can elicit no evidence of any psychopathology. I can find no indication that there exists at this point any aberration, any indication of psychosis, personality disorder or psychoneurosis. From the legal aspect of the McNaughton formula, it is quite obvious that he knew the nature and quality of his acts. . . .

41

October 1973

The day he received Dr. Flicker's report, Robert put David to work on the jury survey.

The survey operated on a simple principle. The final jurors for the case of Lester Zygmanik would be chosen from a list of 300. That list was presumed to be a representative sampling of the citizens of Monmouth County. A jury survey would poll its own sample of the population. Then sympathetic attitudes of respondents would be matched against their corresponding statistics such as age, occupation, and religion. After the data was compiled and analyzed by computer, a profile of the ideal juror for Lester Zygmanik could be constructed.

At Rutgers University, David enlisted the aid of Paul Eckman, sociology professor, who had worked on jury selection for the Camden Six conspiracy trial. Eckman was a lean, nervous, slightly frayed, knowledgeable man in his mid-thirties. He introduced David to two young women, now students, one of whom had been arrested and charged with destroying draft records and subsequently tried as one of the Camden Six defendants. She claimed that the jury survey had been a major factor in her acquittal.

With the aid of these two students, David recruited fifteen high-school girls to conduct the telephone survey. The girls were told it was a "secret project." Eckman designed a questionnaire to acquire basic information on age, sex, marital status, political affiliation, education, occupation, religion, and nationality. Then he added further attitudinal questions designed to separate open-minded and sympathetic respondents from rigid traditionalists dedicated to law and order. The questions included:

If people work hard at their jobs, they will reap the full benefits of our society. (1) Strongly Agree. (2) Agree. (3) Disagree. (4) Strongly Disagree.

If a person is suffering from a fatal disease, the person or his family has a right to ask the doctor to end his suffering.

The findings of science may someday show that many of our cherished beliefs are wrong.

Under unusual circumstances, a person might be justified in breaking the law.

Police should not hesitate to use force to maintain order.

David mimeographed the questions at Temple Beth El. The Monmouth County voting list contained 225,000 voters. Every 111th name was culled, constituting a random sampling. Telephone calls were conducted from a rented room at an oceanside motel. Throughout October, 700 calls were made, 576 questionnaires were answered.

Jury surveys had been used, for the most part, in political trials, such as the Ellsberg trial, where the defendants had been Vietnam War protesters. In these cases, defense lawyers claimed that public prosecutors often used public investigators, FBI, and police to gather information on potential jurors, while the defense remained dependent on intuition and knowledge of human nature. A jury survey, they contended, balanced the scales. The current concern was that the practice of jury surveys might produce juries so biased that the entire system could be undermined. Others doubted the effect of either psychiatrists or social scientists, or the impact of a survey. Robert said, "We'll wait and see."

David Silver made a call to Dr. Roger Gould, Los Angeles psychiatrist who had aided attorneys in selecting the Ellsberg jury. Gould said, "There's no such thing as the ideal juror. What you have to look for is a juror who's capable of changing his mind."

Robert took out insurance with his own method. The list of 300 prospective jurors provided names and addresses. He sent David, Arlene, and Karen out to drive by as many addresses as possible, scouting for signs of rigidity such as chain-link fences or American flags. The information from these "drive-bys" was recorded.

On October 28, the Sunday before the first day of trial, Robert and David drove to Middleton, New Jersey, to learn the survey results from Professor Paul Eckman. It was a gray, cold day. The meeting took place at Eckman's brother-in-law's house. In front of the house, an American flag waved in the wind. In a basement room, Eckman presented the outcome of his cross-tabulation. He had computerized the data from the 576 questionnaires. His correlations resulted in a demographic profile of the ideal juror in terms of predilection for sympathy and open-mindedness.

In the case of Lester Zygmanik, the sex of the person made no significant difference, nor did marital status or nationality. The deciding factors would be age, occupation, religion, and political affiliation. Each variation rated a number of points:

A Democrat rated 4 points; an independent, 2 points; a Republican, 1 point.

Under 30 years of age scored 5 points; 31–40 scored 3 points; 41–60, 2 points; over 60, 1 point.

A Jew rated 6 points; a Baptist, 2 points; a Catholic, 1 point.

Professionals scored 3 points; blue-collar workers, 2 points; technical workers, 1 point.

According to Eckman's rating scale, the ideal juror should score 18 points. Any prospect who scored less than 13 points should be eliminated from the jury box.

A basic problem remained. In the state of New Jersey, lawyers no longer questioned jurors directly. The process of *voir dire* was the prerogative of the Judge. It would be impossible to discover the age, occupation, religion, and political affiliation of each potential juror unless the Judge agreed to ask such questions.

Eckman wanted to sit at the Defense table during jury selection. Reluctantly, Robert agreed. "But if it's my intuition against your technology—"

"Sociology," David corrected.

"Don't expect miracles," Robert said.

42

October 1973

While Lester waited for trial, Watergate continued, three astronauts set a record in space, and the twenty-eighth anniversary of the bombing of Hiroshima went by. Vice President Spiro Agnew resigned after being investigated for graft, extortion, and income-tax evasion. Twenty-seven bodies were discovered in Houston, Texas, the victims of a homosexual murder ring. Food prices skyrocketed, Burton and Taylor split, and Harold de Pasquale of Atlantic Highlands, New Jersey, was arrested for feeding a cat on the Asbury Park boardwalk.

Between June and October, Lester resumed an ordinary life. Through July and August, late afternoons and weekends, while painting the house, he heard a radio newscaster say, "Opinion remains strong in Monmouth County about twenty-three-year-old Lester Zygmanik, now in seclusion on the family farm in Perrineville," and he found it comical that they called it a farm. In September, the rains came, turning earth to mud. Wearing George's old army boots, he constructed a fuel tank and filled it with oil, though he failed to get the heating installed and he worried about another winter around the cellar stove. October brought wind. He cleared out twelve acres of autumn woods, mowed five acres of grass for the final time, and put up the storm windows, though most of the month remained warm and dry. Then what he had left was a weekend, three days.

On Friday, the 26th of October, he purchased a corduroy suit with narrow lapels—cheap, rough corduroy the color of school ink.

On Friday, Ansell told him the local Polish Defense Fund had raised $360 toward the expenses of his trial.

He had never been in a courtroom.

On Saturday, Ansell said, "Okay—there's a rail that divides the spectators from the Judge, and once you walk through that rail, you'll have everybody's attention. That's how it works. There'll be twelve people in the jury box. Their eyes will be on you. If their average age is only twenty, that's more than two hundred years of experience looking at you. You can't fool them. I don't want you to try to fool them. I just want you to be yourself. Be Lester."

"I don't know if I can do that." He had one day left.

Sunday dawned cold as reality, still as a corpse, the first day of winter. Diane arrived early, before breakfast. Jean went to church. Lester played ball with little Georgie. Late afternoon brought a wind that spilled tarnished leaves on the gravel road. His mother wept, on and off, until sundown. At six o'clock, David Silver showed up to wish him luck. Lester said, "I expect to walk out of that courtroom a free man."

It was just after midnight when the rain began, big, spattering drops assaulting his windowpane. All night long, the wind blew and the beagles howled from the dog shed. He had made a deal with Dan Parrotino to take the dogs if they sent him to prison.

At 7:00 a.m. on Monday, October 29, the Exxon station was bleak and deserted—closed since Labor Day, when tourists vanished from East Jersey side roads. A cold rain drizzled. Parked at the rear, Lester waited for Ansell. A hundred days had passed. On Saturday, he had said to Ansell, "When this is over, I'm definitely gonna quit smoking. When this is over, I want to live a long time."

He was half an hour early. In the rear-view mirror, he saw his face had grown thinner. Ansell had instructed him to lose twenty pounds —with effort, he had lost fifteen. Unaccustomed short hair made him dizzy and lightheaded—Ansell had ordered it cut. Most of all, he missed the mustache, gone since July—Ansell had insisted. If anyone asked, he was supposed to say he had shaved it because of the heat.

The result of Robert Ansell's instructions would appear in an artist's sketch to be done at the trial, surreptitiously, against the Judge's orders. The drawing would show a young man wearing an urchin haircut, a choirboy's face, a plaintive expression. Present in the courtroom would be those who saw Lester that way—his mother, his girlfriend, his brother's wife, his boss. The Prosecutor would see him differently. Malcolm Carton would rise, face the jury box, and say, "Ladies and gentlemen of the jury, the State maintains that this case consists of a willful, deliberate, and premeditated murder. It is murder in the first degree, and based on the facts of this case, it can be nothing else."

Not until that moment would Lester really understand that his life might be taken away.

43

October 29, 1973
Freehold, New Jersey

Outside, it continued to rain. In front of the Freehold Courthouse, oblivious to weather, a statue of Molly Pitcher presided over the site of British defeat in the 1776 Battle of Monmouth. Nearby, the Freehold Racetrack turned as muddy as the Vegas rumor which claimed all Freehold horses were drugged except the winners, the only ones tested. On Monday morning, fog and rain obscured both the glory of history and present corruption.

Inside, the arena was small, one-quarter the size of a city courtroom, and beautifully kept. Along paneled walls hung portraits of judges, impartial, deceased. It was a windowless place, soundproof, both awesome and intimate—a civilized arena where no man battled for his own life, but depended, instead, on the shrewdness of strangers.

At 10:30 a.m., court convened, an hour and a half late. In the hallway, together, they had lined the benches and paced the corridor, appraising each other—Defense lawyer and Prosecutor, witnesses for the Defense, witnesses for the Prosecution, defendant, defendant's family, interested friends, reporters, and curious observers. It was less than the ideal arrangement.

Thirty minutes ago, in the Judge's chambers, Prosecution and Defense had agreed to select fourteen jurors, including two alternates who would be eliminated by lottery at the end of the trial. Judge M. Raymond McGowan agreed to ask Robert's questions for prospective jurors, questions which included Eckman's as well as his own. The Prosecutor then made a request which was also granted— throughout the trial of Lester Zygmanik, the term "mercy killing" would be forbidden.

Now the dozen pews filled up with veniremen. The press had been instructed that nothing might be reported beyond what appeared in the record. Spectators had been temporarily barred—but, a moment ago, Victor Kazma, Jean Zygmanik's father, had forced his way in, shouting, "I have to take care of my daughter's interests!"

At the Prosecutor's table, Malcolm Carton wore a banker's pinstripe and an air of impatience. His dark, curly hair had been severely plastered down. He was short, wiry, barely thirty years old, Monmouth County's most eligible bachelor. In the first row were half a dozen long-legged girls who had already come to be known as Malcolm Carton's "groupies." The Prosecutor's table was not, as custom required, nearest the bench. In the Freehold Courthouse, in the forties, Malcolm Carton's father, County Prosecutor, had been assaulted from the rear by an irate defendant—and though Carton, Sr., had survived and flourished, the seating was forever after reversed. So, on Monday morning Malcolm Carton's position gave him an unobstructed view of Lester Zygmanik.

At the Defense table, Steve Delaney and Professor Paul Eckman sat opposite Lester. He was wearing the navy-blue corduroy suit. He seemed passive, frightened—above all, bewildered. Robert, in a neat gray suit with stovepipe trousers, looked grave and slightly Victorian. In the past few years, women had begun to find him attractive—attention he attributed to his bristly mustache and lack of response, though, as the veniremen filed in, he was not above saying to Steve, "Eighty percent of this trial is going to be getting into the jury's pants."

Dennis Jacobs, a twenty-three-year-old technician at an army hospital, excused himself from the jury box. Judge Raymond McGowan's question had been, "Will you agree to follow my instructions regarding the law?" Translated beforehand, the question was: *If I tell you the law requires that Lester Zygmanik be imprisoned for life, will you abide by my instructions regardless of personal feelings, philosophy, or beliefs?*

"I'm sorry," Jacobs said. "I can't do that."

"Excused."

Judge McGowan, in his early sixties, had a rosy complexion, a shock of white hair, and a theatrical manner. Robert had tried cases before in front of McGowan. In this case, he had the distinct impression that McGowan hoped for conviction, and so would be severe but fair enough to avoid errors in the record in case of appeal.

The squirrel cage revolved. Another name was drawn. Prospective juror Dennis Jacobs was replaced by a sixty-seven-year-old retired upholsterer, eighth-grade education, Catholic, Knights of Columbus, Republican.

Robert exercised the fourth of his twenty allotted peremptory challenges.

The upholsterer was replaced by a sixty-six-year-old minister's wife. "Sourpuss," Steve said.

Eckman scribbled notes on a pad, adding and subtracting points. "No good," Eckman said. Lester was silent.

The minister's wife was replaced by Mrs. Jenny Carpenter, a middle-aged dietician's assistant, two years of high school, Catholic, score on Eckman's scale: 8 points. "Terrible," Eckman said. Robert checked through his own notes. David had done a "drive-by" on Mrs. Jenny Carpenter, Freehold, New Jersey. David had written: *Lots of plants and flowers, development neighborhood, neat, potential juror wearing loud paisley dress; ugly dog.*

"I like her," Robert said. Part of his criteria was whether or not the prospective juror's tone was appropriate to the content of what he said. Any sign of exaggerated vanity was bad. Signs of individuality such as mustaches, beards, or bright colors were good. Signs of conformity or a need to please the Judge and the system were bad. A tanned complexion, an indication that the juror spent time outdoors, was good. Any sign of *machismo* in men which permitted an interpretation of Lester's act as manly was good.

Malcolm Carton used a peremptory challenge on the twenty-year-old airline stewardess who had been smiling at Robert. Robert challenged a forty-three-year-old insurance actuary, elder in the church. The Prosecutor challenged a twenty-six-year-old male telephone-installer. No Jews were called, no blacks, a minimum of young people.

Paul Eckman objected to Marcelle Dean, age fifty, inspector in a glass factory, divorced, Catholic, dyed red hair, previous service in the air force as a surgical nurse. Robert decided to keep her. She looked neurotic and tentative. He felt he could sway her.

Steve liked James F. Clark, age fifty-four, elected AFL-CIO union official, Catholic, ex-artillery sergeant, score: 8 points on Eckman's chart. Robert kept him.

At recess, in the conference room provided by the court, Robert gathered with Steve, David, Karen, and Paul Eckman to discuss the prospective jurors. Lester paced the room and remained silent.

"It's terrible," Eckman said. "It's a Medicare jury."

Between recess and lunchtime, the jurors seemed to get worse. Every name called turned out to be Catholic, over forty-five years old, a non-professional, and a Republican.

Over Eckman's protests, Robert decided to keep Frederick Ogden, school custodian, eleventh-grade education, Catholic, member of the VFW. Robert decided to keep him because he was wearing a lavender shirt. Robert kept Diego Batiste, Cuban, Presbyterian, chemist, because he wore a small, pointed beard and a checked bow tie. It was down to instinct and any sign of non-conformism.

In the conference room over lunch—peanut-butter crackers and cartons of milk—the issue became Juror No. 5—Content Peckham, age twenty-six, unemployed art teacher. Steve felt the Prosecutor hadn't challenged her because she looked older. David suggested she had the air of somebody who was recovering from a nervous breakdown. Karen didn't like her mouth. Eckman pointed out Content Peckham had the highest score on the rating scale: 13. Robert liked her. She was wearing a bright, flowered dress.

After lunch, Robert challenged a sixty-three-year-old farmer with a ninth-grade education. He kept Larry Smith, a middle-aged, square-jawed engineer from Bell Labs. He felt Smith was strong-minded, had presence, and, if convinced, might influence the others. Smith's score was 10 points. Robert liked Juror No. 10, Tntien Pei Lee, Chinese, Buddhist, Ph.D. engineer. Lee was the only other juror who rated 13 points. Robert challenged a forty-nine-year-old freight agent, Catholic, Knights of Columbus, another "drive-by"—Karen had written: *Big fence, two German Shepherd police dogs*. He was replaced by Helen Hauke, age fifty, Catholic, two brothers-in-law who were policemen in Newark, wearing a light-brown wig and harlequin eyeglasses. Score: 10 points. Robert liked the expression around her eyes. He left her. Malcolm Carton challenged a twenty-three-year-old man who wouldn't take off his sunglasses.

At 3:00 p.m., of the fourteen potential jurors, Eckman approved only two—Juror No. 5, Content Peckham, the unemployed art-school teacher, and Juror No. 6, the Cuban chemist with the pointed beard. Steve liked Juror No. 1, the fifty-four-year-old union official, and Juror No. 7, a sixty-year-old widow with a hard-worked face. Lester had attached himself to Juror No. 12, Mrs. Jenny Carpenter, the dietician with the ugly dog. Robert liked Juror No. 10, the Chinese Buddhist engineer, Juror No. 5, Content Peckham, and Juror No. 11, Mrs. Concheeta Ponzo, whose husband was a maintenance man for a grammar school, and who had a deceased child. On Eckman's scale, her score was 8 points. Juror No. 8 was a technical writer who worked at Fort Monmouth; Juror No. 9 was Marcelle Dean, dyed red hair. Juror No. 14 was Mrs. Evelyn McElroy, sales clerk for Sears' catalogue department, Presbyterian. She could go either way.

It was Robert's turn. He had six remaining peremptory challenges.

If he exercised another, he gave Malcolm Carton an opportunity to bump one of his decent jurors, and that one might be replaced with an intolerable substitute.

In the back of the courtroom were the remaining veniremen. Robert scanned the faces, a conglomeration of age and severity. One black man, less than a half-dozen young faces, no one who was recognizably liberal or Jewish or nonconformist. He had the feeling that few would turn out to be any better than what he had and many could be worse. As with a political election, the *trend* was set.

He looked over the jury box. There were seven men and seven women. Average age: forty-five. Average point score on Eckman's rating scale: less than 10. The majority were Catholic, Republican, blue-collar—by Eckman's criteria, disastrous.

Robert accepted the jury.

44

Lester ate dinner with his family. Little Georgie made a lot of noise, giving him a headache. All through dinner, he kept seeing the jurors as they stretched out their arms toward the Bible and repeated the oath together.

At the kitchen table, Diane sat next to him, blushing and giggling —periodically, she burst into tears. He had no appetite. He kept hearing an echo of the Judge's voice, saying to the jury, "You have a solemn obligation to be sure justice is done to the State and the defendant." He, Lester Zygmanik, was the defendant. It remained an alien thought.

His mother and Jeannie began to fight. Their voices turned loud. His mother accused his sister-in-law of being on pills. Jeannie grew hysterical. He felt a profound flash of animosity for both of them. The moment surprised him.

He tried not to think about the day. When court was over, he had carried Ansell's briefcase. Reporters had surrounded them. He had wanted to run. He had felt as if he could be somebody else.

In the car, he had said to Ansell, "I really feel I'll be let go. I could be wrong, but that's what I think." He had wanted to shout: *Somebody has made a terrible mistake!*

His mother and Jeannie continued to scream at each other. Little Georgie set up a harsh crying. Lester got up and went out the kitchen door. Diane followed him. Outside, the rain had quit. A pale moon was out. A cold, brisk wind was blowing. When he reached the top of the cellar stairs, he kept walking. Diane said, "Where are you going?"

"I don't know," he said.

A half-hour later, on highway 35, he headed north. Traffic was light. He pushed the truck over sixty, over the speed limit, deliberately fast, the wind on his face. When he reached the cut-off to Perth Amboy, he turned in and drove through town until the streets grew familiar.

The neighborhood looked the same—he could smell the familiar cooking odors, and under a streetlight a mixed group of kids were tossing coins. It was a sight from his childhood that made him feel calmer, less frightened.

He found a parking space. He locked the truck. It was a neighborhood where he used to worry about making it to and from school. There had been at least one fight a day. He had liked math and mechanical drawing, nobody studied—he had quit studying.

He began to walk. He recognized most of the houses, duplexes and multi-family dwellings, always too small. Those they had lived in had always been dirty until his father repaired and painted everything. He passed houses that were neatly kept, but most were in disrepair, all were piled one on top of the other, not enough room between them to catch a glimpse of his own shadow.

He went past the church on the corner, Jehovah's Witnesses. Beyond Gracie's Grocery Store and John's Bar were a few boarded-up buildings. Behind dingy curtains, dull lights shone. Somebody had cleaned off all the graffiti. An old Spanish woman was walking a small, deformed dog.

Memories flooded back.

He walked until he reached the red brick four-plex. In front of 396 Market Street, he stopped. A slim, dark kid, Cuban, about sixteen years old, sprawled on the stoop, smoking. The kid said, "Who are you, man?"

"I used to live here." He looked up. There were no lights where he used to live.

"Yeah? What's your name?"

"Lester Zygmanik."

"Who?"

"I belong to the Angels," Lester said. "A couple of years ago, we had a big fight on the waterfront. Thirty-five guys on each side. A lot of people got hurt."

"I never heard of it," the kid said.

"It was a big fight," Lester said.

"Listen good, man," the kid said. "You got a white face. You talk good American. You don't live in this shitplace no more. So, don't come back lookin' for trouble."

The highway was empty, a bright stripe of road rolling under his headlights. He threw out a lighted cigarette butt and watched it fly like a lonely, falling star. He felt tired and vaguely disappointed, as if what he had expected to find hadn't been there—his father and his brother. He picked up speed. Cold air whipped his face. He had walked the streets like a kid. The thought made him angry. He pressed down on the accelerator, taking refuge in speed, the feeling of no ground beneath him, the illusion of freedom. But the moment had no duration. Directly behind it came the sense of despair, and the fear.

He turned on the radio. He hurtled through the darkness, wrestling with loneliness and the knowledge that wherever he went, he would feel lonely. Then he heard the siren and he became aware that he had been listening to it for the past few minutes.

He slowed the truck. In the rear-view mirror, he could see the flashing red light. He pulled over and stopped, and turned off the radio. Up ahead, he could see a neon sign flashing on a roadside motel. In the silence, he could hear his heart beating.

The cop was angry. The cop didn't seem to recognize the name. Holding a flashlight, the cop looked at his license and registration, and said, "You know what they're gonna do, buddy? They're gonna take your license away."

It was after eleven o'clock when he got home. In the dark, he drank a glass of orange juice. Then he sat at the kitchen table, smoking, trying to put off calling Ansell. Finally, when he dialed, he got the wrong number. He had the feeling his mother was awake in the bedroom, listening. He tried the number again. When Ansell answered, he said, "This is Lester. I did somethin' really bad."

Ansell said, "What's the problem?"

"I got another ticket—for speeding. I'm gonna lose my driver's license."

"Don't worry about it," Ansell said. "They can't take your license until they get you to court, and they can't take you to court for a long time. I'll take care of it."

"Why do you think I did somethin' like that?" Lester said.

"It's nothing to worry about," Ansell said.

"I mean—listen," Lester said. "Like maybe I wanted to do somethin' bad, like maybe to myself?"

"Forget the psychiatry," Ansell said. "Get some sleep. We've got a big day tomorrow."

45

October 30, 1973

The rain had stopped. Beyond the Freehold Courthouse was a cold, clear autumn of incredible color. This morning, on the way to court, Lester had talked about rabbit-hunting.

It was Tuesday morning, the second day of trial. Shortly, the jury would listen to opening speeches. Traditionally, the Prosecution opened first and closed last. The theory was, the burden of proof was on the State. The fact that in Lester's case the evidence was stacked and the burden of proof lay with the Defense had not reversed tradition.

The jury was quiet, attentive, as Malcolm Carton rose. An opening speech was a restrictive framework. No arguments could be made. Neither Defense nor Prosecution could do more than outline to the jury what each intended to prove. For Carton, the task was simple. The facts were open and shut. Going in, the State of New Jersey could prove Murder One in thirty seconds.

The Prosecutor's manner was confident, if slightly petulant. His words were shrewd and to the point. He delineated the damaging evidence and described the testimony that would shortly back up the set of shocking facts. He reminded the jury of its oath, the ethic of duty, and the definition of justice. He acknowledged that "this is a sad and pathetic case, difficult for everyone involved." The fact remained that Lester had committed a "willful, deliberate and premeditated murder." It was the law, more binding than mercy, which demanded conviction.

Members of the jury cast glances at Lester. To the defendant, murder was not a reckless act. This morning he had said, "If my brother asked me, I would do it again."

Seated among the spectators was Lester's family. Sonia Zygmanik wore black crepe, high heels, a jaunty brown felt derby. Victor Kazma whispered constantly in his daughter's ear. Jean retained a permanently startled look.

Robert rose and began to prowl. It was his first direct contact with the jury—the moment when he would establish, or fail to establish, the tenuous emotional connection that would be Lester's lifeline for the rest of the trial. Carton had constructed his opening speech from the facts. Robert attempted to create a context in which the jury might interpret those facts. The Defense denied nothing. The Defense conceded all damaging evidence. The Defense, however, would present Lester's actions within their proper emotional framework. On the day of the shooting, Lester had gone through a series of "highs and lows," of "ups and downs." Robert coined a phrase to describe the events—"Lester's roller-coaster behavior."

Robert said, "You will hear testimony about behavior changes in Lester. He began to have substantial problems with reality, alternating between depression and optimism—and, after a period of almost total sleeplessness approaching four or five days, he came apart. . . ."

The jury remained cautious.

Robert reiterated the facts, saying, "At one moment, Lester would be compulsively, methodically, sawing off a shotgun. At the next moment, he would be totally out of touch with reality. . . ." He paused before he said, "—and the next moment, Lester would be calmly sitting in front of witnesses and doing something which—to this day— the State of New Jersey doesn't know about."

Robert stopped pacing. The jury leaned forward, interested. In a calculated move, Robert described the waxing of the bullet, presenting the act as further evidence of Lester's confusion. Had Lester chosen a higher-powered rifle, the waxing would have been unnecessary. Lester waxed three shells—but took only two to the hospital, one of which was not waxed.

The jury remained attentive, though Robert felt few, if any, were aware of the daring nature of this disclosure.

In closing, Robert pointed out that most criminals were tried for "greed and hate and selfishness"—but Lester was a young man who was overwhelmed by "grief and love and selflessness." He said, "There is emotion in this case; we ask for your collective heart. There is morality in this case; we ask for your collective conscience. There is reason in this case; we ask for your collective mind. . . ."

He felt it was an effective speech. He felt he had reached them. He had tried to humanize a tragic deed, create a sympathetic canvas, and provide a benign perspective which was predicated, in part, on his own personality. By his own analogy, he had taken the first step from the bottom of the Grand Canyon on the climb toward the summit of Mount Everest from where the Prosecution had imperiously been viewing the proceedings. The size of this step remained to be calculated.

46

October 30, 1973

The first witness for the Prosecution was young, tall, antiseptic, neatly dressed in a burgundy blazer and a matching tie. He stated his name: Gregory Carver. Age: twenty-six years old. Occupation: Anesthesiology student at Jersey Shore Medical Center. It was Robert's first look at the anonymous doctor-in-the-cafeteria.

Carton didn't approach the witness stand. He directed his questions to the witness from a standing position at his table.

"Directing your attention to last June, can you tell us where you were employed?" Carton asked.

"The Anesthesia Department, Jersey Shore Medical Center."

"How long had you been employed at that point?"

"Since October prior," Carver answered, robot-like.

"Did you participate in surgery on George Zygmanik?"

"Yes, sir. I was involved in administering anesthesia."

"Can you tell us the date, please?"

"June 20," Carver said.

"Did you see the patient before the operation?"

"Only that morning, when we went to pick up the patient from Intensive Care."

"Did you see the defendant, Lester Zygmanik, before the operation?" Carton pointed at Lester.

"That morning, when we picked up the patient," Carver said in the tone of a man who had done a lot of rehearsing.

"Did you have any conversation with the defendant at that time?"

"No, sir."

"Did you have any conversation with the defendant at a later time?"

"Yes, sir. That afternoon, after surgery, I was downstairs in the snack bar, having lunch, and I talked to him at that time. . . ."

". . . Your first conversation, then, with Lester Zygmanik was in the afternoon after surgery? In the coffee shop? Is that correct?"

"That's correct. . . ."

". . . Would you relate that conversation to us, please?"

Carver's voice waned. Judge McGowan interrupted the testimony to ask the witness to speak closer to the microphone. The court reporter repeated the question. Robert studied Carver. Fear and discomfort became evident just beneath the rigid control.

"The defendant approached me," Carver said, "and asked if I had been involved in the operation. He explained the patient was his brother. I said yes, as far as anesthesia was concerned. He asked me what I had found, and I—I can't relate anything about surgery. My involvement was strictly with anesthesia." Carver paused, then went on.

"The defendant said Dr. Kreider had found a bruised spinal cord, and I said yes, that's what they found.

"He asked me, I believe he asked me—if I had been in the service and seen injuries of this nature before. I said yes, but on a long-term basis I didn't know how they turned out because I was overseas, and the patients were shipped back to the States. . . .

". . . The defendant asked me what I would do in his position. I said there was no way to answer that question." Carver lowered his eyes.

"Was there any discussion of the possibility of recovery?" Carton asked.

"Yes. He asked me that. I said it would just depend on time. There was no way I could know that." Carver kept his eyes lowered.

"Can you tell me approximately what time this conversation took place?"

"It was a short conversation—I have to admit I was uncomfortable, I got up and left. Probably around 1:00 o'clock in the afternoon."

"In this conversation, did the defendant indicate anything further about how he felt about his brother? Or what he felt should be done?"

"He said—the smart thing for him to do would be to go up and shoot him in the head and get it over with."

The jury reacted. Carton turned to look at them. Robert understood that Carver had been called as the Prosecution's first witness for the purpose of showing blatant premeditation. Carton's look said to the jury: Here is a witness who is testifying that, eight hours before the shooting, Lester was talking about killing his brother. Ladies and gentlemen, this was no spur-of-the-moment impulse.

To Robert, Lester said, "That sonofabitch is lyin' through his teeth."

Robert rose to cross-examine. His tone was pleasant.

"Mr. Carver—you weren't comfortable?" he inquired.

"No. I was not comfortable. No," Carver said.

"You were uncomfortable?" Robert looked directly at the witness as if there were no judge or jury, only the two of them.

"Yes."

"And is it safe to say Lester was also uncomfortable?"

"I'd say he was definitely uncomfortable."

"You and Lester discussed what happens when someone is paralyzed from the neck down?"

"Yes." Carver stared at a point at the rear of the courtroom.

"You discussed that in the context of war victims?"

"Yes. He asked me if I had seen this overseas."

"Did you also discuss that in the context of Veterans' Hospitals?"

"Veterans' Hospitals? I don't believe so," Carver said.

"Did you discuss it in terms of life-span?"

"Yes. He asked me what the long-range outlook was. I said I didn't have any idea."

"Lester told you something else, didn't he? About what his brother was saying?"

Carton objected. "Hearsay."

Robert argued that the purpose of the witness was to testify to his conversation with the defendant.

McGowan allowed Carver to continue.

"Yes, sir," Carver said. "He said his brother had been begging him to kill him."

"Did he say this whole situation might kill his mother?" Robert's tone hardened.

"Yes, sir."

"Did he say he didn't know what would happen to his brother's wife and child?"

"That's correct. He said that. Or to himself, either."

"Lester said he couldn't stand the pressure any more? Is that correct?"

"Yes, sir. I believe he did say that."

"He appeared nervous to you?"

"Extremely nervous," Carver said. "His speech was stuttered. As I recall, he was smoking one cigarette after another. His hands were very shaky."

"Then he turned to you and said: the smart thing for him to do would be to go up and shoot his brother?" Deliberately, Robert repeated the harsh statement.

"Shoot him and get it over with," Carver said. "I was very upset about it. . . ."

"Did you reach out a hand to help him?" Robert said sharply. "Did you reach out a hand to Lester?"

He knew the question was out of bounds. Predictably, the Prosecutor objected. Predictably, McGowan sustained. Yet, without launching a frontal attack, Robert knew he had achieved his purpose. The jury now understood (1) they would hear more about this cafeteria conversation, (2) there would be a dispute as to what was said, (3) whatever was said had an adverse effect on Lester, and (4) Carver, like others, did nothing when faced with a Lester who was behaving irrationally.

McGowan said, "That's an improper question, Mr. Ansell. Don't ask that kind of question again."

Robert chose to rephrase the question.

"Mr. Carver—after the defendant said these things to you, and in view of your observation of his condition, did you do anything for Lester?"

Carton objected. McGowan sustained.

The bailiff called Juanita Johnson.

47

June 20, 1973

On that Wednesday morning, June 20, three days after his brother's motorcycle accident, the sky threatened rain. It seemed fitting.

Outside the hospital, thunder rolled when they came to take George. Then Lester watched his brother grow smaller as they carried the stretcher down the corridor. Finally, George disappeared behind elevator doors, and all that was left was the flickering light that stopped at surgery.

After that, a summer rain began on the window, and the clock moved slowly. Jeannie wept. Victor kept saying, "It's in God's hands."

Lester left the hospital. He took Jeannie's car. He drove around aimlessly, feeling helpless and frightened. Traffic enveloped him. Horns honked, brutal, impersonal. He drove erratically, assailed by waves of fatigue and disorder. Once, he heard grotesque laughter. Once, he found himself on the rainy highway, propelled by a wish to flee.

He returned around noon. He was told his brother had been taken to recovery. In the corridor, the surgeon's voice echoed: "Your brother will never use his arms or legs again." The surgeon's face blurred. "We may never be able to remove the tracheotomy."

The hallway grew cavernous. He was overwhelmed by intolerable pain. Then an eerie silence encompassed him, and he felt nothing.

He took the elevator downstairs. In the cafeteria, he talked to Victor, but he couldn't feel the muscles of his mouth. The counter was crowded. Sitting nearby was the doctor who had come in the morning to take George to surgery. The doctor was still wearing his green cap.

The doctor frowned. "If you want to know what your brother will be like, go over to the East Orange Veterans' Hospital. There are men there, deteriorating. . . ."

He felt something shatter, like breaking glass. Fear assaulted his body. He found it difficult to breathe.

The doctor pushed at his cap. "I saw cases like your brother in service. These people dry up. They turn to skin and bone. They get terrible bedsores. Somebody has to be with them twenty-four hours a day."

He tried to protect himself from a roaring darkness.

The doctor shook his head. "I'd rather be dead than like your brother."

Then the doctor was gone, and, behind him, Victor said, "It's in God's hands."

He turned on Victor, cursing.

On October 30, under the Prosecutor's questioning, Juanita

Johnson would say, "It was sometime after eleven p.m. I was working the night shift with Mr. Blannett. I saw the defendant come into the room. I said, 'Good evening.' He didn't answer me. He went past me. He went over to his brother's bed and he stood there. Then we heard this loud noise."

It stopped raining in the afternoon. The air turned warm. He paced the parking lot, sweating. After a while, he lost the boundaries of his body. Once, he found himself at the ocean, running.

It was late afternoon before they let him see his brother. With his mother, he stood beside his brother's bed. His brother slept, swollen, distorted by pain. He turned away, trembling. In his head, the doctors' voices condemned his brother to a wasteland. He closed his eyes. He willed himself into the glassy silence where he felt nothing, heard nothing beyond his brother's demand: "I want you to promise to kill me. I want you to swear to God."

He went down to the lobby and asked Victor to drive him home.

Victor stayed with him. Victor kept saying, "Give God a chance."

He couldn't sit still. He kept moving around the kitchen, back and forth, feeling dizzy, as if his legs might collapse. Finally, he shouted, "Do you think God's gonna help my brother?"

He began to make telephone calls, but he found hearing difficult—and, after a while, he couldn't remember whom he was talking to, or what he was saying, only that he was shouting.

After sundown, his mother and Jeannie came back—and Victor said, "I'm tired. I have to go home."

He followed Victor out to the car, saying, "Please—go with me."

Long after Victor's taillights vanished, he stood in the darkness, crying. Then the air turned still, and the fog enclosed him in a silent world where nothing existed beyond his brother's need.

He moved automatically.

At half past nine, he crossed the land, heading toward the woods. Once, he stopped because he thought he heard somebody call him, but there was only darkness, so he moved on. Then the dogs heard him coming and began to bark.

When he reached the clearing, he chose his spot, far from the house and the women. It took a few minutes to anchor the shotgun. Then he marked the barrel, twelve inches from the tip. The beagles fell quiet. Harsh and shrill, the handsaw struck metal. He had chosen his weapon, a smooth-bore shotgun, the one he used to shoot rabbits. Sawed off, it would kill a man.

The air was damp. Pale shafts of moonlight pierced the fog. He worked patiently, steadily. Once, he stopped because he thought he heard somebody crying, but there was nothing. Then the gun barrel shuddered and broke. Severed, twelve inches of cylinder lay at his feet. The dogs set up a howl. He couldn't remember whether or not he had fed them.

He left the gun in the car. When he entered the kitchen, the women were sitting there. "The dogs need water," he said. His mother rose, weeping. It took him a moment to remember why Jeannie was staring at him.

Last night, his brother had said to her: "I want you to promise not to interfere. I want you to swear to God."

From a long way off, he seemed to hear the church bell ringing.

On October 30, Katherine Kealy, a registered nurse with gentle brown eyes, would testify for the Prosecution. In a soft, breathless voice, she would say, "I saw Lester in the hall. I was on my way to Room 322. He was outside of Room 321, Intensive Care. There was no conversation. I was in the next room when I heard a loud noise. I checked to see what happened. At first, I didn't realize—because Lester was still there. Then, looking at the patient, I realized he had been shot."

His mother filled the dog pail. Then the screen door slammed and he heard her climb the cellar stairs. He took a seat at the table, waiting for something, he didn't know what. Then he remembered his mother would probably find the pieces of the sawed-off gun.

He picked up a newspaper. Then his mother came back. Jeannie got a flashlight and, together, they left. A long time went by. Finally, the women returned and Jeannie began to shriek, "What are you going to do?" Over and over, "What are those pieces? What are you going to do?"

Jeannie went upstairs to check the guns. When she came back, she said again, "Where's the gun? What are you going to do?"

Finally, he shouted, "You know what I'm going to do!"

He found himself outside. He seemed to be floating. It was difficult to remember where he had hidden the gun. When he came back to the kitchen, his mother was waiting to take the gun. Relieved, he watched her put the gun on the bureau. Then she lay down on the bed and closed her eyes. He was tired. He wanted to lie down and close his eyes.

Barbara Petruska came in. Then the telephone began to ring. His head began to clang with jarring sounds. On the phone, his own voice disappeared. All he could hear was Jeannie saying, "He's got a gun. I don't know what he's going to do."

When Barbara Petruska touched his shoulder, he pushed her across the room, shouting, "If my father was alive, he'd kill all of you!"

After that, the kitchen turned quiet.

He said, "Where's a candle?" His voice was calm.

"In the garage," Jeannie said. "What are you going to do?"

He found the candle.

At the kitchen table, Jeannie and Barbara watched him empty the shotgun shell into the ashtray. Then he lit the candle and melted wax into the shell, adding some of the pellets. He was aware the women were shouting, but no sounds penetrated. He was aware his mother was lying on the bed with her eyes closed.

He went upstairs and put on a jacket.

When he came back to the kitchen, he concealed the shotgun under his coat, turned his back to the women, and asked, "Does it show?"

Somebody said, "I can see it."

He switched the shotgun to the other side. "Can you see it now?"

Somebody said, "No."

He turned around. He stood a moment, waiting for something, he didn't know what. Then he said to Jeannie, "I want you to go to the hospital with me. Please, come to the hospital with me?"

On October 30, twenty-five-year-old Robert Blannett, a graduate nurse who wore a Fu Manchu mustache, would draw a diagram of Intensive Care for the jury. He would sketch a desk, six beds, six patients. Near the window, the bed which had been occupied by George Zygmanik would be marked with an X. Then Blannett would testify, "After he shot his brother, he shook his head."

It was a twenty-mile drive.

Beyond his windshield, fog created ghostly shadows. Then the illusion of his father's presence was dispelled by darkness—and he understood he was alone.

The road was deserted. Once, he slowed because he thought he heard a police siren. Then night enveloped him—and the world contained only the two of them, he and his brother.

The parking lot was desolate, empty. It was raining again, a light, drizzling rain. He had the feeling he was somewhere else, watching himself. He began to see images and strange, blinding lights.

Then he found himself in the elevator, no longer able to recall why he had come. So he decided he was simply taking an elevator. Then the elevator stopped, and he heard his brother say: "You're the man now."

He walked slowly down the corridor. He remembered that the neurosurgeon had said, "Your brother has a head, he has eyes, ears, and a mouth—he's not better off dead." Then the doctors had disappeared. Everybody had disappeared. Last night, he had given his promise.

He found himself standing in front of Room 321, waiting for something. But nobody came. His choice became clear. He could run. Or he could do what his brother had asked him to do.

The room was dark. At the far end, his brother was suspended in air. There was a light on his brother. He crossed the room. "Are you in pain?" he said.

His brother nodded. His brother opened his eyes and closed them again. Behind his brother's bed was a window. Reflected in the glass was a desk. Two people were at the desk. He wondered why they weren't looking at him. He wondered why they weren't crying.

He loaded the shotgun. "I'm here to end your pain," he said. "Is that all right with you?"

His brother nodded. His brother's eyelids flickered.

"Close your eyes, George," he said, "I'm going to kill you." Then he raised the shotgun to his brother's temple.

He felt no pressure from the trigger, heard no explosion, felt nothing. In the silence afterward, he listened to the air in the tracheotomy still being pumped into his brother's throat.

He pulled the tracheotomy.

He laid his hand on his brother's chest and said, "I love you, George. God bless you, George."

Slowly, he turned and walked out.

48

Robert Ansell

Once you get to trial, the least important person in the courtroom is the client. He has nothing to do with the case. He's not even involved. Only in the sense that he's there for the jurors to look at while they think: Does he really look capable of doing what that witness just said he did?

If a witness testifies to a fact that helps the State, there's nothing we can do about it. What they're saying is true. There's no way I can shake them. The only way to fight is to try to draw from them facts or attitudes or implications that might help us—try to use them to support my own theory, my own concept of temporary insanity. For instance, if I can spend five questions with Carver showing Lester was nervous, I can keep that in the minds of the jury for five seconds —or if I can stretch it to twenty seconds, I'm going to. Or with Juanita Johnson—I got a good description of Intensive Care from her. I wanted to hammer home to the jury the fact that George wasn't in some quiet little private room somewhere, that Lester was stewing around in front of the world—technicians, employees.

The problem is, you don't know what effect you're having on the jury. The jury can't talk back. They never let you know (a) whether they understand what you're doing, or (b) if they approve of what you're doing. Jurors know they're onstage. In a case I tried last year, there was a guy on the jury who always smiled and responded and was terrific. I discovered later that in the jury room the other jurors were telling him, "Everybody's looking at us. You've got to sit there straight and not show any emotion or do anything." Then, there's that old cliché about the juror who smiles, but who knows?—maybe he's smiling because he's happy about convicting somebody. We've got one on this jury—she's a crotch-gazer. Does that mean she likes me?—Or is my fly open? How can you tell?

49

October 30, 1973
Freehold, New Jersey

Lester stared at the American flag in the lefthand corner of the courtroom. Throughout the proceedings, he didn't look at the jury.

Behind him, in clear view of the jurors, was the sawed-off shotgun, entered into evidence by the Prosecution during Katherine Kealy's testimony. Robert saw this piece of material evidence had effected a greater impact on the jurors than any of the verbal testimony.

The Prosecution was moving swiftly. Before morning recess, Malcolm Carton had presented four witnesses. His questions had been simple and forthright. Each witness had been brief.

In succession, two hospital security guards had testified. Each had said: After the shooting, Lester was discovered in the corridor near the personnel elevator; and Lester said, "I'm the one you're looking for."

Now, the bailiff called Detective Sergeant James A. Ward. The witness was sworn. He was thirtyish, tanned, weather-beaten, dressed in a horse-blanket plaid sportcoat. He was handsome, vacuous, likable. His bond with the Prosecutor was evident. They were both professionals.

"Sir, by whom are you employed and in what capacity?" Carton asked.

"Neptune Township Police Department, Detective Sergeant."

"How long have you been with the Police Department?"

"Nine years." Ward's manner was easy, relaxed, yet professional.

"Did you have occasion to be called to work on the 20th of June?"

"Yes. I was called around 11:55 p.m. to come to Headquarters."

"And—what did you do after you got to Headquarters?"

"I interviewed the defendant, Lester Zygmanik, in Cell No. 7." Ward began to direct his answers to the jury.

"Can you tell me what was said."

"I advised Lester Zygmanik of his constitutional rights, Miranda warning."

"Did you have a conversation with him at this point?"

"Yes."

"Relate the substance of that to us, please."

"I spoke to Lester and asked him what had taken place at Jersey Shore Medical Center. He advised me that his brother, George, had been involved in a motorcycle accident and was paralyzed from the neck down. He said he had taken a shotgun up to the Intensive Care Ward of Jersey Shore Medical Center around 11:00 p.m., and walked over to the bed, put the gun up to his brother's left temple and pulled the trigger—shot his brother."

Robert saw Juror No. 3, the square-jawed engineer, appraise Lester. The rest of the jury seemed passive and respectful. To most of them, Ward appeared to represent the protection of ordinary citizens, of life and property. Robert's task would be not to crack Ward, but to crack the jury's acceptance of Ward.

"What did you do at that point?" Carton asked.

"I called Detective Sergeant Martin into Headquarters to help with the investigation. We went up to the hospital. We returned about twenty minutes to 1:00."

"What happened when you returned?"

"The two of us advised Lester Zygmanik again of his constitutional rights. At that point, he gave the same story again. Earlier that day, June 20th, at his home in Millstone Township, he had taken a 20-gauge gun, cut this gun down at both ends, and drove to Jersey Shore Medical Center. He walked into the Intensive Care Unit, he put the gun to his brother's left temple and pulled the trigger."

"Do you know the approximate distance between the hospital and the Zygmanik home?"

"I would estimate 20 miles."

"Was there anything else said at that time?"

"Lester was asked if he would give a written statement to this effect. At that time, he wished to consult with an attorney and he was given a phone call—he called home."

It was cold, factual testimony. In a murder trial, Robert knew the deletion of emotion often resulted in the most dramatic kind of accusation.

Robert began cross-examination. His method always was: (1) Never ask a question you don't know the answer to, and (2) it's the question that's important, not the answer. Though he addressed Ward, he kept one eye on the jury, hoping to supersede their bond with Ward by his own.

"Officer, you studied your report before you came to testify?—to refresh your recollection of these events?"

"Yes, sir."

"Do you have it with you?"

"Yes, I do. It's back here, at the desk."

"Will you get a copy of it, please?" Ward rose, retrieved the report, and took the stand again.

"Now—about this initial conversation with Lester," Robert said, "I think you said it occurred in Cell No. 7. Was that in Neptune Township Police Headquarters?"

"That's correct."

"Lester was quite confused at this point, wasn't he? Did you observe that confusion?"

"I couldn't tell if he was confused."

"Didn't he tell you in that first interview that he had shot his brother in the *right* side of the head?"

"Yes. I have the right side of the head in my report."

"You have that in your report?"

"Yes."

"And that report was typed up, when?"

"The early hours of June 21st."

"Directly after you talked to Lester?"

"Directly afterwards, yes."

"And it was obvious from what you saw at the hospital that George had been shot in the *left* side of the head?—but Lester told you he had shot him in the *right* side?" Robert turned directly toward the jury.

"That's what I have here in my report," Ward said.

Quickly Robert crossed the courtroom and picked up the sawed-off shotgun. He handled it easily, in a deliberate attempt to dilute its effect on the jury.

". . . You are familiar with shotguns, aren't you?" he asked Ward.

"Yes, sir."

"What is this?"

"I'd say it was a 20-gauge, used more or less for birdshot."

"Have you fired shotguns?"

"Yes, I have."

"Is it dangerous to fire this one? In this condition?"

"Yes, sir."

"And is it also dangerous to fire a shotgun around oxygen?"

"It sure is," Ward said. Robert nodded. Two jurors nodded imperceptibly in response. Lester had fired the shotgun under circumstances dangerous to himself.

Detective Sergeant Martin—tanned, fortyish, dark eyebrows, wearing a coat and matching vest—confirmed Ward's testimony.

Then Carton called Dr. Sheldon Lang, the pathologist who had performed the autopsy on George Zygmanik. In the same way that Ward had represented an orderly society, Dr. Lang seemed to be a civil servant of death. He was short, overfed, moon-faced. The Prosecutor began by establishing Lang's credentials:

Downstate Medical School, class of '57; internship at Bellevue, New York City; residency training at Michael Reed Hospital in Chicago, Stanford University in California, and St. Joseph's Hospital in Syracuse, New York. Next to Robert, Lester began to watch Dr. Lang attentively.

"Are you a pathologist, doctor?" Carton asked.

"Yes, sir."

"What is a pathologist?"

"A pathologist is a physician who studies the effects of diseases and injuries on the human body."

"What is your present position?"

"I am the Medical Examiner for Monmouth County, and I am also a pathologist at Monmouth Medical Center," Dr. Lang answered, not without a note of vanity.

"What do your duties include as first assistant Monmouth County Medical Examiner?"

"My duties include investigation of deaths that would come under the jurisdiction of the Medical Examiner's office—and performing autopsies when it is deemed necessary to determine the cause of death," Dr. Lang said.

Lester remained mesmerized by Dr. Lang.

"Can you tell us approximately how many autopsies you have performed?" Carton asked.

"It would be in the thousands," Lang said, again with visible pride.

"Did you perform an autopsy on George Zygmanik last June?"

"Yes, sir."

"Did you determine when George Zygmanik died?"

"He died at 2:05 a.m. on June 22nd, 1973."

"Can you tell us what your external examination revealed?—please."

"My external evidence revealed a young adult-like male, five feet nine inches in length, and weighing 173 pounds. When I examined him, his head was extensively covered by bandages. When I removed the bandages, there was a wound in his left temple region 4 by 3 centimeters which is about 2 inches by 1¼ inches. Surrounding this region were black marks resembling powder burns."

Lester began to tremble. "Take it easy," Robert said, as Lang described the details of his findings.

Lang said, "Through this wound, portions of the brain protruded.

"There was also evidence of a wound in his neck which resembled a tracheotomy. And a wound which was a surgical incision, approximately 12 centimeters which would make it about 5 inches, in the back of the head.

"There was also evidence of contusions or black and blue marks around the eyes."

"Now," Carton asked, "would you tell us briefly what your internal examination consisted of?—and what the significant discoveries were?"

Precise, methodical, devoid of emotion, Lang answered, "My internal examination consisted of a complete autopsy.

"My examination of the head revealed that this wound, through which the brain was protruding, extended into the cavity of the cranium, the space where the brain is. In this wound, there was hemorrhage, multiple lacerations of the brain, fragments of bone in the brain, shotgun pellets and a portion of the plastic wadding which looked like the 'following' from a shell. And every bone in the cranium was fractured at least once.

"In fact, the scalp was holding some of the fractures together.

When the scalp was removed, portions of the bone came away leaving the brain protruding from the inside of the cranium. This was unrelated to the actual wound—I'm just using this as an example of how badly fractured the neck was."

"Would you explain that to us, please?"

"Well, when the scalp was removed to examine the skull, there were multiple fractures, and pieces were being forced up by the underlying brain tissue—the brain was exposed without further removing the brain manually."

"Were there any further findings, doctor?"

"The original wound to the back of the neck was examined, and the fracture which appeared to have resulted from the motorcycle accident was examined, and palpated—which means felt in the vertebra, the fifth cervical vertebra. And the spinal cord in this area which had been previously operated on was examined also, and there was severe damage to the spinal cord in this area."

"All right, doctor, would you tell us what your diagnosis was, please?"

"As to cause of death?"

"Yes."

"The wound to the skull," Lang said.

50

October 30, 1973

On Tuesday night, Scott, Brian, and Kevin came to dinner, shrieking, in dress rehearsal for Halloween—one ghost, one chimneysweep, and one ape.

At 8:00 p.m., Robert pulled out of the driveway into a cold moonless night. A brisk wind scattered autumn leaves.

Tomorrow morning, Lester's defense would begin. All preparations were complete except the construction of a hypothetical question for Klagsbrun and Motley. Mulling it over, he seemed to get no further than: *Doctor, I want you to assume the following facts*. . . . He found himself caught in the vague depression that had begun this afternoon in court. . . .

The Prosecution had rested.

The jury had been dismissed. The courtroom had emptied of all spectators who had come for the drama. Only the reporters had remained as Judge McGowan arbitrated the legal battle between the Defense and Malcolm Carton.

Robert had made the first of a series of motions for acquittal: "It is fundamentally unfair to try Lester Zygmanik within the same framework as a bank robber who shoots a teller."

The Prosecutor had argued vigorously. McGowan had ruled that the Defense could continue through the rest of his motions.

Number two had been: "The prerequisite of a common-law crime is the absence of the consent of the victim."

McGowan had remarked, "That would be a revolutionary change in the law, wouldn't it?"

The Defense had conceded the point, then argued its third motion: "This case is not the taking of a life; this case involves the right to die."

McGowan had denied the motion. The Defense had then argued for Number four: "The proper grounds for this case are the grounds of manslaughter, a murder under provocation—not Murder One."

Finally, Robert had argued for jury-nullification, asking McGowan to instruct the jurors to disregard the law.

Three of Robert's motions had asked for a change in the law of homicide, one had attempted to reduce the degree of the crime, and the last was a procedure that had never been used in New Jersey.

McGowan had ruled against all of them, saying, "On Wednesday morning, the trial will continue."

Bangs Avenue was deserted. In front of the telephone company, under a streetlight, a lone patrolman stood, smoking, waiting to escort the operators home. At night, nobody walked the streets of Asbury Park alone.

The office was empty. Robert stopped in the hallway to study a photograph of his father as a young attorney. His father's silence had been the loudest voice of his childhood. He wondered if he loved his father as much as Lester had loved George. He wondered if he loved anybody as much as Lester had loved George.

Lester envied him. In Lester's eyes, he had everything. He had a wife with class, a big house, an assured career, an insured future. Lester saw him as the possessor of the ultimate, the illusive, dream. Yet, was his reality any different from Lester's? Wasn't his life as rigidly structured—whatever the structure? Hadn't the values been passed from father to son—whatever the values? Hadn't he, in fact, exercised as little real choice about his own life as Lester? Was it a case of one man's dream being another man's nemesis? Or had Lester simply provoked a lot of questions that had been lying around for a long time?

He reminded himself that he had not expected to win any of the motions he had proposed to McGowan this afternoon. He had simply wanted to cover the record in the event of appeal. Then, suddenly, he understood the emotional underpinning of his thoughts— an acknowledgment of the real possibility of defeat.

51

October 31, 1973
Freehold, New Jersey

A few years ago, when the body of Vito Genovese, "Mafia king," was returned from federal prison to Atlantic Highlands, New Jersey, for Catholic rites, hundreds attended the services. Notably absent was

Genovese's ex-wife, Freehold resident, who claimed that Genovese had once broken her nose and set fire to her hair with a cigarette—to which Genovese had replied in the press, "Why did she step on my heart?" Genovese's legacy included four decades of crime, thirteen indictments, and a multimillion-dollar crime empire. At his funeral, a local policeman described Genovese to reporters as "a good father who raised his children to be honest, well-behaved, and religious."

In the spring of 1970, in Long Branch, New Jersey, five patrolmen, a police detective, a juvenile officer, and five firetruck drivers were dismissed for holding a "gang-bang" in the West End Firehouse. The girl was seventeen years old. A local councilman said, "This situation is worse than the Mafia."

So went New Jersey. . . .

It was Wednesday morning, the third day of trial. In a few minutes, Robert would begin his defense. At 9:25, the jurors filed in, fourteen representative citizens of the Garden State.

It was a state that had a tolerance for corruption, particularly when executed with style, brashness, or grandeur. At the same time, Jersey maintained a solid belief in the respectable and the Biblical. The contradictions appeared to be the result of the enclaves of Mediterranean and Slavic immigrants who superimposed their passions and needs onto a place already steeped in Anglo-Saxon righteousness. If so, no reconciliation ever occurred—Jersey continued its tradition of selective morality.

It had been, more or less, the principle of selective morality which had permitted Robert to apply the concept of sleep-deprivation to the case of Lester Zygmanik. Yet by Wednesday morning the theory had been refined and transformed into a cornerstone of his defense.

At 9:25, opposite the jury box, Robert set up a chart which embodied weeks of preparation.

He believed in visual aids, and so had searched for some kind of demonstrative evidence that would give impact to the effects of lack of sleep. Two weeks ago, he and David Silver had begun to design a graph. He had consulted Klagsbrun as to psychological effect; should the graph run up and down or left to right? Finally, he had called on a client, a graphic artist, who had aided in the construction.

Now the result dominated the courtroom—approximately four feet by two feet, running left to right, covering the hours from the Saturday before George Zygmanik's motorcycle accident to the time of the shooting. As each witness testified, the chart would be marked— Lester's sleeping hours in blue, his waking hours in red. As each witness completed his testimony, that page would be flipped backward so that the following witness could not be influenced by previous markings. At the end of the trial, all pages would be restored to their original position, so arranged that the total amount of sleep-deprivation, marked in red, would be clearly visible to the jury.

The chart represented a gamble.

It was deliberately dramatic, certainly not unobtrusive. Yet Robert hoped to defer immediate disclosure of its purpose, fully aware that sleep research was controversial, a leftfield tactic, one that invited the Prosecutor to produce a qualified rebuttal witness to shoot the theory out of the courtroom.

At 9:35, the jury waited. Robert began briskly, requesting that George Zygmanik's hospital records be entered into evidence. Immediately, Carton interrupted to call McGowan's attention to the graph.

"What is this?" McGowan asked.

"It's a blank chart," Robert said. "It has names and dates on it. I intend to use it when the witnesses take the stand."

McGowan considered the chart. Finally he said, "All right," and then, "hospital records are marked D-1."

Quickly, Robert called Diane Haus to the stand.

Diane, as first witness, had been another expedient choice. Scheduled afterward was Al Harper, who would describe the events of the Saturday night before George's accident. Al Harper would testify that Lester took a girl home to Trenton, beginning the chronology of Lester's sleep-deprivation.

Al Harper involved another risk. Robert understood that the reference to a sexual escapade might alienate some of the jurors, but he hoped these implications would be overcome, later, by the importance of his sleep theory. Then the strategy had left him with the problem of Lester's "steady girl"—a dilemma he had solved when he scheduled the order of witnesses: Diane Haus would take the stand before she heard Al Harper's testimony.

Diane was sworn. She wore eyeshadow, mascara, bright lipstick, a short gray shepherdess dress, dark stockings, chunky shoes, and a large silver cross. Her mass of ginger hair framed a face that was rosy, nervous, and wide-eyed.

Robert leaned against the rail, his back close to the spectators. He was a dozen yards from Diane. In a gentle voice, he said, "Diane, you talk very quietly, so lean into the mike and try to talk to me way back here. All right?"

"Okay," she said.

"Make your voice carry back to me."

"Okay."

"Now—do you know Lester Zygmanik?"

"Yes."

Briefly, Robert glanced at Lester. It was the Diane Haus/Al Harper aspect of the trial that had troubled Lester most.

Quietly, he said, "For about how long have you known Lester Zygmanik?"

"Three years," Diane said.

Robert saw that Lester had closed his eyes.

52

October 31, 1973

". . . Okay, Diane," Robert said, "from 2:00 in the afternoon on Sunday until 2:00 in the morning, you were with Lester almost all that time?"

"Yes."

"Did you see Lester sleep at all on Sunday?"

"No."

Lester opened his eyes. Ansell was marking the sleep chart.

Lester looked at the jury. A man at the rear, the butcher, looked as if he had gone to sleep.

On the stand, when Diane began to answer Ansell's questions again, he remembered telling Klagsbrun, "She's going crazy." He had told Klagsbrun, "I made up my mind to tell her I couldn't see her any more. She ran out of the car in the middle of the highway. She ran through the woods. I looked for her for four or five hours. Finally, I found her. She cried and cried. . . ."

"What time did you see Lester on Monday night?" Ansell asked.

"About 10:30 that night. We went to the hospital to pick up Jeannie. I waited outside. In the car, going home, Lester was depressed and crying. He kept saying, 'What are we going to do about George? What's going to happen to George?' " Diane said. Lester could hear the emotion in her voice.

"Did you go back to the house?" Ansell asked quietly.

"Yes."

"Do you recall what time you left the house on Monday night?"

"Between 2:00 and 2:30 in the morning."

"Did you see Lester sleep at all during that period?"

"No."

Lester watched Ansell cross the courtroom and mark the sleep chart again. He only vaguely understood its purpose, though Ansell had explained it to him on the way to court. Then he watched Diane. He realized she was trying to help him. He remembered telling Klagsbrun, "I can't be with one girl for a long time. I like a lot of women, you know? I go about it very, very calmly. I never push the issue. I've been turned down, but the reason is that I didn't spend enough time. . . ."

"On Tuesday, June 19th, did you have occasion to see or talk to Lester?" Ansell asked.

"I spoke to him on the phone. About 9:30 in the morning," Diane answered.

"What did Lester say to you?"

"He told me not to come to his house, he was going to stay all night with Jeannie at the hospital."

"All right. Now, let's get to Wednesday, June 20th. Did you have occasion to talk to Lester that day?"

"Yes."

"What time was that?"

"About a quarter after five—he called me at my office."

"Would you tell us about that conversation on Wednesday?"

"He was screaming on the phone and yelling and saying, 'You don't know what they did to my brother!' He said he was talking to a doctor in the cafeteria and the doctor told him George would never come home any more," Diane said. Lester heard her voice break. She didn't look at him. Still, he knew she was doing a good job for him.

"Was he speaking any differently on Wednesday than he was on Monday, or Tuesday?" Ansell asked.

"Yes," she said.

"What was different about him?"

"He kept screaming—and talking and talking."

"Did he go into any detail?"

"He said they would put George in a Veterans' Hospital with people just like him and his body would waste away—and everything like that." Diane began to weep, softly.

"Was there anything unusual about the way Lester was talking to you—from the Lester you had known for three years?"

"Yes. Usually, Lester is very calm." She brushed at her eyes.

"Did you make any plans to meet Lester in that conversation?" Ansell asked her, gently.

"Yes. He told me to come around 11:00 o'clock."

"Did you come down that night?"

"Yes, about a quarter to 11:00," she said. Lester tried not to think about how she would feel when Ansell put Al Harper on the stand.

"Who was at the house when you got there?"

"Jeannie, Sonia, and Barbara," she said.

"Did you ask for Lester?"

"Yes. They told me he left and they thought he went to the hospi-

tal. They told me not to go there and then I just went anyway."
Diane shook her head. Lester closed his eyes again.

"What happened when you got to Jersey Shore Medical Center?"

". . . Two nurses came out and told me there had been some trouble."

"Where did you go then?"

"I went to the Police Station."

"Did you eventually see Lester?"

"Yes. The police were walking him out. So, I said, 'Lester'—you know? And then he just looked at me like at first, like he didn't know who I was—and then he said, 'Diane?' . . ."

When Lester opened his eyes, he saw Diane was still crying.

Then Al Harper took the stand, looking like a young schoolteacher with slicked hair, dressed for church.

". . . Did you see Lester on Saturday, June 16th?" Ansell asked.

"Yes, I did."

"Where?"

"I met him at the Manor. A bar on Route 130."

"How long were you together?"

"Approximately between 11:00 p.m. and 1:30 in the morning."

"Did Lester leave with you?"

"No, he did not," Harper said.

"Who did he leave with?"

"He left with a female companion."

"And that's the last time you saw Lester on Saturday night?"

"That's correct."

Ansell marked the sleep chart. Lester looked back at Diane. He saw most of the jury turned to look at her. She was sitting in the third row. She held her head erect and was no longer crying.

53

At 10:15 a.m., Nathan Acari, fifty-four-year-old heart patient in the bed next to George, testified to George's condition. He said, ". . . When I was laying down, I seen George laid up, not in a bed, but on a table, and with weights hanging down in the back of his head. They also had him on intravenous and quite a few other pipes that led to all parts of his body, and they also had a breathing apparatus which made quite a bit of noise"—Acari clapped his hands to demonstrate the sound—"and George kept saying, 'I want to die, I want to die.'"

"Did you see George on Wednesday when they brought him back from the operating room?" Robert asked.

"Gee whiz—what a sight he was. He had this breathing apparatus. He had this pipe that looked like a football around his neck, and he had blood plasma—it was an awful sight to look at him, even as a healthy person myself, as anybody would be healthy to look at him—"

Carton objected. McGowan said, "The question, sir, is what you saw, not what you felt."

Acari described "blood plasma and pipes all over him." Robert had made his point.

"Mr. Acari, you were operated on?" Carton began.

"Yes."

"When?"

"Tuesday morning."

"Were you on medication from that point on?"

"Yes."

"What kind of medication?"

"I don't remember. They were giving me needles and medication."

"That was all day Tuesday, Tuesday night, and Wednesday—is that correct?"

"Yes," Acari said. It was a stand-off. Carton had made his point.

Robert called "Mike" Akins, twenty-five-year-old graduate nurse, wearing close-fitting white nylon pants, white nylon shirt, scissors in the pocket, chewing gum. Robert brought him a paper cup for the gum. Akins testified that George Zygmanik occupied what they called "the fifth bed."

"Do you recall what his condition was?" Robert asked.

"It was critical. He was in cervical traction. He had what are called Vicki Tongs—these are placed in the skull and retracted back with weights. He had motor and sensory deprivation from the neck down. By Tuesday, they had done a tracheotomy."

"Did he talk well with that?"

"Surprisingly well. . . ."

". . . Did you discuss his future with him?"

"He wanted to know if he'd ever be able to walk again," Akins said, "and I always told him I didn't know. On a couple of occasions, he expressed that if he had to live like that for the rest of his life, he didn't want to live. . . ."

". . . Now, did you see the defendant during these three days?"

"Yes."

"Did you notice any changes in Lester's condition over the period of time you observed him in the hospital?"

"He seemed to be getting more tired each time I saw him, more drained," Akins said.

Carton asked one question: "During the course of your conversations with the patient, isn't it true that surgery had not yet taken place?"

"Correct," Akins answered.

Robert calculated the distance to the peak of Mount Everest. It seemed closer—but he was still a long way from the top.

54

October 31, 1973
Freehold, New Jersey

Robert called Victor Kazma.

Victor settled into the witness chair and turned to face the jury as he took the oath. The jury saw a small, spidery man dressed for the occasion in a frayed undertaker's suit, a wrinkled shirt, a shoestring tie. In the hallway, at recess, Lester had said to Robert, "I don't know how to tell you this, but Victor just said he's gonna do something sensational."

Victor was a necessary witness. He had overheard the conversation between Lester and Gregory Carver in the hospital cafeteria. He could, also, confirm some of the hours that Lester had been awake. Robert planned to move quickly through these two points. Within thirty seconds, however, the entire courtroom was aware that Victor had no intention of conforming to anyone's plan.

Robert established Victor Kazma as Jean Zygmanik's father, George's father-in-law, grandfather of George's son, whom Victor called "the Champ." Victor grinned at the jury, making an obvious attempt at alliance which the jury visibly rejected.

Then Robert began with Sunday, June 17, Father's Day, and the fact that Victor was present at the time of the motorcycle accident. Victor's answers were voluble, erratic, irrelevant, and self-dramatizing. It took forty-nine questions to make Robert's point.

His fiftieth question was, "During that time, on Sunday, between 7:30 p.m. and midnight, did you observe Lester to sleep at all?"

"No, sir," Victor answered.

Robert marked the sleep chart.

Under further questioning, Victor continued to grin at the jury.

Through the rambling response he stated he had remained at home on Monday and Tuesday, in contact by telephone with the Zygmanik family. On Wednesday, June 20, however, the morning of George's operation, Victor went to Jersey Shore Medical Center. Twenty-six questions later, Ansell finally established Victor in the cafeteria.

During this portion of Victor's testimony, Carton objected twice and McGowan admonished the witness five times. The simplest testimony appeared to take an inordinate amount of time, provoking impatience in both jury and spectators.

Victor testified that, after the conversation in the cafeteria, Lester was "like a wild animal, very disturbed." Victor then stated that he took Lester home and remained there until 9:00 p.m. During this period Lester was still "very disturbed."

Robert asked, "During this time, Wednesday, did you see Lester sleep at all?" His tone was angry and firm. Still, Victor refused to conform to the rules of the courtroom.

"No, sir," Victor said. "I don't think anybody slept in that house since—"

Carton objected.

McGowan warned the witness again.

"No more questions." Robert marked the sleep chart.

Under Carton's cross-examination, Victor remained intractable.

"Mr. Kazma, directing your attention to this conversation you told us about in the hospital—what day was this when you overheard Lester and the doctor talking?"

"Wednesday," Victor rasped.

"That was Jersey Shore Medical Center?"

"Yes, sir."

"And approximately what time?"

"At a quarter to 12:00, to around lunchtime."

"Are you sure it was Wednesday?"

"Well, if I wasn't sure, sir, I wouldn't tell you."

"Just answer yes or no, please. Was it Wednesday? Are you sure?"

"Yes, it was Wednesday."

"All right. Now, were you here yesterday in court?"

"Was I here yesterday in court?"

"Right."

"I believe I was."

"Were you here all day for the testimony yesterday?"

"I don't know whether I was here all day."

"Were you here when Gregory Carver, the student anesthetist, testified? Do you recall that?"

"Yes."

"Was that the man having the conversation with Lester in the hospital?"

"Yes."

"Are you sure of that?"

"If I wasn't sure, I wouldn't answer your question, sir."

"Were you sure? Yes or No?"

"Yes."

Carton's cross-examination proved nothing. Yet he kept Victor on the stand as if to expose him fully to the jury, as if he were aware that the value of Victor's testimony for the Defense could be canceled by Victor's own manner.

Finally Carton relinquished him.

McGowan asked the witness to step down. Victor refused to move, saying, "Your honor, can I ask you something?"

"No, you may not," McGowan answered.

Victor repeated, "Can I ask you something?" He refused to move.

"Not here, no, sir," McGowan said.

"I feel I have an obligation to—"

"Get off the stand, please," McGowan said. "If you have anything you feel hasn't been covered, you'll have an opportunity to talk to Mr. Ansell about it."

"I feel I have an obligation to my son-in-law and the court," Victor said. His voice was raspy, loud.

McGowan, visibly angry, said, "Talk to your lawyer, he can explain it to me later."

Victor shouted, "*I think somebody should defend my son-in-law in this courtroom!*"

55

The day turned warm, like Indian summer. By noon, the pigeons were sunbathing on the statue of Molly Pitcher.

Lester hung on to the briefcase. Preoccupied, Robert drove.

The damage was clear. Victor Kazma had intended to give a eulogy for George Zygmanik—but what it sounded like was an attack on Robert's own defense. Whatever valid testimony Victor might have contributed had been negated by his personality and the resulting chaos.

He had spent the morning building an ambiance, creating a bond with the jury. No verdict was ever won or lost on hard evidence—the outcome always depended on a consistent emotional environment and that tenuous bond with strangers.

One personality could blow it to hell.

Victor had done that. Victor had sabotaged everything that went before him, and had left a pall to hang over everything that would come afterward.

Silently, Robert cursed Victor.

In downtown Freehold, Robert parked in front of the American Hotel, a genteel landmark that specialized in Revolutionary pretensions, snow-white tablecloths, and tasteless food. Its main attraction was proximity to the courthouse.

The dining room was sparsely occupied—a couple of traveling salesmen and a handful of refugees from other trials. Robert asked for a table in the corner. The waitress stared at Lester. Robert said, "We're in a hurry."

He watched Lester light a cigarette. Lester's hands were shaking. Around them, he could hear the discreet sounds of glassware, sedate voices. He wondered if he had come here to buy Lester a last proper meal before the symbolic hanging.

"I'm going to put you on this afternoon," he said.

"On the stand?"

"Yes."

Lester toyed with a fork, looking awkward against the faded Victorian wallpaper. The blue suit was at the cleaner's. His brown cotton jacket was already badly wrinkled. "I don't know if I can do it," he said.

"I'm going to try to make it easy for you," Robert said. "I'm going to lay out the entire afternoon so there won't be any surprises. So you'll be absolutely comfortable when you take the stand."

"Suppose the trial wasn't goin' okay? Would you tell me?"

"I've told you, nobody can predict what a jury'll do."

"Right," Lester said.

The waitress brought their order. She hung around, staring. Robert said, "How about leaving us alone?"

Lester ignored his food.

"After lunch, all the testimony will revolve around the events directly preceding the shooting. Every witness is going to pave the way for you."

"This afternoon?"

"That's right," Robert said gently. "You'll go on last."

"Suppose—I can't do it?"

"You can do it."

"I don't know." Lester shook his head.

Robert described the first two witnesses of the afternoon.

"Listen," Lester said. "What would you do if you had to go to jail? I mean, how would you feel?"

"If the verdict goes against us, you won't be there long. We'll *appeal*."

"What about your wife? She's a good-lookin' girl. Would you miss your wife?"

"I don't know," Robert said.

"Right."

"Look," Robert said, "I know you're scared. That's why I'm trying to tell you what's going to happen."

"Right," Lester said.

Quickly, Robert sketched in the next witnesses. "Barbara's going to tell the truth. Then Jeannie's going to tell the truth. Do you understand?"

"Right," Lester said.

"By the time you take the stand, it's going to be easy."

"Listen," Lester said, "if you had to go to jail, would you miss your father? What about your brothers? Would you miss your brothers?"

"Sure, I would."

"What about your house? That's definitely a nice house. Would you miss your house?"

"I'd miss my kids," Robert said.

"Right." Lester shook his head. "That's what I'm talkin' about. I mean, what would I miss? My mother? Like I worry about my mother, but I wouldn't miss her, you know? And it would probably be hard doin' without girls, but I really wouldn't miss Diane. Everybody I would miss is already gone, you know? So I keep askin' myself —what would be so terrible? But I couldn't stand bein' locked up. I definitely can't stand the idea of bein' locked up."

"We're going to fight like hell to keep that from happening," Robert said.

"I don't know. Like—why did you tell them about my waxing the bullet? I don't see any advantage in that."

"That's what a trial's supposed to be," Robert said, "a search for the *truth*. Sometimes it's like that. Not always. But sometimes. In your case, there was no choice."

"Why?"

"Because—there's nothing to lie about. What do you want to lie about? The pressure you were under? The code that exists in your family? Your brother's request? His wife's tacit, if not active, approval? Your mother? Given those circumstances, you did an honorable thing."

Robert saw that Lester didn't understand all the words, but Lester was listening.

"Society calls it murder," Robert said. "The law requires us to call it temporary insanity. But before this trial is over, the jury is going to understand the facts the way I understand the facts. And every juror in that box is going to ask the same questions I've been asking for three months: *Would I ever have the kind of courage Lester had? Do I love anybody as much as Lester loved his brother?*"

Lester was silent. Finally, he said, "Okay. This afternoon—I think, maybe, I can do it."

Robert turned. The waitress was standing directly behind him. He realized that in age and education she was approximately the average juror. He realized she had been standing there for quite a while.

In an angry gesture of disapproval, she slammed the check in front of him.

56

October 31, 1973
Freehold, New Jersey

Robert called Mrs. Jeannette Somer, widow, next-door neighbor on Sweetman's Lane. He asked her to confirm Lester's "roller-coaster" behavior by describing a fifteen-minute telephone conversation she had with Lester at 6:15 p.m., Wednesday, June 20—five hours before the shooting.

She spoke in a soft voice, "Lester was very, very disturbed and very distraught, and it was hard to talk to him. But he said his brother was paralyzed, completely paralyzed. His neck, I think, was shattered, and there were pieces of bone they had taken out. He said, 'There is absolutely no hope.' The main thing he said was his brother was in very severe pain. He said it was so severe, it was unimaginable. Then he told me a doctor had said if he had been George, he would want to be dead. Lester was very hysterical. He said he wanted the doctor to give George a needle to kill him. I said, 'A doctor wouldn't do that, he'd lose his practice.'

"Lester said, 'I don't care. If I was a doctor, I wouldn't care.' He was very, very disturbed, you know, very distraught. It was mainly the pain. He couldn't take his brother's pain."

"Had you ever heard Lester talk like this before?" Robert asked gently.

"No. You see, Lester was quiet."

"Were you trying to solicit these comments from Lester on the phone?"

"No. In fact, I didn't really want to hear all that, because I was getting very upset myself. . . ."

". . . Now, did you know George?"

"Yes."

"And did you know John Zygmanik, the father?"

"Yes, yes," she said.

"And Sonia—the mother?"

"Yes—I was pretty close to the family."

"Would you tell the jury what kind of family they were?"

"They were a very, very devoted family. The father was a very proud, handsome man. He was just a lovely, lovely person and he worked with his sons. Anytime he had spare time, he was out in the woods. You see, they lived in the woods and they were clearing it out, and they made their home like a park. They cleared out part of the trees and they put grass there, and they planted a vegetable garden."

"Who was this?—the three men?"

"Yes. The father and the sons were very, very devoted. It was the three men, always together. . . ."

The jury seemed moved.

57

October 31, 1973
Freehold, New Jersey

Orlando Linn, wearing a white plantation-owner's suit, seemed subdued and pliant as he took the stand, awed by the occasion and uncomfortable in the presence of the law. Gone was the black revolutionary. As Linn described his telephone conversation with Lester on Wednesday evening, June 20, his testimony had the tone of a blessing.

"Well, this conversation—Lester was explaining to me his brother's condition. He said he talked to a doctor in the hospital down there, and the doctor told him his brother was going to deteriorate, like dry up—and Lester says, 'I can't stand to see my brother like this.' He says, 'Linn, my brother is suffering.' He says, 'He can't even scratch his own ear.' Like he was very, very excited, talking in a high-pitched screaming voice."

"Was it different from the Lester you had known, and worked with since March?" Robert asked.

"This was not a Lester I had known," Linn answered. Nervously he fingered his polka-dot necktie.

"Will you continue. What did you say to him?—and what did he say to you?"

"I explained to him that it was not up to us who should live and who should die, who should have accidents. I said, 'It's up to God.'"

"What did he say?"

"He says, 'Don't tell me about God.' He says, 'Linn, God took my father.' He says, 'My father was a good man—he never did any harm or any wrong.' He says, 'What God would let my brother lie there and suffer like this?' He says, 'I would rather see my brother dead than to see him suffer like this.' "

"Was there anything else said?"

"I felt he was very upset and nervous, and I tried to convince him the best thing for him to do was to come back to the job. I said, 'If you are not there at the hospital and you don't see these things, it won't bother you as much. Come back—work during the day and then at night, you go see your brother.' "

"What did he say?" Robert faced the jury.

"He said, 'I'm going to the hospital to see my brother tonight, but I promise you, I'll be back on the job tomorrow morning.' "

"Was there anything else?"

"Well, I kept repeating, asking him because, like, even though this tragedy happened to the Zygmanik family, I have a business to operate and I wanted to know should I call for another man to run the machine—and he kept promising me that he will be back tomorrow. He says, 'Don't get another man. I want my job.' He says, 'I promise you, Linn, I'll be back tomorrow morning.' "

The jury seemed unimpressed.

58

October 31, 1973
Freehold, New Jersey

Barbara Petruska occupied the stand uneasily, lowering her eyes as she spoke. She was a big woman with a plain, broad, good-natured face, and a self-deprecating air that canceled out her youth.

Quietly, on the verge of tears, she described George Zygmanik's motorcycle accident. The jury appeared to be affected by her.

Then Robert led her into the hours preceding the shooting. It was a move intended to subtly distribute the responsibility for George's death. To batter at Barbara's guilt, however, would be to admit Lester's, so his questions were careful and contained, allowing the jury to draw its own conclusions.

"Now, would you tell the jury what Lester did when he sat down at the kitchen table?—what he said and what he did."

"He had a cartridge, and he asked Jeannie if she knew where a candle was. Jeannie asked him what he wanted it for, and Lester said, 'Don't worry, I know what I'm doing.' And I believe Jeannie told him where a candle was, and he got it." Her tone was even, her manner straightforward.

"Then he lit the candle and he took the little balls out of the shell, and he dripped wax inside, and he closed it."

"He did this sitting at a table with you and Jean?" Robert asked.

"Yes."

"Did Lester appear unusual to you? Or did you feel he was acting normally?"

"It wasn't Lester. He was upset. His face was very red, and even when I talked to him, it seemed like he didn't hear me."

"What happened then?"

"He got the gun. And he got his jacket. He said he was going to the hospital. He asked Jeannie and me whether we could see the gun under his jacket. He asked if it was hidden. We could see it on his right side. So then he put it on his left side and asked if we could see it, and we said no. Then he left. . . ."

Carton hesitated before beginning his cross-examination. In the course of the trial, Carton had refrained from attacking any of Robert's witnesses except Victor, as if to illustrate to the jury both his confidence and his chivalry. Both he and Robert knew the facts and the law were on the side of the Prosecution. At this point, however, it was clear that Robert had used each witness to build toward Lester's irrational state of mind. So, Carton chose to emphasize the fact that Lester had said he knew what he was doing.

"How many times did Lester say he knew what he was doing?" Carton asked.

"He said it twice."

"And where did he put the gun?"

"On his left-hand side, in his pants. . . ."

"Then he moved it from one side to the other?"

"Yes."

"And he said he knew what he was doing?" Carton repeated.

"Yes."

"And then he left? Is that right?"

"Yes."

"And you did nothing?"

"No."

Carton dismissed her. Subdued, Barbara returned to her seat.

Then, without warning, Carton pointed to the sleep chart. "Your Honor, I object to this third-grade coloring chart. It has not been marked into evidence, yet it has been displayed to the jury throughout this entire trial. I object to its presence."

It was a critical moment. The sleep chart had allowed Robert to send a daily subliminal message to the jurors, who had watched it grow. He had counted on its psychological effect, and on what the chart represented: a simple, understandable, identifiable, physical, non-esoteric reason for the ordinary juror to acquit Lester Zygmanik.

He had hoped to avoid a direct confrontation—a gamble calculated to preclude expert testimony. Authorities and counter-authorities tended to cancel themselves, confuse the jury, and diminish the issue. Now the Prosecutor had challenged him, and the Judge was waiting for a response.

He decided on a light tone, playing for time. "Your Honor," he said, "it's at least a fifth-grade coloring chart."

A few spectators giggled.

McGowan rapped the gavel. "Mr. Ansell," he said, "no explanation has been given to the court. Perhaps you'd like to give one now."

Robert tried evasion. "It's a diagram. I plan to offer it into evidence when it's completed."

"You are fully aware, Mr. Ansell, that we don't mark a diagram and then, at some later point, say, 'I offer it in evidence.' Now, what is it?"

Robert hesitated, then tried to dismiss its importance by using a matter-of-fact tone. "I would represent to the court—and it can be checked against the transcript—that marked in red are the time periods when witnesses observed Lester to be awake. Marked in blue are the time periods when Lester was sleeping. It is a matter of convenience and visual aid."

Carton objected.

Robert argued that visual aids were fundamental and traditional.

Carton objected on the grounds that the accuracy of the chart was in doubt.

Robert argued that the chart could be checked against the transcript.

McGowan dismissed the jury. Then he ruled, "When all Mr. Ansell's witnesses have testified, when the chart is complete, both counsel will confer and go over the diagram and the transcript. If counsel can agree that the chart accurately depicts what Mr. Ansell represents it depicts, it will be entered into evidence at that time."

Robert quickly calculated the number of witnesses ahead of him—four, all of whom would take the stand by tomorrow afternoon. Which meant: If Carton wanted a sleep expert, he had thirty-six hours to come up with one—and thirty-six hours to go through the transcript for an error that could invalidate the sleep chart.

Robert looked at Carton. His own final gamble was to count on Carton to do neither.

59

October 31, 1973
Freehold, New Jersey

In the months preceding the trial, Jean had been unable to talk about her husband's death without breaking down into tears and confusion. As she took the stand, however, she seemed a woman with presence. In contrast to her father's offensive behavior, she was calm and self-possessed. She wore a black, long-sleeved dress, a prominent crucifix, the flowing pony-tail, curls over each ear. There was a marked absence of hysteria as she responded to Robert's questions.

"All right, Jean—now, on Sunday, you saw Lester when he arrived at Freehold Hospital? . . . and then, afterwards, at home? Is that correct?"

"Yes. . . ."

". . . So, on Sunday, you were with Lester from 7:30 p.m. until 2:30 a.m. when he went to his room? Is that correct?"

"Yes."

"Did you see him sleep at all?"

"No. . . ."

". . . And what time did you wake Lester on Monday morning?"

"A few minutes after 4:30."

"Two hours later?"

"Yes." Jean's voice remained steadfast.

"What did you do then?"

"They had moved my husband to Jersey Shore Medical Center. We went there."

During Jean's testimony, Robert marked the sleep chart. On Monday, she said, Lester slept as little as he had on Sunday. On Tuesday, from 7:00 a.m. until the following morning, she and Lester remained beside her husband's bed.

On Monday, she said, "My husband kept crying. He would ask me to kiss him. He would ask his brother to kiss him. He was afraid to be left alone."

"What was George's mental condition on Tuesday?"

"He said they were torturing him. He didn't want to go on living."

"Was Lester present during this conversation?"

"Yes. He said, 'Lester, promise me.' Then he said, 'Swear to God.' He said, 'Swear to God to me that you're not going to let me live like this.' Lester was crying, and my husband was also crying, and I kept saying, 'Don't talk like this.' Then my husband said, 'Jean, you have to promise me you're not going to interfere.' And the look on his face, you know?—and the way he said it, got to me so bad that I had to tell him what he wanted me to tell him. Lester, also." Jean looked directly at the jury.

Robert waited a moment before his next question.

"Did Lester swear to God that he would not let him go on like that?"

"Yes."

"Did you swear to God to George you would not interfere?"

"Yes."

"Then what did you do? . . ."

Jean spoke slowly. ". . . My husband asked Lester to hold one of his hands, and for me to hold the other one, and he wanted us to pray out loud together with him—and the three of us said the Lord's Prayer, and the Hail Mary, out loud."

"This was Tuesday?" Robert said.

"Yes."

"Did something also occur on Tuesday which had to do with George's living, not George's dying—wasn't there an incident with the tracheotomy? The tube George had in his throat?"

"Yes."

"What happened?"

"My husband felt cold, and he wanted Lester to bring the blanket up to his neck because he felt cold. So, as Lester raised the blanket to his neck, the thing that was in his neck, it fell out, and my husband started to gasp for air—because it fell out."

"What did Lester do?"

"He ran to the desk and started yelling, 'My brother can't breathe, my brother can't breathe!' And the nurse ran back to the bed and she put the thing back in his neck and he started breathing all right."

In detail Robert led Jean through the events of Wednesday, June 20, the day of the shooting.

She described Lester's disturbed behavior after his conversation with the "doctor" in the cafeteria.

Like Barbara Petruska, she described the waxing of the bullet, the concealing of the shotgun, the fact that Lester had asked her to return to the hospital with him. Finally, Robert released her.

"No questions," Carton said. He had hammered relentlessly at Barbara Petruska. Now, however, he deferred to the unwritten law: *One must not browbeat the widow of the deceased.*

60

October 31, 1973
Freehold, New Jersey

At 3:00 p.m., it was Lester's turn. As he took the stand, he was not visibly nervous. He appeared, instead, rather casual, offhand, leaning back in a relaxed attitude as he took the oath. The fourteen jury members watched him carefully.

Robert began with background questions, eliciting answers meant to give the jury a picture of the Zygmanik family: The family had always lived together; Lester worked all through school, turned his paycheck over, saved money to help buy the land; Lester and George and their father cleared the trees by hand—it took two years to clear five acres. Carton objected. McGowan cautioned Ansell not to overdo it.

Robert took his time. It became clear that he intended to keep Lester on the stand for as long a period of time as possible in order to gain two advantages: (1) This would not leave time for cross-examination this afternoon—the jurors would sleep on his version of Lester's story—and (2) Lester's brusque manner of talking improved with time.

Robert questioned Lester about the Saturday before George's motorcycle accident. Lester testified that he worked all day, went out that night to a bar, then took a girl home to Trenton, where he stayed until 6:30 a.m. Robert marked the sleep chart. Then Lester described the events of Sunday, Father's Day, the day of his brother's accident. At Freehold Hospital that evening, Lester testified, he spoke to three doctors—among them, a neurosurgeon who said "the bone in my brother's head had exploded and he didn't feel my brother would ever walk again."

Robert asked, "How long did you sleep on Saturday night?"

Lester replied, "A couple of hours."

Robert marked the sleep chart.

Under questioning, Lester described his brother's condition on Monday—the rods in George's head, the weights, the swivel bed, George's increasing pain. Lester said, "My brother felt ashamed of his condition—that he didn't know what his body was doing, that he had no control over his body. He made me raise his hand to show him that at least he had a hand because he couldn't see his body, or feel his body."

"Did you try to give him hope on Monday?" Robert asked.

"Yes, I did."

"And what was his reaction?"

"Well, he was always saying, 'I hope so, I hope so'—but like deep, deep in his mind, like you could see he knew it was a permanent condition." Lester slouched in the chair.

"Towards Monday evening, did things get worse?"

"Yes."

"Did you leave the hospital Monday night and go home?"

"Yes, I did." Lester rested his head on one hand and crossed a foot over his knee.

"Why?"

"Because I couldn't bear to look at my brother any more," Lester said.

"And when you got home, did you go somewhere with Diane?"

"Yeah, I went to get her car from the gas station."

"When you finally got back home after that, was there a call waiting for you from the hospital?"

"Right. Jeannie had called and told me she can't take it any more and that she wanted me to pick her up." Lester shifted position, slouching further in the chair.

"Did you go back to the hospital?"

"Right."

"What was George's condition like at that time?"

"At that time he was screaming and you could hear him down the halls. He was screaming, 'What are they doing to me?' Saying that 'they're making a monster out of me.'" Lester's tone remained his normal one, seemingly offhand and matter-of-fact.

"Did you get Jeannie out?" Robert prompted.

"Yes, I did."

"And did you go home?"

"Right."

"What time did you get home?"

"I'd say around 1:00 o'clock, 2:00 o'clock, something like that."

"What did you do there?"

"We continued to discuss my brother."

"For how long?"

"I don't know—maybe 45 minutes, something like that." Lester frowned.

"Then what did you do?"

"I laid down."

"*And did you sleep?*"

"I wasn't really sleeping, you know? I couldn't sleep."

"Did you stay in bed?"

"Well, no—I was in bed, walking around the house, doing different things."

"What happened the next morning?"

"The hospital called and said my brother had been asking for us."

"What time did that call come in?"

"It was very early in the morning, like 5:00 o'clock."

Robert crossed to the sleep chart and marked the hours of Monday night in red.

Then Lester testified to Tuesday's events. The doctors performed a tracheotomy. Afterward, George kept saying, "Why don't they let me die?"

". . . Did you talk to Dr. Kreider on Tuesday?"

"Yes."

"Did you discuss George's future with him?"

"Right, I did."

"Can you describe that conversation?"

"I said, 'What's going to happen to my brother?' He kept telling me, 'In due time your brother will adjust to this condition and so will your family.' And I told him, 'Listen, this is going to kill my mother.' He said, 'Your mother is not my patient.'

"And then, you know, I told him, 'Why don't you do my brother a favor, do what he wants, just let him die?' And he said, 'What do you want me to do—stick a knife in his chest?' And I believe I told him, I said, 'If you don't, I will.' "

"Was that on Tuesday?"

"Right. I believe it was Tuesday. . . ." Lester faltered.

"Would you tell the jury what happened Tuesday night."

". . . Well, my brother told me, 'Lester, I want you to promise me that you won't let me live like this.' How could I possibly tell him no?"

"Did you swear to God?"

"Yes, I did."

"And did Jeannie swear to God not to interfere?"

"Yes."

"Were you committed to do this at that time, in your mind?"

Carton objected. McGowan sustained, saying, "That's a conclusion which somebody else better make, Mr. Ansell."

Robert took a few moments to establish the fact that Lester spent Tuesday night at the hospital and had no sleep at all. He marked the chart. Then he began to question Lester about the events of Wednesday, the day of the shooting.

"On Wednesday morning, they took George in for a neck operation—is that right?"

"Right—at the back of the neck."

"When did you see George after the operation?"

"About 2:30 probably."

"What was he like?"

"Well, his head was all swollen and he wasn't conscious but you could see the nerves in his face were twisting," Lester said.

"What did you do then?" Robert checked out the jury. Was Lester's childishness coming through? Or did Lester appear brusque and insolent. There was no way to tell.

"I went around the hospital looking for Dr. Kreider to explain this to me, so he could do something, but he could not be found."

"Where did you go?"

"I went downstairs to the cafeteria."

"Did you meet anyone downstairs in the cafeteria?"

"Yes. Across from me, this fellow—what's his name—Gregory Carver sat across from me and I remembered seeing him as one of the people who removed my brother from Intensive Care to be operated on."

"What did you do?" Robert moved closer to the jury box, where he stood quietly and listened.

"I went to him," Lester said, "and I asked him about George Zygmanik's condition and I asked him had he worked with Dr. Kreider on my brother. He said yes he had. And I told him, 'Well, Dr. Kreider says that there's no chance my brother will ever walk again or anything.' And he says, 'Yup, that's about what it is.'

"He told me that's about one of the worst things that can happen to you, that he wouldn't wish that on anyone no matter what, and that he would much rather be dead than to go through what my brother is going through.

"He told me that this situation would continue to grow worse, he would no doubt get pneumonia, that he would start to get sores and due to lack of mobility, any sores he did get wouldn't heal, which, in that case, they might have to amputate things off of him.

"He told me there's people like my brother in Veterans' Hospitals and he had seen around fourteen cases in Vietnam—and there was a lot more but I really can't remember it all."

"Did you leave the cafeteria then?"

"Yeah."

"Where did you go?"

"I went back upstairs to see my brother. Then I went home with Victor."

"When you got home, what did you do?"

"I was talking to Victor and I believe I was on the phone."

"Later on that evening, what did you do?"

"I went to my room and I took a shotgun and got a hacksaw from somewhere and I went out to the dog shed and I cut both ends of the shotgun."

Robert picked up the shotgun—looked directly at the jury. "Is this the gun we're talking about?" he asked Lester.

"Right," Lester said.

"Do you have other shotguns at home?"

"Yes, I do."

"Are they more powerful than that one?"

"Yes!"

Robert paused, laid the gun down, and looked at the jury again, as if to remind them of the point he had made in his opening speech. If Lester had chosen a more powerful gun, there would have been no need to saw it, no need to wax a bullet.

"After you sawed it off, what did you do?"

"I believe I put it in the car."

"All right. Now, did Jeannie come home eventually?"

"Yeah."

"And was Barbara at the house? Barbara Petruska?"

"Yes, she was."

"Do you recall shoving her or pushing her while you were talking on the phone?"

"No."

"Do you recall talking to your boss, Mr. Linn?"

"Yes, I do."

"Do you recall telling him that you would see him at work the next day?"

"I don't."

"Do you recall saying to Mr. Linn that there is no God?"

"I don't remember it."

"Do you believe in God?"

"Yes, I do. . . ."

Robert paused. ". . . When Barbara and Jean were there, did you go outside and get the gun?"

"I can't really remember going out to get the gun, but I can see myself walking into the house with the gun."

"What happened when you entered the house with the gun?"

"My mother took the gun away from me."

"What did she do with it?"

"She put it on the bureau."

"What did you do then?"

"What did I do? I don't know. I got a candle from somewhere and was waxing down a shell."

"Why?"

"Why? I don't know why. It seemed the right thing to do."

"How many shells do you recall waxing?"

"Three."

"Do you recall asking Jean to go to the hospital with you?"

"No, I don't."

"Did you go to the hospital?"

"Yes, I did."

"Did you take the waxed shells with you?"

"Yes. I took two."

"Did you take the gun back from your mother's bureau before you went to the hospital?"

"Yes, I must have."

"And you hid the gun under your coat in front of Barbara and Jean?"

"Yes."

"Why did you do that?"

"Because I knew that the hospital nurses wouldn't let me walk into my brother's room with a gun."

"Was the gun loaded?"

"I don't remember. . . ."

". . . What happened then?"

"Well, I ended up in my brother's room."

"All right. Tell the jury, please, what happened in that room."

"I looked in the room. I saw my brother at the far end of the room. I walked over to him and I asked him if he was in pain. At this time, he couldn't speak at all. He just nodded that he was. He nodded yes. So, I says, 'I am here to end your pain—is that all right with you?' And he nodded yes. And the next thing I knew, I shot him. . . ."

". . . Did you do anything with the tracheotomy?"

"Yes. I also pulled the tube out of his neck."

"Why did you do that?"

"My brother didn't like that tube. . . ."

61

Robert Ansell

I have to bring out all the adverse facts myself. I can't wait for the Prosecutor to bring out something in cross-examination that I haven't even touched on. By the time Carton hits the sawing, or the waxing, or the hiding of the gun, that fact is already familiar to the jury—we've beat him to it, and, hopefully, we've presented that fact in the context of irrationality. So maybe the juror will say to himself, "Sure, I know that fact—it proves Lester was confused, or crazy, or that fact fits this pattern of roller-coaster behavior that Ansell talked about in his opening speech."

So far, everybody's done fairly well. Diane was sensational. Barbara was good. Jean did better than I would have ever imagined. And I think Lester got to the jury before we finished. The one setback was Victor, and I don't feel it had a permanent effect. I feel we offset him.

The real problem is the one we've had from the beginning—the fact that the Prosecution has always had this case wrapped up in a neat little package. How much time did it take Carton to prove his case? Less than two hours. That's a record in a murder case. He hasn't even asked a helluva lot of cross-examination questions. He doesn't have to. It's in the nature of this case that all Defense witnesses corroborate the testimony of the Prosecution's witnesses. There's no dispute about the facts. The dispute is how those facts should be interpreted.

The whole legal-insanity concept is so restrictive and, in a sense, unreal. McNaughton is absurd. There isn't a psychiatrist in the world who believes it. Going in, Lester knows the nature and quality of his act, and he knows it's wrong. He fulfills the McNaughton requirements. Now, I have to prove that he doesn't. The tough part is still ahead. Three psychiatrists are going to get up there and disagree. A lot depends on how that's handled. And before that, Lester's got to stand up to Carton tomorrow. I feel Lester will hold up. But there's always the chance he may not. If he doesn't, nobody will have to worry about what the psychiatrists are going to say. It's all over tomorrow morning.

62

November 1, 1973
Freehold, New Jersey

Court was in session. It was Thursday, the fourth day of trial.

At 9:25, Dr. Samuel Klagsbrun waited for his patient to take the stand again for cross-examination. The Prosecutor's attitude was expected to be tough—no holds barred. This morning, Lester had said, "Doc, I have to hold my head in my hand to keep it from shaking."

Also present this morning was Dr. John Motley, another psychiatrist for the Defense. Absent for now was Dr. David J. Flicker, State psychiatrist. Later this afternoon, they would present contradictory testimony to a panel of laymen—who, traditionally, reacted to psychiatrists with caution, discomfort, and, often, angry dismissal.

As the jury filed in, Dr. Klagsbrun performed an off-the-record exercise—a brief, semi-professional evaluation of these fourteen men and women who would accept or dismiss his testimony in their judgment of Lester Zygmanik.

JUROR:

No. 1, James F. Clark, fifty-four-year-old union official, is "very proper, a problem."

No. 2, Frederick Ogden, fifty-four-year-old school custodian, is "uninvolved, distant."

No. 3, Larry Smith, square-jawed engineer, is "businesslike, fair, ready to do something against the grain."

No. 4, Mrs. Helen Hauke, wearing harlequin glasses and a wig, is "proper, conservative."

No. 5, Content Peckham, twenty-six-year-old unemployed art teacher, is "grossly disturbed."

No. 6, Diego Batiste, Cuban, chemist, bow tie, is "fair, but unassertive, conformist, asleep."

No. 7, Mrs. Dorothy Matthes, sixty-seven-year-old widow, desk clerk, is "sympathetic."

No. 8, Clyde Teters, youngish, technical writer, "leans to the rules."

No. 9, Marcelle Dean, age fifty, glass inspector, divorced, dyed red hair, appears to be "hysterical, but will go for sympathy."

No. 10, Tntien Pei Lee, Buddhist, engineer, is "fair, very involved."

No. 11, Mrs. Concheeta Ponzo, age fifty, blonde, deceased child, is "very possibly the best."

No. 12, Mrs. Jenny Carpenter, dietician, ugly dog, Lester's favorite, "doesn't like whole business."

No. 13, Cyril Skuby, butcher, is "distant."

No. 14, Mrs. Evelyn McElroy, Sears catalogue clerk, is "very positive, if she can be given a reason."

At 9:37, Dr. Klagsbrun watched his patient take the stand. Lester was wearing his navy-blue corduroy suit again. This morning, he had said, "Doc, I don't know why my mother forgot to have my suit cleaned."

63

November 1, 1973
Freehold, New Jersey

During the first half-hour of his cross-examination, Carton attempted to establish the chronology of the three days between the accident and the shooting. It was a technique designed to wear Lester down by sheer weight of detail. Lester bore up well. Then, suddenly, Carton's manner became brisk and threatening.

"Mr. Zygmanik, did you have any further conversations with your brother on Tuesday?—the day before the shooting?"

"Yes."

"And what were they about at that time?"

"He told me, at that time, that he didn't even want to see his son any more—and then to dim the lights so no one would see him in that condition."

"All right—and did you have a conversation with him on Tuesday night?"

"Yes."

"What time was that?" Carton asked.

"I don't know—I was there all night."

"And was Jean there?"

"Yes, she was."

"All right—when did he ask you to promise him that you would not let him stay like that any more?" Carton hammered.

"That was sometime Tuesday evening. . . ."

". . . *When did you make up your mind, Mr. Zygmanik, that you were going to kill your brother?*"

Robert objected. It was a crucial issue. An admission of "making up his mind" to kill would constitute Lester's knowledge of the "nature and quality" of his act as defined by McNaughton.

McGowan overruled Robert's objection. "The witness may answer."

"When did you make up your mind, Mr. Zygmanik, that you were going to kill your brother?" Carton asked.

"There was never any time that I definitely sat down and said that I'm going to do this. It just came about."

"Can you tell me when it came about?"

"It came about sometime Wednesday."

". . . On Tuesday, after your brother asked you to make that promise, did you discuss this with anyone?"

"Yes, I did."

"With whom?"

"I discussed it with Dr. Kreider."

"Was this on Wednesday?"

"I discussed it on Tuesday, also."

"You had a discussion with a nurse, too, didn't you? With Mr. Blannett?"

"Possibly, I don't recall right now—I was talking to quite a few people there."

"When did you make up your mind in relation to your brother's operation on Wednesday?"

"I never said I made up my mind."

Later, under Robert's questioning, Dr. Klagsbrun would testify, "Lester grew up in an old-fashioned, European family. The concept of right and wrong was clearly depicted from the time he was born. It was, however, a family that had a tremendous need to fight off passivity—not to be at the mercy of Fate. The attitude when facing a problem was—by God, go out and find a solution of some kind. It was almost an obsession."

"Do you recall testifying yesterday to a conversation with Dr. Kreider—when he said to you, 'What do you want me to do, stick a knife in your brother?' And you answered, 'If you don't, I will'?"

"Yes," Lester said.

"Do you recall what day that was?"

"I don't recall what day, no."

"You don't know whether it was Tuesday or Wednesday?"

"It must have been Tuesday," Lester said.

". . . You had a brief conversation with Dr. Kreider following surgery, on Wednesday—is that right?"

"Right."

"Didn't he tell you there was still a chance?"

"He never told me there was a chance," Lester said stubbornly.

"There came a point, then, when you were convinced there was no hope for your brother—is that right?"

"I imagine there was, right."

"Do you have any idea when that was?" Carton demanded.

"No, I don't."

"Didn't you indicate, before, that you made up your mind to kill your brother before the operation?"

Robert objected strenuously. "There's no such testimony, absolutely no such testimony!"

McGowan sustained.

Later, under Robert's questioning, Dr. Motley would say, "My diagnostic impression is one of a Reactive Depression—this is specifically associated with the loss of something important, and of clinical importance when an individual's symptomatology begins to interfere in their life, or their adjustment to life.

"In my opinion, Mr. Zygmanik was experiencing a Gross Stress Reaction, brought about by exposure to overwhelming stress."

"Mr. Zygmanik," Carton said, "I believe you testified yesterday that you couldn't remember going outside to get the gun, but you could see yourself walking into the house with the gun? Is that right?"

"Right."

"Where was the gun when you first got it?"

"In my room," Lester said.

"Where did you take it?"

"I took it out by the dog shed."

"And what happened then?"

"I don't remember getting the hacksaw to cut the gun," Lester said.

". . . But you cut both ends?—with a hacksaw?"

"That's correct."

"Is this the gun you sawed at both ends?" Carton showed the gun to the jury. Solemnly they regarded it again.

"Correct," Lester said.

"Do you know how much time that took?"

"I don't know, no."

"Had you made up your mind then?—when you sawed the gun? Had you made up your mind to kill your brother?"

"No," Lester said.

Carton laid the gun down. "After you cut up the gun, what did you do with it?"

"I walked into the house with it."

"Were you concealing the gun?"

"I wasn't concealing anything."

"What happened when you walked in with the gun?"

"My mother took it away."

"Was there any conversation when she did that?"

"No."

"What did she do with the gun?"

"She put it on the bureau."

In answer to Robert's hypothetical question, Dr. Klagsbrun would say, "In my opinion, Lester experienced a psychotic reaction of a temporary nature.

"This is a temporary period of time during which a person shows evidence of bizarre behavior that is clearly different from his normal life-style.

"A psychotic reaction also includes mental aberrations, such as memory loss, periods of amnesia, and distortions of reality—being absolutely sure something happened that did not happen."

Carton asked, "Now, yesterday, you said you had three shells?"

"Three, right." Lester remained stubborn.

"Where did you get the shells?"

"From my room."

"And you explained yesterday, you waxed the shells."

"Yes."

"How long did it take to wax one shell?"

"I don't know."

"Had you ever done that before?"

"No, I haven't."

Carton picked up the shell and held it a few inches from Lester's face. "I show you what has been marked S-6 into evidence, and ask you to look at this, please. Is this shell waxed? Can you tell?"

"Yes, you can see it. There is wax on the outside of it. . . ."

". . . Had you made up your mind to kill your brother when you waxed the shell?"

"No, I didn't say that to myself—I'm going to kill my brother."

"I didn't ask you what you said—I asked if you had made up your mind?"

"No."

"And what about S-5 in evidence, the unexploded shell—was that waxed?"

"No, it wasn't. . . ."

". . . Now, Mr. Zygmanik, what did you do with those shells?"

"I don't remember. . . ."

Under Robert's questioning, Dr. Klagsbrun would testify, "I would date the beginning of Lester's disintegration to the afternoon of the cafeteria interview with the doctor who described the dismal condition of a paraplegic patient.

"In my opinion, the disintegration was compounded by sleep-deprivation. Under normal laboratory conditions, in experiments done with normal subjects, there has been a correlation between people who became mentally sick in a very severe fashion, and abnormal sleep patterns."

". . . What do you remember, Mr. Zygmanik, when you finished waxing the shells?"

"I was at the hospital."

"Do you know where you got the gun before you drove to the hospital?"

"From my room," Lester said.

"Your mother had put it on the bureau, right?"

"Oh, yeah—I don't remember. All I can remember is being at the hospital with a gun."

"Do you remember driving to the hospital?"

"I remember getting out of my car in the parking lot," Lester said.

"Do you know where you parked your car?"

"No, I don't."

"Where did you put the gun?"

"I put it on the side of my jacket."

"Did you do that in the parking lot?"

"Yes, I believe so."

"Do you know where you entered the hospital?"

"I guess, the front door."

"Didn't you go through the emergency room?"

"Yes, I did—yeah."

"Did you take the elevator up to the third floor?"

"I don't recall taking the elevator—but I also don't recall going up any stairs."

"What is the next thing you remember?" Carton asked.

"Entering my brother's room. . . ."

". . . Now, when you entered your brother's room, had you made up your mind to kill him?—at this point?"

"I don't know what I was thinking at this point. . . ."

During cross-examination of Dr. Klagsbrun, Carton would ask, "In your opinion, did Mr. Zygmanik know he was using a gun at the time of the shooting?"

Dr. Klagsbrun would respond, "No, I don't think he knew he was using a gun—in the sense that his cognitive faculties were impaired, his brain was not assessing what he was doing."

Carton would ask, "Can you tell us what he thought he was doing at that time?"

Dr. Klagsbrun would answer, "When somebody is psychotic, you have what is called primary material flooding a person. That means you're flooded with many, many things without a rational thinking pattern superimposed on what's coming up. Also, he was suffering from sleep-deprivation—that means biochemical abnormalities, physiological abnormalities."

"Now, Mr. Zygmanik, you indicated that you hid the gun under your coat?"

"Yes."

"And you said that was because you knew the nurses wouldn't let you walk into your brother's room with a gun?"

"Right."

"Why did you think they wouldn't let you walk in with a gun?"

"Because I had spoken to the doctors there that my brother wanted to die—for them to stop operating on him and cutting him up, and they refused to do that. So, I knew they definitely would not let me relieve my brother from his pain."

"You knew it was wrong, didn't you?—to walk in there with a gun?"

"I don't know. At that time, I really wasn't thinking."

"Did you know it was wrong to shoot your brother?"

"At that time, I didn't think about anything but relieving my brother's pain."

"You had been in the room before?—on several occasions?—is that right?"

"Right."

"Did you see other patients in there on those days?"

"Yes, I did."

"In fact, the Intensive Care Unit was basically full, wasn't it? The five other beds were occupied, weren't they?"

"Yes, I believe they were."

"When you entered the room, did you speak to the nurses at the desk?"

"No."

"Did they speak to you?"

"No."

"You walked over to your brother's bed?—is that right?"

"Right."

"And he couldn't talk at this point?"

"No."

"Do you recall what you said to him?"

"I asked him if he was in pain. I asked him if the pain was real bad. He nodded, yes. Then I told him I was here to relieve his pain. I asked him if that was all right with him. I believe I told him, 'Don't worry, you won't be in pain any more.' And he nodded, yes."

"And then you shot your brother?"

"Yes."

During cross-examination of Dr. Motley, Carton would ask, "How was it, Doctor, that Mr. Zygmanik showed no regret at all the second time he was interviewed by you?"

Dr. Motley would reply, "This is a very complex issue. At the time of the act, his behavior was disorganized, his thinking was disorganized. The subsequent events, the return of more fully conscious control, leaves Mr. Zygmanik with some realistic problems of trying to understand himself in relationship to the act, to put it in a frame of reference that is meaningful to him. I find it very plausible that it's important to him to feel what he did was right."

". . . Mr. Zygmanik," Carton asked, "did you know it was wrong to shoot your brother?"

"No, I didn't think about that. . . ."

". . . You were very upset?"

"Yes."

"And you had lost a lot of sleep?"

"Yes."

"And you felt very badly?—is that right?"

"Yes."

"You have had a long time to think about it from that day until now—is that right?"

"Yes."

"You have had a long time to reflect on this?"

"Right."

"Now, if your brother were in the same condition today, Mr. Zygmanik, would you do this again?"

"I don't know."

"Did you tell Dr. Flicker, on October 4th, that you would?"

"No, I didn't."

"Can you tell us now whether you would?—if your brother were alive and in that condition?"

"I don't know, I don't know."

Robert objected. An argument with Carton began. Judge Mc-
Gowan admonished them. The real nature of the argument was not
verbalized, though each knew the importance of the Prosecutor's
question:

Repentance was the prerequisite for mercy. The absence of
remorse sanctioned any penalty.

"Do you recall going to see Dr. Flicker?" Carton asked.

"Yes."

"Do you recall him asking you the following question: If your
brother were alive today, and in the same predicament, would you do
the same thing?"

"He asked me this. He asked me—had your brother been in the
same condition, and had all circumstances been the same today as
they were then?

"I said—No doubt, it would be done again, because the same
thing would have happened.

"I never told him that had my brother been alive today in that
condition, that I would do it again."

"Will you tell us now—if he were alive and in that condition?—
would you do it again?"

Robert objected again. "If the Prosecutor wants an answer to that
question, he should give the witness time."

Repentance was the prerequisite for mercy. The absence of remorse sanctioned any penalty.

McGowan turned to Lester. "Do you want some time to think
about the question?"

Lester said, "No, I'll answer the question."

Carton waited. The jury waited. Robert waited.

"I don't know," Lester said. "I'm confused. Sometimes, I feel I
possibly did the wrong thing. Possibly, I did the right thing. I don't
know. I really can't give you an answer one way or the other."

64

November 1, 1973
Freehold, New Jersey

With a show of concern, Robert helped Sonia onto the witness stand. She was wearing the black crepe dress, the pointed high-heeled shoes, the pert brown derby. She smiled tentatively at the jury —the smile of a woman who had never had lovers, and so remained in her heart a dazzling virgin; at the same time, her youth had obviously ended in childbirth and she had gone directly to old age. The jury saw only the mother of the accused.

"Mrs. Zygmanik, I have only two points. Do you recall the night this happened?"

"Yes." ,

"Do you remember taking a gun away from Lester? A gun?"

"No."

"Did you?"

"No."

"Did you see that gun?"

"No."

"Did you?"

"No."

On the witness stand, Dr. Samuel Klagsbrun had described Lester's background, his normal personality, and his erratic state of mind as the day progressed toward the shooting. At Robert's request, however, Dr. Klagsbrun had omitted a specific conclusion. "Without his mother's urging, Lester would not have shot his brother."

65

November 1, 1973
Freehold, New Jersey

In these final hours of trial, combat took place in the arena of the human psyche.

The framework of the law, the courtroom, the process of judgment admitted no mysteries. All that was grave and profound had to be replaced by what was logical, passionless, and diligently sorted out. There was room for ingenuity, but not for subtlety. A psychiatrist became a witness who translated human emotions into routine terms.

In the afternoon, Robert had presented Drs. Samuel Klagsbrun and John Motley. They were honorable men, adept, knowledgeable, well-intentioned. Dr. Klagsbrun had described Lester's father's death as a "catastrophical experience which Lester is mourning to this day." He had described hallucination and memory gaps that took place in the course of the three days in question. Dr. Motley had described the "intolerable stress" to which Lester was subjected. Dr. Klagsbrun had described the further effects of sleep-deprivation. It was crucial testimony. The jury had listened earnestly.

To both men, Robert had posed a long hypothetical question which was in fact a summary of the events juxtaposed to illustrate graphically the irrationality of Lester's behavior. At the end of it, he had returned to the ultimate reduction of human complexity— McNaughton: Dr. Klagsbrun had testified that Lester knew neither the nature nor the quality of his act, nor that what he was doing was wrong. Dr. Motley had testified that Lester knew the nature, but not the quality or the difference between right and wrong.

The jury had seemed satisfied with its own ability to be enlightened.

The Defense rested.

A third psychiatrist was called—in rebuttal, by the Prosecution.

Dr. David J. Flicker was a spry, freckled man with a ring of reddish hair and a military bearing. His credentials were impressive. He described psychiatry as "the study of an individual as a unit different from any other individual in the world—his background, his drives, his emotions, his thinking and its detail. . . ."

Carton asked, "Doctor, at my request, did you examine Lester Zygmanik?"

"Yes, sir."

"When was that examination, please?"

"On October 4th of this year."

"Will you tell us what your findings were, please, at that time."

Clipped and precise, Dr. Flicker summarized Lester's background, history, other facts he elicited from Lester, along with his own observation.

". . . He gave his age as 23. He gave his address and described himself as a heavy equipment operator. . . . The household at the time of the alleged offense consisted of five persons—the mother, the two brothers, the wife of the victim and his child.

". . . His past medical history was essentially noncontributory. There had been no illnesses or operations. There had been no hospitalizations, no military service. He described a normal psycho-sexual life. He has had a steady girlfriend for the past three years.

". . . His present difficulty had its onset on, apparently, June 17th, a Sunday, when his brother, George, was injured in a motorcycle accident and was paralyzed. . . . He describes himself and his brother as being extremely close. He is quite certain if George were alive, and he, Lester, were in the same predicament, he would have wanted George to do as much for him. When asked if George were alive today and in the same predicament, would he do the same thing, his reply was yes. . . .

". . . He describes himself as being essentially moderate in his habits. He smokes two packs of cigarettes a day and drinks a six-pack of beer a week. He does not use dope. On a few rare occasions, he has smoked some marijuana.

"He is 70 inches, 197 pounds and essentially a healthy, young, male adult.

"For the purpose of completeness, I did a neurological examination to make sure nothing was overlooked, and because this was essentially within normal range, I will omit it.

"His blood pressure at the time of my examination was 160 over 90 which is a very slight hypertension. His pulse rate was 88.

"In the psychiatric sphere, I felt he was adequately dressed—he was clean, neat, well-groomed. His answers at first were extremely taciturn and laconic. As he went along and a better rapport was established, he became a bit more verbal. His answers were relevant. They were responsive. I could elicit no ideational disturbances. There were no illusions, hallucinations, delusions or phobias. His affect was completely appropriate. His sensorium was clear—his ability to think, remember and so forth. There was no involvement of memory, insight or judgment. Orientation and intellect were good."

"Doctor, as a result of your examination, did you reach a conclusion?" Carton asked.

"Yes, sir," Dr. Flicker said.

"Tell us what that is, please."

"At the time of my examination, I found no evidence of involvement of the central or peripheral nervous system, brain or spinal cord. I didn't expect any. I could elicit no evidence of psychopathology. That is, I could find nothing basically wrong with this man. I could find no indication that there existed any form of psychosis—that is, an insanity pattern, personality disorder or psychoneurosis."

"Are you familiar with the McNaughton rule?"

"Yes, sir."

"Tell us what it is, please."

Robert objected. McGowan overruled, saying, "An expert such as this can be asked matters which constitute an ultimate conclusion under a rule of law."

Dr. Flicker gathered momentum.

"The nature is what the act consists of. Does he know that he is pulling a trigger and that the pulling of a trigger will launch a bullet? The quality is the harmfulness of the act. In this case, if an individual pulls a trigger, does he know this will launch a bullet and this bullet can destroy life?"

"All right. Doctor, do you have an opinion as to whether or not Mr. Zygmanik knew the nature and quality of his act?"

"Yes, I do."

"Would you give us that opinion, please."

"I feel he definitely knew the nature and quality of his acts."

"Would you tell us why?" Carton asked.

"Because there was such purposeness throughout his entire pattern of cutting off a shotgun which would enable it to be (a) more deadly, and (b) more easily concealed, and (c) he carried out the purposeful act of terminating his brother's life which was something he had indicated he wanted very much to do in light of his brother's predicament."

"Can you tell us, Doctor, if Mr. Zygmanik had waxed some shotgun shells several hours earlier, whether he would have known the nature and quality of his act? What I mean is, Doctor—taken some pellets out of a shotgun and placed them back along with wax."

"I believe that Mr. Zygmanik, having owned three guns and hunting, knew the nature and quality of that act and knew how to handle a shotgun."

"What about the act of sawing down the gun? If that act had been done earlier in the afternoon, would Mr. Zygmanik have known the nature and quality of that act?"

"I feel certain that he knew the nature and quality of the act."

"Concealing a gun beneath a jacket prior to going into the Intensive Care Unit—would he have known the nature and quality of that act?"

"Yes, I believe he did, because someone might have questioned him walking in with the gun in its original form and he might not have succeeded."

"Is there any significance, Doctor, to the fact that Mr. Zygmanik, a few minutes after the shooting occurred, announced to the security guards, 'I'm the one you're looking for'?"

"I believe there is. I believe he recognized that even though he felt what he had done was right, what he had done was something for which security guards or the police might be seeking him."

Dr. Flicker's testimony was cold, detached, and implied vast knowledge. It was possible he had canceled Dr. Klagsbrun's benevolence and Dr. Motley's compassion. Robert knew it was in the nature of juries to be impressed by pitilessness.

Carton deferred.

For the first time in the course of the trial Robert attacked head-on. He began by asking, "Doctor, I don't mean to be disrespectful, but do you consider yourself to be a ballistics expert?"

"Expert? No. Reasonable knowledge, yes," Dr. Flicker answered.

"Do you understand that sawing off a shotgun makes it more deadly?"

"I know so."

"How does it make it more deadly?" Robert inquired.

"It causes more of a muzzle blast. It's more deadly at close range." Dr. Flicker's voice remained clipped, like an army colonel accustomed to being obeyed.

"Isn't it a fact that sawing off a gun gives you a wider spread to the pellets because they travel a shorter distance in the barrel?" Robert asked.

"Yes, sir," Dr. Flicker said. "Therefore, at a distance, you would probably miss what you're shooting at. At very close range, however, it produces a tremendous muzzle impact and a greater hole."

"Isn't it in fact inconsistent to saw off a gun and then wax a cartridge? Aren't you doing two opposite things?" Robert asked.

"I don't think so. I think you're making sure there'll be no misfiring of your gun when you wax your cartridge."

"I see. If you wax it, it helps the shell explode?"

"More likely to."

"Isn't the explosive part of the shell in the gunpowder section?"

Carton objected. "These questions are getting very technical about the composition of cartridges."

McGowan overruled.

"I believe the explosive part is in the shell," Dr. Flicker said, aware now that he was under attack, suddenly cautious.

"Do you know where he waxed the shell?"

"No, sir."

"How can you base an opinion on something Lester did when you don't know what he did?"

"Just what I was told by counsel." Dr. Flicker grew visibly uncomfortable.

"What were you told?"

"That the shell had been waxed, pellets had been waxed."

"Do you realize in a shotgun shell there's a separation between the chamber that holds the gunpowder and the rest of the shell which holds the pellets?" Robert asked.

"Yes, sir."

"Will you tell me, sir, how waxing a portion of the shell that holds the pellets helps the gunpowder to explode?"

"It doesn't essentially help the gunpowder to explode. It makes sure the shell will propel more definitely—especially through a sawed-off shotgun where there might be some difficulty in otherwise expelling the shell."

Robert paused. "Do you know when the shot was fired, Doctor?"

"When?"

"Yes."

"In time I don't know. It was fired when the man was in the room, right after his brother had made the statement he wanted to die. He was going to take him out of his pain and then he fired the shell. At least, that's what I was informed."

"What date was the shot fired?"

"The gun was fired on the date that he took—" Dr. Flicker blustered. He tried to recover. "I don't know how to answer that. The date he took the gun into the hospital. He states this was some four or five days after—he described the sequence of events. He took the gun into the hospital under his coat. He asked—"

"Excuse me, Doctor. Please try and listen to the question I'm asking you. If you know the answer, please tell me. If you don't, please tell me. Do you know the date the shot was fired."

"The date? No, sir," Dr. Flicker said.

"Do you know the day of the week?"

Carton objected. McGowan overruled.

"No, I don't know what day of the week it was." Dr. Flicker squared his shoulders in an attempt to remain imperious.

"Do you know how many days after the accident it was?"

"I think—all I could gather from the patient is some four or five days after the accident. The patient recounts that this was four or five days after the incident which now placed him in his problem with the law. So, I didn't pursue it any further because I didn't feel it was pertinent to my examination."

"Would you tell me what your report indicates?—page 2, the last paragraph."

Dr. Flicker read from the report. ". . . On Monday immediately following the accident, his brother could still speak. At that time, he extracted from Lester a promise he would not permit George to continue to live as an invalid. He went home. He described taking a 20-gauge shotgun, sawing it off in the dog shed."

"Is that the information you have?—that on Monday, the promise was extracted and on Monday, Lester went home and got the shotgun?"

"I don't know the exact time sequence," Dr. Flicker said. "This is what I got from the patient. I don't know. I don't know when he went home and sawed off the shotgun. I don't know whether it was the day that the incident happened, or if it was on Monday—but he sawed off the shotgun."

"Have you finished, sir?"

"Yes, sir."

"If you don't know the exact time sequence, do you know the approximate time sequence?"

"Nothing more than the period of these few days in which these occurrences took place. I don't know whether he sawed off the gun the day in which the act was carried out, or whether he sawed off the gun on Monday after he spoke to his brother. . . ."

Abruptly, Robert changed the subject of questioning. ". . . Is it true, Doctor, that on October 4th, Lester walked into your office at 12:15 p.m. and left at 1:05 p.m.?"

"I don't know. I think I said my examination was over an hour. I don't know how long."

"What time did he spend there?" Robert asked.

"I don't have it in time. I think he was due at 12:00. I have no memory of his being late. I think it took somewhat over an hour for the examination."

"What is somewhat over an hour?" Robert turned toward the jury as Dr. Flicker answered.

"Over an hour, I don't know, Counsel."

"Whatever length of time it is, would you say ten or fifteen minutes was spent on a neurological examination?" Robert faced the witness again.

"Yes, but during the neurological examination, the psychiatric goes on. I am still appraising the patient as to his reactions, his behavior. Very often it is during that period that I can establish one of the best rapports."

"You agree, do you not, Doctor, that the relationship between patient and physician influences the patient's motivation to reveal the nature of his problems and their sources?"

"When you are dealing with therapy, yes. But not necessarily in this picture. But even then, I suppose the relationship does enter in, in whether or not patients are inclined to reveal things that are helpful."

"And your judgment or diagnosis or opinion is only as good as the information upon which it is based?"

"No. It is a little better than that," Dr. Flicker countered, though his composure threatened to fail him and his authority was clearly diminished.

"It does decrease your chances of being right, if the information is erroneous?"

"It depends upon the situation," Dr. Flicker hedged.

"How about if the information is incomplete?"

"It would depend upon whether or not it is that incomplete as to affect the final conclusion. . . ."

". . . Did you inquire, sir, as to the effect that his father's passing had on him?"

Dr. Flicker hedged again. "As to the effect, in detail, no."

"In any way?"

"No. I assumed it was the normal human reaction when one loses a father. He didn't indicate anything special about it."

"You didn't ask him, did you?"

"No, sir. I didn't ask him."

"Can the death of a parent have an effect on a person's mental condition?"

"Temporarily, it will almost always have an effect, without exception. But I don't think it produces insanity . . . ," Dr. Flicker said angrily.

". . . You assumed this was normal when he lost his father, that he had a normal response to it, and you didn't inquire into that?" Robert glanced at the jury again. He felt a palpable connection.

"That's correct," Flicker said.

"Would it have been significant if he had had an abnormal response to it?"

"It depends upon what the abnormal response was," Dr. Flicker hedged again.

"Are there circumstances when an abnormal response to the loss of a parent can be important in your work as a psychiatrist?"

"There are always possibilities of that type."

Robert changed tactics. "You conducted this examination on October 4th?"

"Yes, sir," Dr. Flicker said.

"And what you were attempting to do, was it not, was to flash back to June 1973, is that correct?"

"Yes, sir, in part. Part of the time."

"And how did you do that?"

"I asked him questions. . . ."

". . . Let's suppose that Lester was hallucinating at the time of the shooting and what he recalled wasn't at all true. How would you find out it wasn't true?"

"I wouldn't."

"How did you find out about his behavior back in June?"

"From what he told me. And, at a later point, Mr. Carton gave me other data."

"When did Mr. Carton give you other data?"

"Last week or so, I think."

"Last week?"

"Yes."

"In what form was that, sir?"

"I don't know. He showed me the Police Report, et cetera," Dr. Flicker said.

"What is et cetera?"

"I think there was some other data. I don't remember. . . ."

". . . You got no independent material, Doctor?—other than what Lester told you and some Police Reports you looked at a few weeks after you submitted your report?"

"That's correct."

"Do you know how much time Lester spent at his brother's bedside between the time of the accident and the time of the shooting?"

"No, sir."

"Do you know how much sleep he had between the time of the accident and the time of the shooting?"

"No detail, no. I assume it was very little."

"Did you ask him how much sleep he had?"

"No. It wasn't pertinent."

"If he went without sleep for five days, would that be pertinent?"

"No, sir. People can go without sleep for five days and still be logical and coherent."

"Do you agree that people can go without sleep for five days and be psychotic under laboratory conditions?"

"Under laboratory conditions, it's more likely than under stress conditions where the individual has an outside stimulus constantly keeping him awake."

"Sleep-deprivation does have an effect on mental condition, does it not?"

"Yes. Sleep-deprivation hurts us all. . . ."

". . . Did you make a determination as to whether or not sleep-deprivation played any role in Lester's mental condition in June of 1973?"

"Seeing him in October, it would have been absolutely impossible to make a determination, except that his statements indicated sleep-deprivation did not enter in any way into his thinking processes."

"He didn't tell you very much about his behavior in June, did he, Doctor?"

"He told me of the pattern in which he reacted to the stress of his brother's request to terminate his life. . . ."

". . . Did he tell you about approaching the security guards and stating, 'I'm the one you're looking for'?"

"No, sir. I did not find that out until a short time ago when Mr. Carton told me."

". . . Do you know what his appearance was?—in June 1973?"

"I presume he showed stress reaction, that he was on edge, that he was unhappy, that he was tense."

"You presume that?"

"Yes."

"Do you know that?"

"No, I don't . . . ," Dr. Flicker said.

66

November 2, 1973
Freehold, New Jersey

The couple looked like playing cards—a robust Queen of Hearts, a slender Jack of Clubs. The boy was young, still clumsy, marred by acne, swimming in a shiny double-breasted suit. He clasped a Bible. The woman, thirty years older, was massive, rosy-cheeked, dressed for the opera. Together, they moved along the crowded corridor toward Sonia Zygmanik.

For the participants of the Zygmanik trial, it was morning recess on Friday, the fifth day of trial. Against the window, the family lined the benches, crow-like silhouettes, smoking, talking quietly, waiting for court to resume. Apart from the others, Sonia gazed silently out at the cold gray sky. Then the boy touched her shoulder and she turned, startled.

"Do you know Jesus Christ, your Savior?" the boy said. Behind him, the woman smiled.

Sonia shook her head.

The boy knelt and opened his Bible. "Matthew fifteen," he said. "*'For out of the heart come evil thoughts, murder, adultery, fornication, theft, false witness—'*"

"Go away," Sonia said.

"My name's Bishop," the woman said. "Sylvia Bishop. The Lord sent me."

It was 11:10 a.m., Friday, the final day of trial. Testimony was complete.

Yesterday, the jury had heard conflicting descriptions of Lester

Zygmanik's state of mind at the time of the shooting. Yesterday, the Defense had rested. Dr. David J. Flicker, State's psychiatrist, had given the last testimony of the day.

This morning, the Prosecution had produced two rebuttal witnesses. Gregory Carver denied Lester's version of the conversation in the cafeteria. Then Dr. Clement Kreider, surgeon, denied telling Lester his brother's condition was hopeless. He further stated that George Zygmanik was not in pain, adding that after the tracheotomy on Tuesday, George would have been unable to speak and, therefore, unable to request his death at Lester's hand.

In his rebuttal, Robert, quoting from hospital records, had established the fact that George had continually been given medication for pain. Then Robert had called Detective Sergeant Vincent Martin, whose report, dated June 21, included an interview with Dr. Kreider who had admitted telling Lester "his brother would probably be paralyzed for life."

The final argument now belonged to the lawyers. What remained were summations, Judge McGowan's charge to the jury, and the jury's retirement. Whether these would take place this afternoon or be deferred until Monday was still in doubt.

Pacing, Robert awaited the Judge's decision on this matter of timing. "If McGowan lets the jurors go home over the weekend, they'll attend church, and every preacher in East Jersey is going to give a euthanasia sermon on Sunday."

The Queen of Hearts pinned Sonia down. "Honey," she said, "you see this boy? In Vietnam, a hand grenade exploded right in front of him. He's livin' proof that the Lord sends miracles."

Sonia turned away.

The boy flipped through his Bible. "Luke six," he said. " '*For no good tree bears bad fruit, nor again does a bad tree bear good fruit; for every tree is known by its own fruit—*' "

"You go away," Sonia said.

The woman laughed. Her earrings jangled. "Honey, you gotta believe in miracles," she said. "This boy here is livin' proof of *two* miracles. One in Vietnam, and one that happened just three weeks ago in the Church of the Redeemer. You see, eighteen years ago, my current husband—he *impregnated* this poor little girl. The baby was a boy, but the girl, poor soul, she gave the child away. My current husband grieved for eighteen years. Then the Lord *intervened*. Ain't that right, Arnie?"

"That's right," the boy said.

"You see, three weeks ago, these long-haired kids came in for Sunday services in the Glad Tidings Church." She patted the boy's head. "I took one look at this boy here, and I said to my current husband, 'Bishop, that's your son.'"

"That's right," the boy said.

"God brought this boy back to his father." The woman's hands fluttered around Sonia. "You see, honey," she said, "that's why we're here—to change this boy's name from Cronin to Bishop."

At 11:25, court convened.

The Prosecutor moved to defer summations until Monday.

Robert objected.

McGowan ruled, "In my opinion, the ends of justice and the interests of justice will be better served by having this matter continued until Monday. Summations and my charge to the jury will be made at that time."

67

The weekend passed slowly, like scenery through a train window. Sometimes an hour picked up speed, careening toward Monday—or halted, as if suddenly out of fuel, and Lester found himself standing motionless in the same thought for a long time.

He spent the two days outdoors. Halfway through a chore, he stopped to remember that his life belonged to strangers. In the middle of a reverie, he reminded himself he had no future plans. His mind skipped around, touching briefly on a memory, a face, some old resolution—one recurring phrase: *I'll work out something.*

Saturday was cold. The stove blazed all day in the kitchen. In his mother's bedroom, the ceiling had been mutilated to make room for the installation of heating ducts, but all week no units had arrived and no workmen. So he spent three hours on Saturday driving around in the truck in a futile attempt to locate the bastard who had taken his last $2,000 of savings for the job.

Diane stayed all day. Little Georgie said to her, "I don't want Lester go get married, Lester's my friend."

At sunset, alone, he walked down the road to St. Joseph's. Inside the empty church, he stood where the choirboys stood on Sunday, watching the shadows play over the crucifix. No childhood prayers came to him. In the graveyard, Jeannie had left a handful of flowers. He stooped, pulled out a few weeds on the unmarked graves, then patted the earth over his brother and father, saying, "Are you okay? I hope you're okay."

On Sunday, he checked out the storm windows and touched up a place on the barn-red house. Diane followed him everywhere. Then David Silver arrived and everybody sat in the kitchen, talking and, strangely, laughing.

"Ain't that somethin'?" he said. "Twelve people are gonna tell me what to do with my life."

Diane giggled. Jeannie joined her. Sonia poured coffee for everybody.

"I predict that jury's gonna be out for twenty-two minutes," Lester said.

"Twenty-one minutes," David said.

"That's definitely possible," Lester said. "Look at what Ansell did to Dr. Flicker. 'Doctor, are you a ballistics expert?' I liked that. Those jurors were lookin' at Dr. Flicker like he was some kinda *god*, then right away he turned into a—"

"An idiot," David said.

Sonia smiled. Jeannie laughed again. Diane curled up, giggling.

Lester slapped the kitchen table. "Listen—if anything goes wrong, I'll take off, right? Leave the country. I'll go to Mexico or Canada, right? Maybe I'll go to South America."

"Brazil," David said. "There's no extradition in Brazil. I think it's Brazil."

"I'll write you a letter," Lester said. "And then if anybody asks you, you can say, 'And then he disappeared.'" Lester roared with laughter.

"Into the horizon," David said.

"Somewhere, anywhere."

"Maybe it's Argentina," David said.

"Brazil," Lester said. "I bet you wish you were part of that jury? Right? You could go in there with six-guns, right?"

"Right," David said.

"Like you'd let me off in a minute, right?"

"Sure."

"Because you know how I feel, right?"

"Right," David said.

"Wrong," Lester said. "Like if I was you—free, and goin' to college, not worryin' about money, not worryin' about anything—I know how I'd feel. But if you was me, you wouldn't know anything about how I feel. You see what I mean?" Lester laughed.

"Maybe you're right," David said.

"Like your mother talks English, right? And you were born in this country, right? And you would never be sittin' in this house right now if I hadn't killed my brother, right? That's pretty funny, don't you think?"

"That's not funny," Jeannie said.

"Listen, David," Lester said. "My father believed anybody who worked hard could make it. Do you believe that?"

"No," David said.

"Maybe you can tell me somethin'," Lester said. "How come, by the time my father came lookin' for this country, it was already gone?"

David was silent.

Lester rose and opened the kitchen door. Outside, the setting sun cast fiery shadows on the autumn landscape. "Yeah," he said. "Brazil." His laughter filled the kitchen.

At nine o'clock, the stove went out. Everybody went to bed. Diane went home. At midnight, Lester came down to the kitchen and dialed Ansell's number. "Hey," he said, "what are you doin'?"

"I was thinking about calling you," Ansell said.

"Yeah? Anything in particular?"

"Nothing in particular," Ansell said.

"Listen—I have to tell you somethin'."

"Go ahead."

"No matter how it turns out, you know? No matter what happens tomorrow. I wanted you to know that I think you definitely did a good job. I mean, nobody could've done what you did for me. I just wanted to tell you that. No matter how it turns out. . . ."

Robert hung up and stared at the phone, but he didn't pick it up again. Tomorrow, before the jury returned with the verdict, armed guards would enter the courtroom to take Lester away in the event of conviction. Yet, he hadn't been able to say to Lester, "Don't drive your own car tomorrow, in case the jury convicts. . . ."

68

November 5, 1973
Freehold, New Jersey

On Monday, the final day of trial, the air no longer bristled with the excitement of murder. Instead, a sober hush prevailed. The courtroom, which had served as a backdrop to drama, now reclaimed its stature as a court of law. Perhaps bromidic, but no less real, was the knowledge that a courtroom represented, not justice, but judgment.

It was 10:00 a.m. In a moment, summations would begin. It was Malcolm Carton who would have the final word.

The jury—mostly blue-collar, conservative panel members—had been judged by the standards of sociology and psychiatry, and been found to be less than ideal. Yet, the jury constituted the one human element in what would otherwise be a blood-letting. In any jury resided any possibility.

The final weight lay, always, with the system. The hierarchy was fixed, self-protective, inviolate. Against it, Lester seemed frail. He was neither a corporation nor a hardened criminal. He was the perpetrator of a single violent act. At the rear of the courtroom, the armed guards would soon appear. That morning, without being told, Lester had left his car at home.

Robert began proceedings with a motion. "Your Honor, I would suggest that to this day the State's psychiatrist, Dr. David J. Flicker, doesn't know what this trial is about. He doesn't know the sequence of events, he doesn't even know when the shot was fired. His testimony as a qualified witness is therefore improper, and I ask that it be stricken."

Carton argued. McGowan denied the motion. Robert had intended it clearly for the benefit of the jury.

At 10:17, Robert began his summation. He hit hard at the psychiatric interpretation of the facts. He went through the witnesses who had reported behavior, psychiatric conclusions, and data for the sleep chart. He stressed the fact that the *evidence* demanded acquittal. Woven through these elements of his final argument was a moving description of the tragedy.

"This case involves many people, many lives. You have met these people and you have some idea of their lives. . . ." He gestured toward the spectators. In the third row, Jean was flanked by Sonia and Victor.

"This case is the story of Sonia Zygmanik, the mother, who, in February 1973, was surrounded by three men devoted to her and to each other. In February of 1973, she lost her husband. In June of 1973, she lost her first-born. Now," Robert said, "she stands on the threshold of losing her last-born."

"This case is the story of Jean Zygmanik, who married a family as well as a man, and who kept her word. . . ." He paused to give the jury a few moments to absorb his words. Then he said, "It is the story of doctors who did, medically, everything they could do for George Zygmanik, but who could do nothing for Lester. . . ."

He paced, slowly, then stopped and laid a hand on the rail of the jury box.

"More than anything else," he said, "this case is the story of two young men bound to each other as only brothers can be bound—by love and shared experience, common hopes and common goals. It is the story of the destruction of these two young men—the physical destruction of one and the mental destruction of the other."

He began to pace again.

"Ladies and gentlemen, the law attempts to distinguish between those who are sick and those who are bad. The law uses psychiatrists for this purpose. In this case, the State's psychiatrist, Dr. Flicker, knew nothing of Lester's roller-coaster behavior on Wednesday afternoon. He did not know that Lester made announcements by telephone to anyone who would listen. That Lester believes his mother took the gun away from him, when in fact she did not. Dr. Flicker doesn't know about the fluctuations in Lester's behavior from the hysterical to the mechanical—the hallucinations, the memory lapses. Dr. Flicker used the word 'purposeful,' when in fact Lester was so confused he took the wrong gun, thereby necessitating the waxing of the bullet. When in fact Lester was so disoriented that he took two shells to the hospital.

"Ladies and gentlemen, did Lester think he was going to get a second shot?"

Juror No. 5 responded with a slight smile.

"The State's psychiatrist, Dr. Flicker, sees nothing unusual in the fact that Lester had only four hours' sleep over a period of four days." Robert approached the sleep chart and began to flip the pages. "Yet, this chart graphically depicts that loss of sleep, and we have presented solid testimony that sleep-deprivation alone can alter a person's mind." The red crayon boldly testified to Lester's almost total sleeplessness.

"We all understand that when exposed to sufficient stress, a leg will snap. Why not the mind? We are all familiar with the army motto, 'Every man has his limit.' How many men, in battle, when subjected to loss of sleep and to stress, have cracked? Combined with stress, sleep-deprivation can—and did—precipitate a psychotic episode."

Robert returned to the jury box and let his eyes sweep the panel.

"I would like, for a moment, to contrast your situation with Lester's. You operate now with hindsight. Lester couldn't. You have all the time you want to make your decision. Lester didn't. You can consult with each other, you can argue, you can debate—you have each other. Lester had always counted on George—but every time he turned to George, he found the same begging, the same question."

Juror No. 11 shifted position—perhaps in discomfort, perhaps in acquiescence.

Robert said, "Lester was also operating in a very permissive atmosphere. He made these announcements to the world—to Carver, a total stranger; to his boss on the telephone; to George's father-in-law; to Barbara, who was present when he waxed the shells; to Jean, George's wife. I don't know what the law intends to do with all these people—but we'll leave that to the Prosecutor. . . ."

Two of the jurors glanced at Carton. Ten sat at attention. One kept her eyes lowered. One appeared to be dozing.

Robert said, "This is an unusual case. There is something here today that is not often found in a criminal courtroom. That element is love. It's almost as if a difficult stranger had walked in here. But it belongs here." Robert's tone grew impassioned. "The element of love was in this case from June 17th. It was in this case from the time Lester was born. It belongs here as much as that gun we like to keep out on the table so everyone can look at it. It could have been marked into evidence as well as any other piece of evidence. It's the core of this case.

"We all understand that hate moves men. We should understand that love moves men. Love can be the greatest corrupter of man— not of his soul, but of his reason. What is the target of love, always? Man's power to reason. And when love attacks our reason, are we not almost always helpless? We recognize the strength of love in our platitudes. We talk about love conquering all. We know men die for love. We know hate and greed makes men covet a throne—but only love can make a man give up a throne. We are taught to reject hate, malice, evil, greed. But love is one emotion we have no defenses against. It is the one emotion we are most vulnerable to. We think of love as a friend even when it comes to attack our reason, as it always does. . . ."

Quietly Robert said, "Lester was strong enough to have resisted a physical assault. Lester had the moral upbringing to be on the defensive against hate or malice. The one thing Lester was most vulnerable to was love. And, in his state of sleeplessness, of stress, of anxiety and emotional pain, it was love that attacked his reason. The only crime Lester is guilty of is having his reason overwhelmed by love. We plead guilty to that, but that is not a crime punishable in this state."

At 11:00 a.m., Robert completed his closing argument. He stood still a moment, as if reluctant to give the floor to Carton. He seemed aware that Juror No. 4, Mrs. Helen Hauke—wearing harlequin glasses and a wig—had kept her eyes fixed on her lap. It was possible her mind was made up and she didn't want to be influenced; it was also possible that listening was painful.

Robert returned to the counsel table. Lightly, he patted Lester's arm as the Prosecutor rose to begin his final and most lengthy accusation.

Whatever her reason, Juror No. 4 continued to gaze at her lap.

"Ladies and gentlemen," Carton said, "if we could all stand under Niagara Falls and turn the water into sympathy, grief, and sorrow, you couldn't have more of it than you have in this courtroom. But that isn't what this case has to be decided on—nothing belongs here but the evidence."

Carton didn't pace. He stood firm, as if planted on the rock of his evidence.

"Let us look at Mr. Zygmanik, and at his background. Mr. Zygmanik has been a good, upstanding citizen for most of his life. He has no criminal record—he's been calm, cool, and he's done nice things for people. That's the general picture. Mr. Ansell has expressed to you some dismay that someone in this position can be subjected to the criminal system—that, somehow, the law does not apply to Mr. Zygmanik because of his background."

Next to Robert, Lester stared fixedly down at the counsel table.

Carton said, "Ladies and gentlemen, there is nothing in our law that says if you have an unblemished record and an outstanding background, therefore you can take the law into your own hands for one brief moment—as Mr. Ansell has said repeatedly—one brief moment when he went over the edge."

Carton paused, sipped at a glass of water, then continued. "What we need here is a hard, objective look at the evidence, an acceptance of the law, and a decision based on that.

"Mr. Ansell has made numerous references throughout this trial to the type of shotgun used, and I assume that because Lester used a 20-gauge shotgun instead of a more powerful type, we are supposed to conclude that he didn't know the nature and quality of his act. Now, if you are blasted in the head by a shotgun, it doesn't make a lot of difference what kind it is. The testimony from Dr. Lang is quite clear—there were 24 pellets taken out of George Zygmanik's head, and every bone in his cranium was fractured at least once."

Carton hammered for several moments at the brutality of the act. Then he said, "Mr. Ansell has also made numerous references to the fact that Mr. Zygmanik went without sleep. I assume a good part of the defense is tied to the fact that Mr. Zygmanik was tired at the time of the shooting." Carton's sarcasm was evident. "Dr. Flicker indicated his experience in this area and testified that people who are exhausted can still act in a very rational manner. Being tired, or exhausted, as the defendant allegedly was, doesn't mean you don't know what you're doing."

"What the defendant did in this case," Carton reiterated, "was to take the law into his own hands, and to do so without giving anyone a chance. Eleven hours after critical surgery, he shot his brother."

Carton paused dramatically. Four of the jurors seemed to react. Robert watched them, no longer able to gauge either his own or Carton's impact.

Carton said, "We all know the victim was his brother. What about the victim? Was he really in any condition to ask to be killed? George Zygmanik was in pain, he had severe injuries and was under heavy sedation. Is someone in that position truly able to say, 'I want to die'? Was he really in a position to make a reasonable, rational request for death?

"I'm sure everybody in this courtroom, at one time or another, has been in the position of watching a loved one suffer—some for a long period of time, a lot longer than the three short days we're talking about here. The accident happened on Sunday, and it was all over by eleven o'clock on Wednesday night. Those are the facts. You are the judges of the facts. I hope you will say to yourself: No, I did not allow myself to be swept by emotion, sympathy, compassion, grief. I hope you will say to yourself: Yes, I decided the case on evidence—I returned a true verdict according to the evidence and nothing else."

At 11:45, Carton resumed his seat.

The spectators stirred, temporarily released from tension.

McGowan called a fifteen-minute recess. To the jurors, he said, "Under no circumstances is there to be any deliberation in the jury room at this time. This case is not finished until I instruct you with respect to the law."

To Robert, Lester said, "That's it, isn't it?"

"That's it," Robert said.

For Robert, it was a moment of loss—that moment in every trial when there was nothing more to be said, nothing more to be done. Now the case had passed into the Judge's hands, and McGowan would hold Lester's destiny only briefly before relinquishing it to the jury.

Robert sat quietly while the spectators dispersed. He stared at the sleep chart—it looked suddenly weary, like old confetti. Then he realized Lester was waiting.

"I need a pack of cigarettes," Lester said. It was a question.

Robert nodded. Then he watched Lester move down the aisle with the feeling that Lester was clearer, more familiar, than anyone in his life—and with the knowledge that Lester would eventually fade into the faces of other clients.

He rose and walked out into the noisy corridor. At the end of the hallway, removed from the crowd, he stood, smoking, looking out at the golden autumn. After a moment, he felt someone touch his arm, and when he turned, he found Sonia standing quietly behind him.

She said, "There was no promise. Between Lester and my Georgie, there was no promise."

He stared at her. Sonia shook her head, then turned quickly and walked away. He started to follow her. Instead, he turned back to the window to watch the leaves scattering in the November wind.

69

November 5, 1973
Freehold, New Jersey

Judge Raymond McGowan was a big man with a ruddy complexion, blazing white hair, and a streak of the patriarch. For six days, he had been monitor, referee, host, and authority symbol in this murder trial. Now the last moments of trial belonged to the bench as he addressed the jurors in a rich, booming voice.

"The State must prove willfulness, deliberation, and premeditation. The State is not required to prove a motive. If the State has proved the essential elements, the defendant must be found guilty, regardless of motive or lack of motive."

McGowan had been a trial lawyer, a municipal judge, a member of the bar since 1936—he had spent most of his life in the courtroom. Like the majority of the jurors, he was Catholic, Republican, conservative, counted among those on the side of law and order, but known to be fair. His instructions were couched in that opaque legal rhetoric originally invented by lawyers to instill fear in the layman— nevertheless, the words seemed solemn and chilling.

"Under our law, all persons are presumed to be sane and therefore responsible for their conduct until the contrary is established.

"An accused may have absurd or irrational notions on some subjects, he may be unsound in mind, but, at the time of the deed, if he had the mental capacity to distinguish right from wrong, and to understand the nature and quality of his act, he is amenable to the criminal law.

"In this case, there is a conflict of psychiatric testimony. You, the jury, will have to determine the truth.

"The criteria for judging lay testimony and expert testimony is the same. You must give consideration to the demeanor of the witness, his manner, his method of testifying, appearance, mental capacity, power of observation, his frankness or evasiveness, his logic, his inconsistencies or contradictions. Testimony to be believed must not only proceed from the mouth of a credible witness—it must be credible in itself, and must be such as common experience and observation of mankind can approve as probable in the circumstances."

In the final portion of his instructions, McGowan outlined the jurors' choices. These had been mimeographed for the jury's benefit, to be used while deliberating and, later, to be marked as a final ballot.

"The State contends that this killing was intentional, and it was willful, deliberate, and premeditated. This is a murder in the first degree. All other kinds of murder are murder in the second degree. The Defense admits the killing, while contending the defendant was temporarily insane at the time of the deed.

"The possible verdicts are listed on this sheet. You are to assume no significance whatever to the order in which you find these questions."

STATE V. LESTER MARK ZYGMANIK
INDICTMENT NO. 1197–73

( ) 1. We find the defendant GUILTY of murder in the first degree.

( ) 2. We find the defendant NOT GUILTY of murder in the first degree.

( ) 3. We find the defendant GUILTY of murder in the second degree.

( ) 4. We find the defendant NOT GUILTY of murder in the second degree.

( ) 5. If you have found the defendant NOT GUILTY of murder, did you find him NOT GUILTY by reason of insanity at the time of the commission of the offense alleged?

( ) 6. If you have placed an X in the box designating "Yes" alongside of No. 5, then proceed to answer this question: Does such insanity still continue?

"There will be a new selection of jurors at this time. There will be twelve of you remaining. Those twelve will deliberate. The number-one juror in the box will be the foreman."

Throughout the trial, there had been fourteen jurors. Now all their names were placed in the squirrel cage to spin. The two names drawn would not retire with the rest to the jury room, nor participate in the verdict.

The bailiff called, "Juror No. 7, Mrs. Dorothy Matthes"—then, "Juror No. 11, Mrs. Concheeta Ponzo." These two had been described by Dr. Klagsbrun as "sympathetic" and "very possibly the best."

The foreman, fifty-four-year-old James F. Clark, had been described as "very proper, a problem."

Neither the eliminated jurors nor the appointed foreman represented the kind of luck for which the Defense might have wished.

"You are not to permit any prejudice, passion, sympathy, or bias of any kind to enter into your deliberations. Nor are you to permit any considerations of anger, revenge or hostility of any kind, nor any verdict based upon conjecture or suspicion. You are to reach your verdict without regard to any possible penalty that might be imposed in the event of a guilty verdict.

"Inasmuch as this is a criminal case, the verdict must be unanimous—that is, all twelve of you deliberating must agree. Otherwise, there is no verdict.

"Again—it is your duty and obligation to decide this case based on the facts presented and in accordance with the law given by this State.

"Now, when you have arrived at a verdict, you will knock on the jury-room door and announce to the officer who responds that you have arrived at a verdict—whereupon you will be returned to the courtroom, and you will hand up and deliver this written list of questions.

"When you knock on the door, please don't keep up a continuous rap. It may be that we will be engaged in other business in the courtroom, and we will get to you as soon as we can. We'll hear you—please keep that in mind."

70

November 5, 1973
Freehold, New Jersey

At 1:21 p.m., the courtroom emptied.

In the corridor, Lester found himself surrounded by strangers. He wanted to shout: *Who are you? What are you doing here?* Then the waiting began, indefinite, maybe hours, maybe days.

He didn't like things that weren't definite.

Ansell said, "We'll stick around until eight o'clock, then we'll go somewhere for dinner and come back. If the jury's not out by ten, we can assume nothing's going to happen tonight."

Lester stared through the window. On the ground, the television cameras were set up, waiting—which meant he couldn't go home. He wanted to go home. Only ten days ago, he had ordered a pair of new dogs—they weren't used to him yet. And a month ago he had bred his prize bitch, thinking she'd have to have her puppies somewhere and he'd be with her somewhere.

He believed in luck. Every time something bad happened, something good happened next. He believed in that. Still, he wondered how long it would take. Time was heavy. He wished himself into tomorrow. Then he saw that the idea of prison was something like the idea of death. You went away.

Ansell said, "Let's take a walk."

They climbed the stairs. On the next floor, the corridor was empty. Their footsteps echoed, up and back. He waited for Ansell to say something, but Ansell was silent.

When he came back downstairs, the crowd was still there—and Jeannie was sitting with Victor and his mother, the three of them, side by side. He looked at them as if they were strangers, as if he had never seen them before, seeing them clearly, feeling some thought, some piece of truth emerge from his own desperation. Then he lost it—the sudden clear view of his own past and the knowledge that his life, somehow, had never been his own; that his choices, somehow, had never been his own.

Downstairs, in the snack bar, Robert bought his usual pack of peanut-butter crackers. Directly in front of him, Malcolm Carton purchased a container of milk. Neither spoke. Carton waved at a table occupied by a female quartet and left. The clock said 3:15.

Robert took the stairs. He climbed slowly, struggling with the doubt and fatigue that always descended at the end of a trial. If the verdict was favorable, recuperation would be instant. If not, he knew the sense of failure would haunt him for months. The facts of the case had been complicated. From all of it he had forged a particular truth for the practical purpose of the law, the courtroom, the jury. Two questions remained. Would it work? And: What was the law—his own function in the law? A rash of unresolved, long-deferred questions surfaced. Pushing them down again, he promised himself enough time to wrestle with his own life.

The corridor was crammed.

Sonia sat alone, her derby on her lap, her eyes closed. Robert could hear Victor's raspy voice talking to Jean. And Diane, holding Lester's hand, looked strangely like a china doll.

A few minutes before 4:00 p.m., the bailiff appeared in the hall. "The jury has reached a verdict." At the same moment, a loudspeaker summoned all involved parties back to the courtroom.

At 4:01 p.m., the courtroom was packed. Those who had come earlier for the fever of battle, or the pleasure of entertainment, remained for the verdict. Malcolm Carton's groupies returned. Those to whom the trial had been work and those to whom the trial had meant personal anguish returned: Jean, the victim's widow; Victor, the victim's father-in-law; Sonia, the victim's mother. These were not homespun people. They had been tough, fierce contenders for the American dream. They had provided an incubator for violence.

At 4:01 p.m., the jury had been out for two hours and forty minutes.

McGowan said, "All right, bring the jury out."

At the counsel table, Lester looked quickly back at the spectators. In the third row, Diane Haus thrust a handkerchief to her mouth.

Robert sat quietly, waiting.

The first juror to emerge was Juror No. 9, Marcelle Dean, age fifty, divorced Catholic, dyed red hair—Dr. Klagsbrun had dubbed her "hysterical." She hurried to her place, looked directly at Robert, and smiled. It was possible that the smile was a sign of acquittal; it was also possible that the smile was nervous and contrite, a signal of imminent conviction.

The other jurors followed, grave, austere, eyes lowered.

McGowan said, "Before we proceed any further in connection with the verdict, the audience is reminded that there will be no outbursts of any kind permitted in the courtroom, regardless of the verdict."

In the silence that followed, the bailiff called the roll. Then the final ritual began.

"Ladies and gentlemen of the jury, have you reached a verdict?"

"We have, Your Honor."

"Will you pass the interrogatories to me, please."

McGowan took his time. Aloud, slowly, he reread each question on the mimeographed sheet. Finally, he paused. The courtroom was silent.

"The verdict of the jury is a verdict of—*Not Guilty*."

Sonia began to cry, softly.

Jean gasped. Victor grinned. Diane whimpered.

Lester stared at Robert.

"You made it." Robert grabbed Lester's arm and shook him. "You made it!"

Lester smiled.

In the parking lot, television cameras converged. Somebody held up a microphone, saying, "How do you feel?"

"I feel pretty good," Lester said.

"What are you going to do now?"

"I don't know," Lester said.

In the American Hotel, the jurors occupied a table at the far end of the darkened bar. Out of the courtroom, they looked smaller, more ordinary, less heroic, beautiful. McGowan had left them with a final instruction: "The solemnity of what took place in the jury room is something no one else is entitled to know about. Do not discuss this case with anyone. I make this direction in the form of an order. . . ."

Robert sent them a round of drinks.

At the table, George, Jr., climbed on David Silver's lap. Next to Jean, Victor talked about his childhood—his mother had been a Romanian immigrant, a domestic servant for a Jewish family in Brooklyn. "I always knew Jews were smart," Victor said. He embraced Robert and kissed him solidly. Diane giggled. Lester roared.

The jury sent a round of drinks back.

Lester leaned over to Robert. "Listen," he said, "you know what you did for me?"

"No," Robert said.

Lester grinned. "You did for me what I did for my brother."

71

July 1974

On July 7, one year after the shooting, Robert Ansell stepped out of his office into a blazing noon sun. The street was noisy, under repair. The racket accompanied him as he walked toward the corner coffee shop. Then he heard someone call him, and when he looked up, he saw it was Lester, twenty feet off the ground, straddling a bulldozer. "Ain't that somethin'?" Lester shouted. "I'm fixin' up *your* street."

"Come on down," Robert called back. "I'll take you to lunch."

Robert Ansell
July 1, 1974

There was Lester's act, which was obviously very real. There was the amount of love that encouraged it, or the amount of exploitation he was subjected to, if you want to look at it that way. Or even, in its worst light, that maybe after George couldn't work—he was expendable. But the thing I started to ask myself was, Why can't you love somebody as much as he loved his brother?

That was the point where I started. And then death, naturally—reading about death, and wondering, Why do people fight for life? Is life that good? And if it's not that good, can you make it that good? What it came down to, of course, was, What is my life? Am I doing anything real? I'm totally committed to my profession—I assume, unshakably. But I assumed that about my personal life, too. And all those unshakable assumptions I had indulged in, I found not to be true. After that, my marriage split.

Now I have to think about whether the absence of reality in my life is a function of my personality or my character—or is it a result of the work I do? Am I so used to dealing with scripts, fabricating truths, manipulating reality, that I end up doing that in my life because I'm so used to doing that all day in court?

Lester Zygmanik
July 1974

Like my father wanted to make it. He thought he made it. But he didn't make it, did he? Like this may be the land of opportunity, but you have to have a lot of breaks. If you don't get the breaks, this country'll break you.

My brother, he also worked too hard. He didn't like his job, you know? He said that people used to boss him around there. Used to work him to the bone. But George didn't think like I did. He might've thought this country was all right. Like he used to say, "If we can make it, other people can make it." But did we really make it? You know what I mean? We didn't really make it. A dead brother and a dead father—so we've got a nice house, so what?

And I've got a lot of responsibility, you know? Like there's nobody around any more to take care of things except me. So I've been givin' it a lot of thought. And what I think is, my next step is gonna be a big step. I know that. Like my next step is gonna mean somethin'. It's gonna mean a lot. I haven't figured it out yet. But I will think of somethin'.

February 1975

Since his acquittal, Lester has been living with his mother in Perrineville, New Jersey. He had continued to work in various areas of construction, but current economic conditions have precluded steady employment. Because Sonia does not like to be left alone, Lester rarely goes anywhere socially; he sees Diane less and less.

Jean and her son, George, Jr., now live with her father, Victor Kazma, in Fords, New Jersey. Twice a month, Jean drives to Perrineville so that Sonia may see her grandson. Soon these visits will cease. In March of 1975, Sonia sold the house and the land for $92,000. Sonia plans to move back to Perth Amboy. Lester's plans are indefinite.

Robert Ansell, now divorced, lives alone in an oceanfront apartment in Sea Bright, New Jersey. He has remained with the law firm of Anschelewitz, Barr, Ansell & Bonello. For the most part, his relationship with Lester has been confined to occasional phone calls. Recent events, however, may provide a backdrop for a dramatic reunion of all those involved in the premature death of George Zygmanik.

A civil suit against the motorcycle company has been filed by Jean for herself and her minor child. The suit seeks damages not only for George's injuries, pain, and suffering, but also for his death. In response, the motorcycle company has filed a third-party complaint against Lester, Barbara Petruska, and Jersey Shore Medical Center—on the theory that if the company is responsible for George's death, then Lester, Barbara, and the hospital are also responsible and should help in the payment of any award.

Lester's trial in criminal court has no bearing whatsoever upon this civil action, nor will the outcome of this civil action have any bearing upon the validity of his acquittal. Robert Ansell says, "The civil courts and the criminal courts are two ships that pass in the night."

Shortly, the case of Lester Zygmanik—and all involved—may come to trial again.

72

March 1975

On June 17, 1973, Father's Day, George Zygmanik attended mass at St. Joseph's Roman Catholic Church. There, Father Valentine, a bony old eagle who drove a pick-up truck on weekdays, delivered a fire-and-brimstone sermon which contained the prophetic lines, "It is a good idea to think about death. We should be able to live our lives in the presence of death. It can happen. It can happen this morning. . . ."

Whether or not George acted on an unconscious wish when he mounted Barbara Petruska's motorcycle on that Sunday afternoon, and why he selected his brother as the instrument of his death, leaving Lester to face a murder charge, are questions for a psychiatrist to explore. That Lester's act was an attempt to claim his own manhood seems obvious. That he loved his brother seems incontrovertible. George's death occurred because nothing else seemed possible.

Lester was not a ghetto kid engaged in the thrill of senseless murder as an antidote to a dead-end life. He believed in America. It was not a trivial killing—nor can it be separated from Lester's conditioning, his culture, and his environment. He lived in an area of the country where the middle class and the underworld are indistinguishable—only the poor are distinguishable. He lived in a country where no provisions had been made for the dilemma he faced.

He faced the practice of medicine, where only in private has an adjustment been made to the specter of protracted human suffering. As far back as 1969, in a poll of the American Association of Physicians, 80 percent admitted having practiced *passive* euthanasia. Yet, when Lester confronted George's surgeon, Dr. Clement Kreider's angry response was, "What do you want me to do, stick a knife in him?"

Cruelty always accompanies a disowned reality. Every day, doctors face the enormity of those diseases which destroy all semblance of normal life, those which produce constant pain, those which cripple the mind—while the tyranny of modern technology prolongs a minimal biological existence in that twilight between living and dying. The one means of release lies in a secret path with a decent physician, a close relative, a loving friend. Every day, the right to die is being dealt under the table.

A comparable schizophrenic discrepancy existed between the actual truth and what was presented when Lester faced the law. He was tried on a charge of Murder One. Under the law, the facts were so intrinsically damaging that the Prosecution presented a staccato case in less than two hours. Then, between the lines of a brilliant psychiatric defense which paid its dues to the law, Robert Ansell inserted the details of the real tragedy—in effect, offering temporary insanity as a strategy, as a "legal excuse" for acquittal.

Throughout the trial, the term "mercy killing" was never used. Unacknowledged by law and forbidden by judicial order, the issue nevertheless pervaded the courtroom.

The panel of tough, conservative, blue-collar, over-thirty jurors were not seduced by a parade of utterly charming witnesses nor by an obviously appealing defendant. Did the jury respond, then, to the issue of euthanasia which was blatantly dramatized in spite of the restrictions of the law? Was the ultimate verdict in fact based on a consideration of the circumstances and the motive which prompted Lester's act? Was the verdict predicated on a human recognition which implied, with its decision to acquit, a desire to absolve? Was the right to live given back to Lester under the table?

This denial of reality, this discrepancy between action and creed which surrounds euthanasia in both law and medicine, and the growing public concern with cases like Lester's appear to indicate a need for some kind of legislation. In Belgium, France, Germany, and the Netherlands, a "compassionate" or "altruistic" motive for killing is recognized by law. In Switzerland, Czechoslovakia, Uruguay, and Peru, the request of the victim is an extenuating circumstance, and often no penalty is provided. Anglo-Saxon jurisprudence permits for no such considerations. The solution to this human dilemma appears to be left to those who would assume the responsibility and take the risk. The dilemma itself is left in the hearts and minds of those thousands who find themselves confronted with it.

The temptation, then, is to align oneself with the public groundswell pushing for euthanasia legislation. It is not a writer's task, however, to indulge in easy identification, to assume automatically the prevailing "enlightened" viewpoint. It is a writer's task to question.

A description of the present reality must include the problems of aging, the sick, the poor, the energy crisis, the rising costs of Medicare, and the increasing threat to the American standard of living. Can we be certain that this sudden concern with euthanasia is due entirely to the marriage between medicine and technology? What portion of this need to define who will live and who will die may have arisen from a cold search for expediency?

Are the following facts pertinent? (1) There are twenty million Americans aged sixty-five or over, 86 percent of whom have serious chronic illnesses. (2) Currently, one out of every ten white Americans and one out of every four black Americans officially designated as poor are eligible for federal medical aid. (3) In the next twenty years, the poor and the aged will have doubled, while American hospital costs, already the highest in the world, are continuing to rise at a staggering rate—resulting in the financial projection of a massive government debt for those who are physically and economically dependent.

Clearly, a national policy on euthanasia would result in a sizable reduction in the cost of federal medical aid. Is it possible that this movement, meant to relieve human suffering, is at least partly politically or economically manipulated?

Modern technology has been used heedlessly, without concern for the ambiance in which we live or the ambiance in which we die. Technology, advancing at its rapid rate, as well as producing artificial means to prolong life, has helped to produce a landscape of alienation and, with it, feelings of powerlessness on the part of the average citizen. Has death, not life, become the final area over which we still feel we can claim control?

Euthanasia is a heart-rending issue. It is also complex. What happens when one is incapable of making, or acting upon, a decision to die? Who then has that right? By what authority? By what criteria? What human qualities would have to be officially absent to justify death? Or, in reverse, which qualities would have to be officially present to justify life? And where is the guarantee that the slide-rule of pragmatism which rules modern life will not apply to modern death? That the criteria will not be: Who is dispensable?

To view the prospect of legislation out of the context of the society in which it is being proposed is both nearsighted and dangerous.

In a society fully dedicated to the quality of life, the dignity of dying might be entrusted to humane laws administered by a humane leadership. In a society which reveres its old, the bitterness of final pain might inevitably become a proper political concern. But in a society where the poor remain an embarrassment, where exploitation and dehumanization are common, where profit is crucial, and where personal and national aggression are too often glorified, can the establishment be trusted with the formal power to mediate this profound human problem?